# CHRIST IN ALL THE SCRIPTURES

'AND BEGINNING AT MOSES AND
ALL THE PROPHETS HE EXPOUNDED
UNTO THEM IN ALL THE SCRIPTURES
THE THINGS CONCERNING HIMSELF'

## A. M. HODGKIN

Marshall Pickering

Marshall Pickering Ltd,
34–42 Cleveland St.
London W1P 5FB

First published by Pickering and Inglis Ltd
Reprinted 1908, 1909, 1911, 1914, 1922, 1931, 1936, 1943,
1945, 1949, 1956, 1963, 1969

Re-issued in this format by Pickering & Inglis Ltd in 1985.
Reprinted in 1987
Reprinted in 1989

**British Library Cataloguing in Publication**

Hodgkin, A. M.
    Christ in all the scriptures.
    I. Jesus Christ—Biblical teaching
    I. Title
    232      BT202

    ISBN 0-7208-0676-3

Printed and bound in Great Britain by
Cox & Wyman Ltd, Reading

# PREFACE

ON the glorious resurrection morning Mary went to seek for Jesus. She sought Him in the tomb, but He stood beside her. She thought He was the gardener, but the one word "Mary" revealed to her her Saviour.

As we read some passage in the Old Testament how often our eyes are holden, and we see only the earthly form : we see Aaron the priest, or David the shepherd, or Solomon the king ; but if, like Mary, we are really seeking the Lord Jesus, He manifests Himself to us through the outward type, and we turn in glad surprise, and, looking up, say, "Rabboni"— "*My dear Master.*"

As we continue to seek, we find Him in the least expected places of the Old Testament, until the whole grows luminous with the glory of God in the face of Jesus Christ. "In the volume of the Book it is written of Me." All the lines of history and type, of Psalm and prophecy, converge towards one centre—Jesus Christ, and to one supreme event, His death on the Cross for our salvation. And from that centre again all the lines of history in the book of Acts, of experience in the Epistles, and of prophecy in Revelation radiate out once more to testify that the Father sent the Son to be the Saviour of the world.

After His resurrection our Lord not only "opened the Scriptures" to His disciples, but also "opened their understanding that they might understand the Scriptures." He is ready to do the same for us. The same Holy Spirit who moved holy men of old to write the Scriptures is close at hand to make the words *life* to our souls by taking of the things of Christ and revealing them unto us.

Of the books of the New Testament only a brief summary is here given, partly because they are so much more studied, partly because to treat of them at any adequate length would swell this book beyond the limits of a single volume, and still more because the chief aim of the present Studies is to show that Christ is the Key to the Old Testament Scriptures. To encourage others to seek Him for themselves, under the guidance of the Spirit, in the pages of Holy Scripture, is the object of this book.

I would here gratefully acknowledge the help of Fielden Thorp, B.A., and the Rev. James Neil, M.A., in revision, and of other friends in various ways.  A. M. HODGKIN.

# CONTENTS

# CHRIST IN ALL THE SCRIPTURES

# I. INTRODUCTION

## 1. The Testimony of Christ to the Scriptures

"ABRAHAM rejoiced to see My day." "Moses wrote of Me."
"David called [Me] Lord" (John viii. 56, v. 46; Matt. xxii.
45). We have in these words of our Saviour abundant authority
for seeking Him in the Old Testament, and also a confirmation
of the truth of the Scriptures themselves. To those of us who
believe in Christ as truly God, as well as truly Man, His word
on these matters is authoritative. He would not have said,
"Abraham rejoiced to see My day," if Abraham had been a
mythological character; He would not have said, "Moses
wrote of Me," if the Books of Moses had been written hundreds
of years later; nor would He have quoted from the 110th Psalm
to prove that David called Him Lord, if that Psalm had not
been written till the time of the Maccabees.

With regard to our Lord's reference to the Books of Moses,
the testimony is peculiarly emphatic. It was no mere passing
reference to them. The whole force of the argument again and
again lies in the fact that He regarded Moses, not as a mere
title by which certain books were known, but as personally the
actor in the history which they record and the author of the
legislation which they contain. "Did not Moses give you
the law, and yet none of you keepeth the law?" (John vii.
19). "Had ye believed Moses, ye would have believed Me;
for he wrote of Me. But if ye believe not his writings, how
shall ye believe My words?" (John v. 46, 47). He condemned
the traditions with which the Pharisees overlaid the laws and
teaching of Moses as "*making the word of God of none effect*"
(Mark vii. 13). To the leper He said, "Go thy way, show
thyself to the priest, and offer the gift that Moses commanded"
(Matt. viii. 4). That command of Moses is found in the very
heart of the priestly code which some would have us believe
was framed centuries after the days of Moses.[1]

[1] See *Old Testament Criticism and the Rights of the Unlearned*. J. Kennedy.
M.A., D.D.

1

From a careful study of the Gospels we cannot fail to see that the Old Testament Scriptures were continually upon Christ's lips because always hidden in His heart. In the temptation in the wilderness He defeated the devil, not with any manifestation of His Divine glory, not by a power which we cannot wield, not even by His own words; but He fell back upon written words which had strengthened the saints of many ages, thus showing us how we also may meet and foil our great adversary. It is specially helpful to note that it is out of Deuteronomy that our Lord selects, "as pebbles from the clear brook," His three conclusive answers to the tempter (Deut. viii. 3, vi. 13, 14, vi. 16). For we have been told that this Book of Deuteronomy is a pious forgery of the time of Josiah, purporting to be written by Moses to give it greater weight in bringing about the much-needed reforms. Would our Lord—who is Himself the Truth—have thus countenanced a book full of untruths, and have used it in the critical moment of His conflict with the devil? And would not "the father of lies" have known perfectly well if the book had been a forgery?

When Christ commenced His public ministry in the synagogue at Nazareth with the words of Isaiah, "The Spirit of the Lord is upon Me, because He hath anointed Me to preach the Gospel to the poor," He said, "This day is this Scripture fulfilled in your ears" (Luke iv. 17-21). In the Sermon on the Mount our Lord said, "Think not that I am come to destroy the law and the prophets: I am not come to destroy, but to fulfil. For verily I say unto you, Till heaven and earth pass, one jot or one tittle shall in no wise pass from the law, till all be fulfilled" (Matt. v. 17-19).

In these days we have many books *about* the Bible, but very little searching of the Scriptures themselves. A careful study of what Jesus Himself says about the Old Testament Scriptures, asking for the light of the Holy Spirit upon the pages, would well repay the Bible student. Very few realise how abundant are our Lord's quotations from the Old Testament. He refers to twenty Old Testament characters. He quotes from nineteen different books. He refers to the creation of man, to the institution of marriage, to the history of Noah, of Abraham, of Lot, and to the overthrow of Sodom and Gomorrah as described in Genesis; to the appearing of God to Moses in the bush, to the manna, to the ten commandments, to the tribute money as mentioned in Exodus. He refers to the ceremonial law for the purification of lepers, and to the great moral law, "Thou shalt love thy neighbour as thyself," both contained in Leviticus. To

the brazen serpent, and the law regarding vows, in Numbers.
We have already dwelt upon His threefold quotation from
Deuteronomy. He refers to David's flight to the high priest at
Nob, to the glory of Solomon and the visit of the Queen of
Sheba, to Elijah's sojourn with the widow of Sarepta, to the
healing of Naaman, and to the killing of Zechariah—from
various historical books. And as regards the Psalms and the
Prophetical writings, if possible the Divine authority of our
Lord is yet more deeply stamped on them than on the rest of
the Old Testament.[1] "Have ye not read?" or "It is written,"
is the ground of Christ's constant appeal; "The Scripture
cannot be broken," "The Scriptures testify of Me," "The
Scripture must be fulfilled," His constant assertion. Questioned
concerning the resurrection, Jesus answered, "Ye do err, not
knowing the Scriptures. *Have ye not read that which was spoken
unto you by God,* saying, I am the God of Abraham, and the God
of Isaac, and the God of Jacob? God is not the God of the
dead, but of the living." Our Lord here attributes the scepticism
of the Sadducees partly to their not understanding the Scriptures,
He proves from the Bible the fact of the resurrection, and He
asserts that the very words uttered by God are contained
therein (Matt. xxii. 29-32).[2]

As He drew near to the Cross, our Saviour's testimony to
the Scriptures has a still more sacred import. "Behold we go
up to Jerusalem, and all things that are written by the prophets
concerning the Son of Man shall be accomplished" (Luke xviii.
31). "For I say unto you, that this which is written must be
fulfilled in Me,—And He was reckoned with transgressors: for
that which concerneth Me hath fulfilment" (Luke xxii. 37,
R.V.). On the night of His betrayal, in the shade of Olivet,
three times our Saviour points to the fulfilment of these Scriptures
in Himself (see Matt. xxvi. 31, 53, 54; Mark xiv. 48, 49).
Three of His seven utterances upon the Cross were in the words
of Scripture, and He died with one of them on His lips.

But perhaps the strongest testimony of all which Christ
bore to the Old Testament was after His resurrection. On the
very day that He rose He said to the two disciples going to
Emmaus, "O fools, and slow of heart to believe all that the
prophets have spoken! Ought not Christ to have suffered these
things, and to enter into His glory? And beginning at Moses
and all the prophets, He expounded unto them in all the
Scriptures the things concerning Himself" (Luke xxiv. 25-27).

[1] See *The Continuity of Scripture.* Wm. Page Wood, Vice-Chancellor.
[2] *The Saviour's Bible.* Newman Hall, LL.B., D.D.

Not only did He sanction the Scriptures, but also that method of interpretation which finds throughout the Old Testament a witness to the Messiah of the New.   Thus on the very first day of our Lord's return He resumed His former method of instruction even more emphatically than before, proving His claims not so much by His own personal victory over death as by the testimony of the Scriptures.   After this Jesus appeared to the eleven and said :  "These are the words which I spake unto you, while I was yet with you, that all things must be fulfilled which were written in the law of Moses, and in the Prophets, and in the Psalms concerning Me.   Then opened He their understanding, that they might understand the Scriptures, and said unto them : Thus it is written, and thus it behoved Christ to suffer, and to rise from the dead the third day " (Luke xxiv. 44-46).   Even those who would seek to place limits upon Christ's wisdom and knowledge during His life on earth would surely not extend this to the period of His risen life.   And it is during this period that He sets His seal upon the Law, the Prophets, and the Psalms, the threefold division of the complete Old Testament Scriptures according to the Jews, the very same Scriptures that are in our possession to-day.

But, lest even this should not be enough to confirm our faith, we are given in the Book of Revelation a glimpse of our glorified Saviour, still "this same Jesus," still quoting from the Scriptures, and still applying them to Himself.   He says : "Fear not ; I am the first and the last : I am He that liveth, and was dead ; and, behold, I am alive for evermore, Amen ; and have the keys of hell and of death" (Rev. i. 17, 18).   And again: "He that hath the key of David, He that openeth, and no man shutteth ; and shutteth, and no man openeth " (Rev. iii. 7).   Here He quotes from the two parts of the one Book of Isaiah, from chapter xliv. 6, which says : "Thus saith the Lord, the King of Israel, and his Redeemer, the Lord of hosts : I am the first, and I am the last ; and beside Me there is no God. . . . Fear ye not," and from chapter xxii. 22 : "And the key of the house of David will I lay upon His shoulder ; so He shall open, and none shall shut ; and He shall shut, and none shall open."

Truly the key—not only of life and death, but the key to the Scriptures—is laid upon His shoulder, and He still unlocks the meaning of the book to those who are humble enough for Him to unlock the understanding of their hearts.

## 2. THE TESTIMONY OF THE SCRIPTURES TO CHRIST

Looking forward into the future from the earliest ages, God's servants saw One who was to come, and as the time approached this vision grew so clear that it would be almost possible for us to describe Christ's life on earth from the Old Testament Scriptures, of which He Himself said, " They testify of Me."

There was one central figure in Israel's hope. The work of the world's redemption was to be accomplished by one Man, the promised Messiah. It is He who was to bruise the serpent's head (Gen. iii. 15); He was to be descended from Abraham (Gen. xxii. 18), and from the tribe of Judah (Gen. xlix. 10).

Isaiah looked forward and saw first a great Light shining upon the people that walked in darkness (Isa. ix. 2). And as he gazed he saw that a child was to be born, a Son was to be given (ver. 6), and with growing amazement there dawned upon him these names, as describing the nature of the child. "*Wonderful.*" Wonderful, indeed, in His birth, for the advent of no other child had ever been heralded by the hosts of heaven. His birth of a virgin (Isa. vii. 14), and the appearance of the star (Num. xxiv. 17), were alike wonderful. Increasingly wonderful was He in His manhood, and most wonderful of all in His perfect sinlessness. "*Counsellor.*" "Christ, in whom are hid all the treasures of wisdom and knowledge" (Col. ii. 3). "*The Mighty God, the Everlasting Father.*" There dawned upon Isaiah the consciousness that this promised One was none other than God manifest in the flesh, "Immanuel, God with us" (Isa. vii. 14). As Jesus Himself said, "I and my Father are One" (John x. 30). The next name, "*The Prince of Peace,*" specially belongs to Jesus, for "He is our Peace." His birth brought Peace on earth, and leaving it He bequeathed Peace to His disciples, "having made Peace through the blood of His Cross." Then the prophet sees the child that was to be born seated on the throne of His father David, and he sees the glorious spread of His kingdom. Though born of a royal house, it was to be in the time of its humiliation. "There shall come forth a shoot out of the stock of Jesse, and a branch out of his roots shall bear fruit" (Isa. xi. 1, R.V.). We have in this a glimpse of His lowliness and poverty.

And now the prophets, one by one, fill in the picture, each adding a fresh, vivid touch. The prophet Micah sees the little town where Jesus was to be born, and tells us it is Bethlehem

(Micah v. 2 ; Matt. ii. 6) ; Isaiah sees the adoration of the Magi (Isa. lx. 3 ; Matt. ii. 11); Jeremiah pictures the death of the innocents (Jer. xxxi. 15 ; Matt. ii. 17, 18); and Hosea foreshadows the flight into Egypt (Hos. xi. 1 ; Matt. ii. 15) ; Isaiah portrays His meekness and gentleness (chap. xlii. 2 ; Matt. xi. 29), and the wisdom and knowledge which Jesus manifested all through His life from the time of His talking with the doctors in the Temple.   Again, when He cleansed the Temple, the words of the Psalmist came at once to the memory of the disciples, "The zeal of Thine house hath eaten me up" (Ps. lxix. 9 ; John ii. 17).   Isaiah pictured Him preaching good tidings to the meek, binding up the broken-hearted, proclaiming liberty to the captives, and giving the oil of joy for mourning, and the garment of praise for the spirit of heaviness (Isa. lxi. 1-3 ; Luke iv. 16-21).   Mourning was turned into joy when Jesus came into the presence of death.   The poor woman whom Satan had bound, lo, these eighteen years, was loosed at His word. His gospel was indeed the message of good tidings.   Isaiah pictured even that sweetest scene of all, the Good Shepherd blessing the little children, for "He shall gather the lambs in His arms, and carry them in His bosom" (chap. xl. 11 ; Mark x. 16).   Then Zechariah sings, "Rejoice greatly, O daughter of Zion," for he sees her lowly King entering Jerusalem, riding on an ass's colt ; another Psalm adds the Hosannahs of the children. "Out of the mouths of babes and sucklings hast Thou ordained strength because of Thine enemies, that Thou mightest still the enemy and the avenger" (Zech. ix. 9 ; Ps. viii. 2 ; Matt. xxi. 4).

The prophets foresaw something of the character and extent of the Saviour's work.   The light that was to shine forth from Zion was to be for all the world, Jew and Gentile alike were to be blessed.   The Spirit of God was to be poured out upon all flesh (Joel ii. 28).   "All the ends of the earth shall see the salvation of our God" (Isa. lii. 10).   The picture of a victorious, triumphant Messiah was a familiar one to the Jews of our Saviour's time.   So engrossed were they with this side of the picture that they did not recognise Him when He came, and John the Baptist said, "There standeth One among you *whom ye know not*." " Had they known it they would not have crucified the Lord of glory."   But they ought to have known it, for the prophets who foretold His glory had spoken in no less certain tones of His lowliness, His rejection, and His sufferings.   "Behold," says Isaiah, "my Servant shall deal prudently, He shall be exalted and extolled and be very high " (chap. lii. 13)—when suddenly, what does he see in the next verse ?   " As many were astonied at Thee, His visage was so marred more than any man, and His form more than the sons of men." And how shall we picture the astonishment of the prophet as the vision of the fifty-third chapter dawns upon him with all the majesty of the suffering Messiah? From the root of Jesse was to spring up a tender plant who was to be rejected by Israel. "He is despised and rejected of men; a man of sorrows, and acquainted with grief" (Isa. liii. 3).

As the prophet's steadfast gaze is fixed upon the future, he sees this Holy One led "as a lamb to the slaughter, and as a sheep dumb before her shearers, so He openeth not His mouth (ver. 7; see Matt. xxvii. 12, 14). He sees Him dying a death by violence, for "He was cut off out of the land of the living" (ver. 8). Daniel takes up the same thought and tells us, "Messiah shall be cut off, but not for Himself" (Dan. ix. 26). And now once more a chorus of the prophets unite their voices to tell us the manner of His death. The Psalmist sees that He is to be betrayed by one of His own disciples,—"Yea, Mine own familiar friend in whom I trusted, which did eat My bread, hath lifted up his heel against Me" (Ps. xli. 9). Zechariah tells us of the thirty pieces of silver that were weighed for His price, and adds that the money was cast to the potter (Zech. xi. 12, 13, Jer. xix., Matt. xxvii. 3-10). He also sees the sheep scattered when the Shepherd was smitten (chap. xiii. 7; Matt. xxvi. 31, 56). Isaiah sees Him taken from one tribunal to another (chap. liii. 8; John xviii. 24, 28). The Psalmist foretells the false witnesses called in to bear witness against Him (Ps. xxvii. 12; Matt. xxvi. 59, 60). Isaiah sees Him scourged and spit upon (chap. l. 6; Matt. xxvi. 67, and xxvii. 26-30). The Psalmist sees the actual manner of His death, that it was by crucifixion, "They pierced My hands and My feet" (Ps. xxii. 16). His being reckoned with criminals and making intercession for His murderers were alike foretold (Isa. liii. 12; Mark xv. 27; Luke xxiii. 34). So clear did the vision of the Psalmist become that he sees Him mocked by the passers-by (Ps. xxii. 6-8; Matt. xxvii. 39-44). He sees the soldiers parting His garments among them, and casting lots for His vesture (Ps. xxii. 18; John xix. 23, 24), and giving Him vinegar to drink in His thirst (Ps. lxix. 21; John xix. 28, 29). With quickened ear he hears His cry in the hour of His anguish, "My God, My God, why hast Thou forsaken Me?" (Ps. xxii. 1; Matt. xxvii. 46), and His dying words, "Father, into Thy hands I commit My spirit" (Ps. xxxi. 5; Luke xxiii. 46). And, taught by the Holy Ghost, the Psalmist writes the words, "Reproach hath broken My heart" (Ps. lxix. 20). John tells us that though the soldiers brake the legs of the two thieves to hasten their death, "when they came to Jesus, and saw that He was dead already, they brake not His legs : but one of the soldiers pierced His side, and forthwith came there out blood and water. . . . For these things were done, that the Scriptures might be fulfilled, A bone of Him shall not be broken. And again, They shall look on Him whom they pierced" (John xix. 32-37 ; Exod. xii. 46 ; Ps. xxxiv. 20 ; Zech. xii. 10). Isaiah tells us that "though they had made His grave with the wicked"—that is, intended to bury Him in the place where they buried malefactors—yet it was ordered otherwise, and He was actually buried "with the rich in His death." "For there came a rich man of Arimathæa named Joseph . . . and begged the body of Jesus . . . and laid it in his own new tomb" (Isa. liii. 9 ; Matt. xxvii. 57-60).

But the vision of the prophets stretched beyond the Cross and the tomb, and embraced the resurrection and ascension and final triumph of the Saviour. David sings : "Thou wilt not leave My soul in hell; neither wilt Thou suffer Thine Holy One to see corruption. Thou wilt show Me the path of life : in Thy presence is fulness of joy ; at Thy right hand there are pleasures for evermore" (Ps. xvi. 10, 11). And Isaiah, after he has prophesied the humiliation and death of the Messiah, closes the same prophecy with these remarkable words : "When Thou shalt make His soul an offering for sin, He shall see His seed, He shall prolong His days, and the pleasure of the Lord shall prosper in His hand. He shall see of the travail of His soul, and shall be satisfied" (Isa. liii. 10, 11).

From the remotest past the saints looked forward to events which still lie before us in the future. "Enoch also, the seventh from Adam, prophesied of these, saying, Behold, the Lord cometh with ten thousands of His saints, to execute judgment upon all" (Jude 14). The patriarch Job said : "I know that my Redeemer liveth, and that He shall stand at the latter day upon the earth . . . whom I shall see for myself" (Job xix. 25, 26). Zechariah had a vision of the Mount of Olives with the Lord standing there, King over all the earth, and all the saints with Him (Zech. xiv. 4-9).

And as the prophecies of the past have been fulfilled, so certainly shall also the prophecies of the future. "Now we see not yet all things put under Him, but we see Jesus, crowned with glory and honour" (Heb. ii. 8, 9). And He says, "Surely I come quickly. Amen. Even so, come, Lord Jesus."

## II. CHRIST IN THE PENTATEUCH

### 1. GENESIS

GENESIS is in many respects the most important book in the Bible. Almost all the truths of God's revelation are contained here in germ.

"*In the beginning God.*" The very first word gives God His right place.

"*In the beginning* God created the heaven and the earth . . . And God said—Let Us make man in our image, after our likeness" (Gen. i. 1, 26). Here we have the verbs *created* and *said* in the singular, the name of God in its plural form—*Elohim*—and the plural pronoun *Us.* "*In the beginning* was the Word, and the Word was with God, and the Word was God. The same was *in the beginning* with God. All things were made by Him, and without Him was not anything made that was made" (John i. 1-3). "The Lord possessed Me *in the beginning* of His way, before His works of old. I was set up from everlasting *from the beginning*, or ever the earth was. When He prepared the heavens I was there . . . when He appointed the foundations of the earth" (Prov. viii. 22-29). "Thou lovedst Me before the foundation of the world," Jesus said to His Father when He was about to lay down His life for us (John xvii. 24). Thus in the beginning of all things we see our everlasting Saviour, the Son of God, "whom He hath appointed heir of all things, by whom also He made the worlds" (Heb. i. 2).

Genesis is "the book of beginnings," as the name implies.

(1) *The beginning of Creation.* The account of creation reveals the unity, power, and personality of God. It denies atheism—in the beginning *God*. It denies polytheism—*one* God, not many. It denies pantheism—God is before all things and *apart* from them. It denies materialism—matter is not God. It denies the eternity of matter—in the beginning God!

9

*created* it. It denies fatalism—God, here as everywhere, acts in the freedom of His Eternal Being (Murphy).

" 'In the beginning God created the heaven and the earth.' In that simple statement we have the Bible declaration of the origin of the material universe; and it is one in which faith finds reasonable foundation. Interpretation of method may vary, but the essential truth abides. In its dignified and sublime statement reason may rest as it cannot possibly do in any theory which leaves God out of the question and then finally declares that the first cause was more or less the result of accident, or the existence of laws without mind, or of order without thought." [1]

"As time goes on and thoughtful men come to know more about the truth of this marvellous universe in which we dwell, they approach closer and closer to Moses' record. Never perhaps in the history of scientific investigation did Genesis i. stand out so solidly and triumphantly as now." [2]

If the harmony is not yet seen to be complete it is because we have still so much to learn. The *theories* of Science are continually changing and may clash with Scripture, the ascertained *facts* never do. In the same way our interpretations of the Bible may clash with Science because we may not interpret it aright, but the Divine record in Scripture will one day be seen to agree absolutely with the Divine record in nature. Meanwhile it is remarkable how one scientific discovery after another is proving the accuracy of the Scripture statements, clothed as they are in exquisitely simple language.

For instance, Herbert Spencer speaks of five factors as "the most general forms into which the manifestations of the Unknowable are re-divisible." These five forms are Space, Time, Matter, Motion, Force. The Holy Spirit has given us these five manifestations of God's creative power in the first two verses of the Bible :—

| | |
|---|---|
| In the beginning | Time |
| God created the heavens | Space |
| And the earth | Matter |
| And the Spirit of God | Force |
| Moved | Motion. [3] |

"Through faith we understand that the worlds were framed by the word of God; so that things which are seen were not made of things which do appear " (Heb. xi. 3).

[1] *The Analysed Bible.* G. Campbell Morgan, D.D.
[2] *Outline Studies in the Books of the Old Testament.* W. G. Moorehead, D.D.
[3] *The Conflict of Truth*, p. 136. F. Hugh Capron, F.R.G.S.

Thus God prepared our planet to become the home of man, and, above all, the scene of His supreme revelation of redemption through Christ Jesus.

Genesis gives us—

(2) *The beginning of the Human Race* (i. 26, 27, ii. 7). The outline of the divisions of the race, as given in the tenth chapter of Genesis, is in harmony with the latest theories of ethnology.

(3) *The origin of the Sabbath.*

(4) *The origin of Marriage.*

(5) *The beginning of Sin and Death.* We are introduced at the very beginning to man's great enemy, the devil, and his true character is revealed—subtilty and deceit. The result of the Fall of our first parents is manifest in Cain's hatred of his brother, ending in murder. "And wherefore slew he him ? Because his own works were evil and his brother's righteous" (1 John iii. 12). "This Cain-spirit is seen in the whole line of unbelievers unto this day. It refuses to obey God itself and hates those who do. Cain hated Abel. Ishmael hated Isaac. Esau̅ hated Jacob. The children of Jacob hated Joseph, and this Cain-spirit culminated in the hatred by the world of Christ, the true Abel, who offered Himself a sacrifice for sin. Still to-day the Cain-spirit hates all who seek salvation through that One offering." [1] The enmity of the human heart to God found its culmination in the Cross. All the world was then united. "The kings of the earth stood up, and the rulers were gathered together against the Lord, and against His Christ. For of a truth, against Thy Holy Child Jesus, whom Thou hast anointed, both Herod and Pontius Pilate, with the Gentiles, and the people of Israel, were gathered together" (Acts iv. 26, 27). The inscription over the Cross was written in Greek and Latin and Hebrew—the three great languages of the day, the language of the Gentile nations, the language of the Gentile rulers, and the language of the chosen people—as if to involve the whole world in the guilt. It was also a prophecy of the universal dominion of the King of kings.

(6) *The beginning of Grace,* as shown in the promise of a Redeemer, in the institution of sacrifice, and in God's Covenant. As the redemption of man—the restoration of God's image which he had lost in the Fall—is the great object of God's revelation in the Bible, we find its beginning here in Genesis.

"The first two chapters of the Bible speak of man's *innocence,* what he was before the Fall. The last two chapters

[1] *In the Volume of the Book.* Dr. Pentecost.

of the Bible speak of man's *holiness*, what he shall become; sin is not mentioned in them except the fact that it is absolutely excluded from the Holy City. All the chapters between— the whole Book right through—speak of the conflict between God and sin " (C. L. Maynard).

(7) *The beginning of the Chosen Race.* Genesis shows us the utter failure of man. Adam failed. God gave the race a new start in His servant Noah. But the new race failed, and ended in universal idolatry. Then God called Abram, and from this time He deals with mankind through the chosen race. But the chosen race failed, and in the end of the Old Testament history we see Him dealing with only the faithful remnant.

The Book of Genesis falls naturally into two parts :—

Part I. chapters i.-xi., a very brief but comprehensive history of the world from the creation to the confusion of tongues.

Part II. chapters xii.-l., which narrate the history of Abraham and his family to the death of his great-grandson Joseph.

I. PROPHECIES. We have the glorious promise (in Gen. iii. 15) of *the Seed of the woman* which was to bruise the serpent's head, though the serpent should bruise His heel. The fulfilment is summed up in Heb. ii. 9-14 : " We see Jesus, who was made a little lower than the angels for the suffering of death, crowned with glory and honour. . . . Forasmuch then as the children are partakers of flesh and blood, He also Himself likewise took part of the same; that through death He might destroy him that had the power of death, that is the devil." There were the promises repeated to Abraham of blessing to the whole world through his Seed. "In thy Seed shall all the nations of the earth be blessed" (Gen. xxii. 18, also chap. xii. 3, xvii. 7, xxi. 12). This promise was renewed to Isaac (Gen. xxvi. 4), and again to Jacob (xxviii. 14). Then again there was the blessing of Judah (Gen. xlix. 9, 10), "Judah is a lion's whelp." The Lord Jesus is "the *Lion of the tribe of Judah*" (Rev. v. 5). "The sceptre [or tribal staff] shall not depart from Judah until *Shiloh* come, and unto Him shall the gathering of the people be." Shiloh, "the man of rest, or peace," or "He whose right it is." "He shall be great, and shall be called the Son of the Highest; and the Lord God shall give unto Him the throne of His father David : and He shall reign over the house of Jacob for ever; and of His kingdom there shall be no end" (Luke i. 32).

II. TYPES. In Genesis we have individual men who are types of Christ.

*Adam,* as being the head of the race, and also by contrast. Adam was tempted by the devil and failed (Gen. iii.). Christ was tempted by the devil and triumphed. " As by one man's disobedience many were made sinners, so by the obedience of One shall many be made righteous " (Rom. v. 19).

*Melchizedek.* Gen. xiv. 17-20.

| | |
|---|---|
| Melchizedek—King of Righteousness. | A King shall reign in righteousness. Isa. xxxii. 1. |
| King of Salem—King of Peace. | His name shall be called the Prince of Peace. Isa. ix. 6, 7. |
| King and Priest. | He shall sit and rule upon His throne, and shall be a Priest. Zech. vi. 13. (Both offices united only in Christ.) |
| Made like unto the Son of God. Heb. vii. 3. | A Great High Priest that is passed into the heavens, Jesus, the Son of God. Heb. iv. 14. |
| Having neither beginning of days nor end of life. *ib.* | He ever liveth to make intercession. Heb. vii. 25. |
| Abideth a priest continually. *ib.* | But this man, because He continueth ever, hath an unchangeable priesthood. Heb. vii. 24. |
| Met Abraham after his victory, refreshed him with bread and wine, and blessed him. Gen. xiv. 18. | So Christ draws near to us, and gives us communion with Himself after times of conflict in which He has given us the victory. |

*Isaac.* In *the offering of Isaac* we have one of the most perfect pictures of the great sacrifice offered on Calvary that we find in the Bible. Let us tread softly as we follow it step by step, for we are on holy ground.

| MOUNT MORIAH. | MOUNT CALVARY. |
|---|---|
| Gen. xxii. | |
| Ver. 2. Take now thy son. | Heb. i. 2. God . . . hath spoken to us by His Son. |
| Thine only son. | John iii. 16. God . . . gave His only begotten Son. |
| Whom thou lovest. | John i. 18. The only begotten Son, which is in the bosom of the Father. |
| And get thee into the land of Moriah. | 2 Chron. iii. 1. Solomon began to build the house of the Lord . . . in Mount Moriah. (Thus what was probably the same spot became the place of the Temple sacrifices.) |
| Upon one of the mountains that I will tell thee of. | Luke xxiii. 33. And when they were come to the place which is called Calvary, *there* they crucified Him. |

And offer him there for a burnt offering.

Heb. x. 5-10. Sanctified through the offering of the body of Jesus Christ once for all.

Ver. 4. Abraham lifted up his eyes and saw the place afar off.

Acts iii. 18. God before hath showed by the mouth of all His prophets that Christ should suffer. (The Father knew before the foundation of the world.)

Ver. 6. And Abraham took the wood of the burnt offering, and laid it upon Isaac his son. And they went both of them together.

John xix. 17. And He, bearing His cross, went forth. (See John xviii. 11.)

John x. 17, 18. Therefore doth My Father love Me, because I lay down My life. No man taketh it from Me, but I lay it down of Myself. . . . This commandment have I received of My Father.

Ver. 7. Where is the lamb for a burnt offering?

John i. 29. Behold the Lamb of God which taketh away the sin of the world.

Ver. 8. God will provide Himself *the* lamb. R.V.
So they went both of them together.

Rev. xiii. 8. The Lamb slain from the foundation of the world.

Ps. xl. 8. I delight to do Thy will, O My God.

Ver. 9. Abraham built an altar there, and bound Isaac his son, and laid him upon the altar upon the wood.

Acts ii. 23. Him being delivered by the determinate counsel and foreknowledge of God.

Isa. liii. 6. The Lord hath laid on Him the iniquity of us all.

Ver. 10. And Abraham stretched forth his hand, and took the knife to slay his son.

Isa. liii. 10. It pleased the Lord to bruise Him.

Matt. xxvii. 46. My God, My God, why hast Thou forsaken Me?

Ver. 11. The angel of the Lord called unto him out of heaven.

*Contrast.* (No voice from heaven.)

Matt. xxvi. 53, 54 ; Matt. xxvii. 42. He saved others, Himself He cannot save.

Ver. 12. Thou hast not withheld thy son, thine only son.

Jer. vi. 26. (When God speaks of deep grief He compares it to the loss of an only son.)

Ver. 13. Abraham took the ram, and offered him up for a burnt offering in the stead of his son.

Is. liii. 7, 11. He is brought as a lamb to the slaughter. . . . He shall bear their iniquities.

(No one type can picture all Christ's work for us, the ram is needed here to complete it.)

In *Joseph* we have a picture of Christ's life and character. We can only trace the outline, leaving the details. We see him beloved of his father, sold by his brothers at the price of a slave, taking upon him the form of a servant, resisting temptation, condemned, bound, exalted to be a prince and a saviour, giving the bread of life to the world. In Gen. l. 20, and Acts

ii. 23, we have almost parallel passages showing the great salvation in both cases to be the combined result of human wickedness and Divine purpose.

In *Judah* we have a picture of the *Surety* and Substitute (Gen. xliii. 9, xliv. 32-34).

Coming to other types, we see in Gen. iii. 18 the curse pronounced upon sin, of which *the thorns* were the emblem. This very emblem our Saviour bore upon His brow when He was made a curse for us.

In *Abel's offering* we see the Lamb of God (Gen. iv. 4). We see the same in the various instances in Genesis of *God's Covenant* with man, it was always founded upon sacrifice (Gen. viii. 20, ix. 11-17, xv. 9-18). Jesus is the Surety and the Sacrifice of the better Covenant, of which all these Covenants were the type (Heb. vii. 22). Again, through the Book of Genesis we have repeatedly the record of *an altar*, pointing forward to the One Sacrifice (Gen. viii. 20, xii. 8, xxvi. 25, xxxv. 1, 3, 7). And there, right away at the beginning of God's Book, in Gen. ix. 4, we are told the meaning of *the blood*. "The blood thereof, *which is the life thereof*." Modern science has revealed the vital importance of the blood, but God told it to us from the very beginning. And in the Bible, wherever we read of blood, it is almost always of blood shed; therefore if the blood is the *life*, blood *shed* is *death*, the death of Christ for us as our Sacrifice.

In the *Ark* we see the Salvation God has provided for us in Christ. "*A Man* shall be as an hiding place from the wind, and a covert from the tempest" (Isa. xxxii. 2).

Gen. vi. 5, 7. God saw that the wickedness of man was great in the earth, . . . and the Lord said, I will destroy man whom I have created from the face of the earth.

2 Pet. iii. 6. Whereby the world that then was being overflowed with water, perished.

2 Pet. iii. 7, 11. But the heavens and the earth which are now, by the same word, are kept in store, reserved unto fire against the day of judgment and perdition of ungodly men. . . . Seeing then that all these things shall be dissolved, what manner of persons ought ye to be in all holy conversation and godliness ?

Gen. vi. The Ark was God's plan, it had to be made according to His measure.

Rom. iii. 24, 25. "The redemption" that is in Christ Jesus is also God's plan ; for the next verse says, "Whom *God* hath set forth to be a propitiation through faith in His blood."

**The Ark** was a place of safety.

Heb. vi. 18. That we might have a strong consolation who have fled for refuge, to lay hold of the hope set before us.

| | |
|---|---|
| The Ark bore the storm of judgment. | Ps. lxix. 2. I am come into deep waters where the floods overflow Me. |
| | Ps. xlii. 7. All Thy waves and Thy billows are gone over Me. |
| The Ark had to be entered by the Door. | John x. 9. Jesus said, I am the Door, by Me if any man enter in he shall be saved. |

We have a picture of the Church, the Bride of Christ, *in the Story of Rebekah* (Gen. xxiv.), who was willing to forget her own people and her father's house to go to be the bride of Isaac.

In *Jacob's ladder*—bridging the gulf from earth to heaven —we have a picture of the Cross, which has for ever bridged that gulf for us.

Furthermore, we have in Genesis appearances of Jehovah Himself in human form, under the name of the *Angel of Jehovah.* Surely this is none other than Christ Himself, God manifest in the flesh, who said, "Before Abraham was, I AM." In Genesis xvi. 7-14, He appeared to Hagar saying, "I will multiply thy seed exceedingly." This is language suited only to Jehovah Himself. "And she called the name of Jehovah that spake unto her : Thou God seest me," or as the Jews more correctly render the clause, "Thou art God, visible to me." In chapter xviii. Jehovah appeared to Abraham in the plains of Mamre. Abraham lifted up his eyes and saw three men, he provided food for them which they ate. Verse 22 and chapter xix. 1 show that two of these heavenly visitors ("angels") went toward Sodom, but Abraham stood yet before the third, Jehovah. In Genesis xxii. 11, 15, 16 we find the same Angel of Jehovah calling to Abraham from heaven and saying, "By Myself have I sworn, saith Jehovah," showing again that the names *Jehovah* and *Angel of Jehovah* are used interchangeably. In Genesis xxxi. 11, 13 this same Angel (called this time the Angel of God) speaking to Jacob, says, "I am the God of Bethel." In Genesis xxxii. we have an account of the man who wrestled with Jacob till the breaking of the day. He changed Jacob's name to Israel, a prince of God, "for thou hast striven with God and with man, and hast prevailed. . . . And Jacob called the name of the place Peniel—the Face of God—for I have seen God face to face and my life is preserved."

Surely this is none other than the Son of God, who is the effulgence of the Father's glory, and the express image of His substance (Heb. i. 3, R.V.).

## 2. EXODUS

Exodus is the Book of Redemption. The chosen people are in hopeless bondage in the land of Egypt, having no power to deliver themselves. But God says : "I have *seen* the affliction of My people, I have *heard their cry*, I *know* their sorrows, I *am come down to deliver them* out of the hand of the Egyptians, and to bring them up unto a good land" (Exod. iii. 7, 8). It is a beautiful picture of the soul redeemed from the bondage of Egypt into the glorious liberty of the children of God. God is revealed to us as the Deliverer and Leader of His people, a God near at hand, dwelling among them, concerned with the affairs of their daily life.

His commission to Moses opens with the glorious vision of the Angel of Jehovah appearing in the *Burning Bush.* A common little thorn bush of the desert, ablaze with God! What a picture of the Incarnation. God manifesting Himself in a visible tangible form (1 John i. 1). When Moses asks His Name He says, "I AM THAT I AM; say unto the children of Israel, I AM hath sent me unto you" (Exod. iii. 14). Where do we find that Name again ? Jesus said : "*I am* the Bread of Life; *I am* the Light of the World; *I am* the Door; *I am* the Good Shepherd; *I am* the Resurrection and the Life; *I am* the Way, the Truth, and the Life; *I am* the True Vine." Again, in response to the words, "When Messias cometh, that is Christ," He said, "*I am* He." And once He applies that name to Himself in all its simple majesty : "Verily, verily, I say unto you, Before Abraham was, I AM." It was *then* that the Jews "took up stones to cast at Him." Why ? The answer comes out in the accusation of the Jews to Pilate, "We have a law, and by our law He ought to die, because He made Himself the Son of God."

In the PASSOVER LAMB we have a picture of the Redemption that is in Christ Jesus. With many of the types we feel that we may not have interpreted them rightly, but with some we can have no doubt, for God has told us the meaning. It is so in this case, and in most of the types of Exodus. "*Christ our Passover* is sacrificed for us : therefore let us keep the feast" (1 Cor. v. 7, 8).

Exod. xii. 6. It was a *slain* lamb —not a living one—that availed the Israelites in the hour of judgment.

1 Cor. ii. 2. I determined not to know anything among you save Jesus, and *Him crucified.*

Ver. 5. The lamb was to be without blemish.

1 Pet. i. 18, 19. Ye were . . . redeemed . . . with the precious blood of Christ, as of a lamb without blemish and without spot.

Ver. 7. Its blood was to be shed and applied to the door-posts.

Ver. 46. No bone of it was to be broken.

John xix. 36. That the Scripture might be fulfilled, A bone of Him shall not be broken.

Ver. 3 and 20. In *every* home that night there was one dead, either the first-born or the lamb in the stead of the first-born.

Rom. vi. 23. The wages of sin is death.

Rom. v. 8. While we were yet sinners Christ died for us.

Ver. 2. The Israelites were to reckon their life as a nation from the day of the Passover. "It shall be the first month of the year to you."

John iii. 7. Ye must be born again.

Gal. iv. 3-6. We were in bondage. . . . But God sent forth His Son . . . to redeem them that were under the law, that we might receive the adoption of sons.

Chap. xiii. 2. All the first-born— those who had been redeemed by the blood of the lamb—were to be sanctified (i.e. *set apart*) unto the Lord.

1 Cor. vi. 19, 20. Ye are not your own : ye are bought with a price : therefore glorify God in your body, and in your spirit, which are God's.

The word *pasach*, translated "pass over," in Exod. xii. 13, 23 and 27 is used in three other passages of Scripture, namely, 2 Sam. iv. 4, translated "became lame"; 1 Kings xviii. 21, "halt," ver. 26, "leaped"; and Isaiah xxxi. 5, "As birds flying, so will the Lord of Hosts protect Jerusalem ; He will protect and deliver it. He will *pass over* and preserve it." How does a mother-bird—the word is in the feminine—protect her nest ? Not by passing over it in the sense of passing it by, but fluttering over it, spreading her wings in protection. Thus Jehovah Himself preserved His people on that awful night when the Destroyer was abroad in the land of Egypt. It was by the Lord's command that the Destroyer executed His judgment upon Egypt. "All the first-born in the land of Egypt shall die." Being in Egypt, Israel came under Egypt's doom. But Jehovah Himself stood on guard, as it were, at every blood-sprinkled door. He became their Saviour. Nothing short of this is the meaning of the Passover.[1]

The first-born in Egypt were saved from death by the lamb slain in their stead. God's word to them was: "When I see the blood I will pass over you." The blood of the lamb made them *safe*, their trust in God's promise made them *sure*. In the same way we may have *salvation* through Jesus, the Lamb of God, slain in our stead, and *assurance* through believing God's

[1] From *For Us Men*, chap. ii. Sir Robert Anderson, K.C.B. LL.D.

record that He "hath given to us eternal life, and this life is in His Son" (1 John v. 10-13).

THE LIVING BREAD AND LIVING WATER. Next we have a double picture of Christ as the *Living Bread* and the source of the *Living Water*, and again we are left in no uncertainty as to the application of the types. When Israel murmured, the Lord said to Moses, "Behold, I will rain bread from heaven for you" (Exod. xvi. 4). The Lord applied this type to Himself and said, "I am that Bread of Life. Your fathers did eat manna in the wilderness, and are dead. . . . I am the Living Bread which came down from heaven: if any man eat of this Bread, he shall live for ever: and the Bread that I will give is My flesh, which I will give for the life of the world" (John vi. 48-51). How beautifully this follows on from the teaching about the Passover, which Jesus also applied to Himself when He was eating the Passover Feast with His disciples. He took the bread, which was a recognised part of that feast, and gave thanks and brake it, saying, "Take, eat; this is My body. And He took the cup, and gave thanks, and gave it to them, saying, Drink ye all of it; for this is My blood of the new testament, which is shed for many for the remission of sins" (Matt. xxvi. 26-28). When He spoke to His disciples about eating His flesh and drinking His blood, they murmured and said, "This is an hard saying." And Jesus said, "Doth this offend you? What and if ye shall see the Son of Man ascend up where He was before? It is the Spirit that quickeneth; the flesh profiteth nothing" (John vi. 60-63). We see clearly by these words that it is a personal, spiritual appropriation of Christ in His death which avails, and nothing outward. We also see the vital necessity of this appropriation: "Except ye eat the flesh of the Son of Man and drink His blood, ye have no life in you." We must each for ourselves know the blood which has been shed applied to our souls spiritually for the remission of our sins, and daily—as the Israelites gathered the manna—we must know what it is to feed upon the Bread of Life.

Then in the history of Israel there immediately follows *The Smitten Rock.* "Thou shalt smite the rock, and there shall come water out of it, that the people may drink" (xvii. 6). "They drank of that spiritual Rock that followed them: and *that Rock was Christ*" (1 Cor. x. 4). "Whosoever drinketh of the water that I shall give him shall never thirst; but the water that I shall give him shall be in him a well of water springing up into everlasting life" (John iv. 13, 14).

THE LAW. Moses was a type of Christ, as specially seen in two points. (1) In delivering the whole people from an awful bondage. The bondage of sin from which Christ delivers us is far more terrible than the bondage of Egypt. (2) In the giving of a new law. How much greater that law is Christ Himself shows in the Sermon on the Mount—a law which touches the springs of character and conduct rather than the outcome, a law which He has summed up for us, first in two commandments, and finally in one word—*Love !*

THE TABERNACLE. With the Tabernacle again, and its services, we are not left in doubt as to the true meaning. In the Epistle to the Hebrews we are distinctly told that it was "a copy and shadow of the heavenly things" (Heb. viii. 5, R.V.). It was the outward sign of God's presence in the midst of the camp of Israel—God's tent in the midst of their tents—the meeting-place between God and man. As such it was a true picture of the Incarnation. "The Word became flesh, and tabernacled among us, and we beheld His glory" (John i. 14, R.V., margin). "The Tabernacle of God is with men" (Rev. xxi. 3). As a whole it was a type of Christ, and every part of it shows forth something of His glory (Ps. xxix. 9, margin). Every detail of its design was given to Moses by God in the mount. "As Moses was admonished of God when he made the Tabernacle : for, See, saith He, that thou make *all* things according to the pattern shown thee in the mount" (Heb. viii. 5). And over fifty times it is recorded of Moses, "As the Lord commanded Moses, so did he." What have we each seen in the Tabernacle ? How did it appear viewed from without ? A long, black, unattractive tent of badgers' skins. But when we come inside, we find ourselves surrounded by shining gold : looking up to the curtained roof, we see the wings of the cherubim woven in blue and purple and scarlet and fine twined linen. All the beauty within is revealed by the light of the golden candlestick. So it is with Christ Himself. The natural man, beholding Him, sees no beauty that he should desire Him. But to those who know the Lord Jesus Christ, His beauty satisfies their souls.

The Tabernacle was protected by a court of pure white linen, held up by sixty pillars, and entered by a curtain of coloured material, called the Gate. The walls of the Tabernacle were made of boards of shittim wood overlaid with gold, resting in massive silver sockets sunk into the sand. These sockets were made from the *redemption-money* paid by every Israelite, thus the whole fabric rested upon a foundation of redemption (1 Pet. i. 18, 19). The entrance was protected by a curtain called the Door, and the two parts of the Tabernacle itself—the Holy Place and the most Holy—were divided by another curtain— the Veil. Spread over the solid framework of the Tabernacle were four sets of curtains, which formed its only roof, and hung down over the sides, covering it completely.

Now, draw a straight line from the centre of the Gate to the Mercy-Seat. You go through the Altar, through the Laver, through the Door; you pass the Table of Shewbread on your right hand, and the Golden Lampstand on your left; through the Altar of Incense, through the Veil, to the Ark, covered by the Mercy-Seat, in the Holy of Holies. This is the true Pilgrim's Progress from the camp outside to the immediate presence of God (C. L. Maynard).

The Court was entered by the Gate (John x. 9). This was a curtain. A curtain is the very easiest means of entrance; it is not like a wooden door at which you have to knock, you can lift it silently. At the time no one need know of the transaction which takes place silently between the soul and its Saviour. It may be like Nicodemus, coming by night. But when the curtain is dropped again you are completely inside, not half in and half out as in a doorway—but completely shut off by a sharp dividing line. Inside that Gate you are completely surrounded by the spotless white curtains of the Court. "Complete in Him"; "made the righteousness of God in Him." Here you are immediately confronted by the brazen *Altar of Burnt Offering.* "One Sacrifice for sins for ever" (Heb. x. 12). Then the *Laver.* Cleansing as the result of Atonement (Zech. xiii. 1). Thus far, every Israelite might enter. Have we come thus far? Have we entered by the Gate, and accepted the Sacrifice, and known the Cleansing?

Only the Priests might enter the Tabernacle itself. If we have proved the power of the Cross, Christ calls us to be priests, set apart for His Service. We may enter still farther. The Holy Place is entered by the Door. This again is Christ Himself. He is the means of entrance into every fresh position of blessing. Every spiritual blessing comes with a fresh view of Christ and what He can be to us. He is the one entrance as well for the first step as for the last. The Gate, the Door, the Veil, they were all of the same materials and colours, and the same number of square cubits (20 by 5 or 10 by 10)—though the Gate was stretched out wide as if to emphasise the breadth of the universal proclamation, "Whosoever will may come."

In the Holy Place were two great gifts—Food and Light "I am the Bread of Life"; "I am the Light of the World.' Then the Golden Altar of Incense (Heb. vii. 25); Christ's continual Intercession by which alone our prayers can ascend to God.

So far, and no farther, the Priests might enter. Into the Holy of Holies only one man, only one day in the year, might enter, and that not without blood. "But Christ being come an High Priest of good things to come . . . by His own blood . . . has entered into heaven itself, now to appear in the presence of God for us," as we read in Heb. ix., and also has opened up for us a way of access by His blood into the Holiest, into the very presence of God here and now, as we read in Heb. x.

*The Veil.* Heb. x. 20, "Through the veil, that is to say His flesh." The veil was rent in twain from the top to the bottom at the moment of His death (Matt. xxvii. 51). "From the top to the bottom," the way of access opened by God Himself. *The Ark,* containing the unbroken Law. Here again we see Christ, who alone kept it completely. The Ark was covered by the Mercy - Seat, or, as it should be translated, the *Propitiatory Covering.* The word in Heb. ix. 5 and Rom. iii. 24, 25 is the same. The *Propitiation*—Christ. This is the meeting-place between God and man (Exod. xxv. 22). Above it rested the Shekinah-glory, the symbol of God's presence. It arose from the mercy-seat, a pillar of fire by night and cloud by day, spreading out over the whole camp as a protection, and guiding the children of Israel on their march.


THE GREAT HIGH PRIEST. In Aaron we have a picture of our Great High Priest. His garments were all typical. The three ornaments of his dress, which were engraved with a signet, teach a very precious lesson. The onyx stones on his shoulder and the breastplate on his heart were engraved with the names of the children of Israel, that he might bear them before the Lord continually. The plate of the mitre on his forehead was engraved with "holiness to the Lord" to bear the iniquity of their holy things "that *they* might be accepted before the Lord." On his *shoulders,* on his *forehead,* and on his *heart.* What do we see here but the *perfect strength* and *perfect wisdom* and *perfect love* of our High Priest put forth on our behalf? The Good Shepherd lays the lost sheep "on His shoulder." Christ is "made unto us Wisdom." , "Greater love hath no man than this, that a man lay down his life for his friends."

Many of us see the uselessness of an outward priesthood,—
of any man to come between us and God.   But are we equally
clear in valuing the inner Reality ?   Do we feel our utter need
of the Lord Jesus as our Great High Priest, and recognise that
we cannot draw nigh to God except through His one availing
sacrifice ?

Aaron, the type, fell short, for he was a sinful man.   Jesus
Christ is a perfect High Priest.   As man He was tempted in all
points like as we are, yet without sin.   He is able to sympathise
and to succour because He has been through it all.   He is able
*to understand our need to the uttermost* because He was perfect man.
He is able *to meet our need to the uttermost* because He is perfect
God.   He was able to bear the whole world's sin in His Atonement on the Cross.   He is able to bear the whole world's need
in intercession upon the Throne.

### 3. LEVITICUS

The Book of Genesis shows man's ruin and failure.   Exodus
pictures the great redemption and salvation which God has
provided.   Leviticus follows naturally and is mainly occupied
with the way of access to God in worship and communion.   It
is a book for a redeemed people.   Its teaching in the light of
the New Testament is for those who have realised their lost
condition, and have accepted the redemption that is in Christ
Jesus and are seeking to draw near into the presence of God.
It shows the holiness of God and the utter impossibility of
access except on the ground of atonement.

Such is the main lesson of Leviticus, and it is impressed
upon us over and over again in a variety of ways.   We come
face to face with the great question of sacrifice for sin.   The
stress laid upon sacrifice is no doubt intended to give man a
shock with regard to sin.   This book stands out for all time
as God's estimate of sin.   If we have not studied it at all—if
it looks to us merely like a catalogue of sins and a complicated
repetition of blood-shedding, from which we turn away almost
repelled—even so it conveys the lesson though it be but an
elementary one.   By it God has pointed out for all people in
all ages His holiness and the impossibility for sinful man to
draw near unless his sins have been put away.   It is as a
great lighthouse erected over against the rock of sin.

Ruskin tells us that his mother compelled him, when a
youth, to read right through the Bible, even the difficult
chapters of Leviticus ; these especially held him in the greatest

restraint and most influenced his life. Finney says : "Sin is the most expensive thing in the universe, pardoned or unforgiven—pardoned, its cost falls on the atoning sacrifice ; unforgiven, it must for ever rest upon the impenitent soul." Dr. H. G. Guinness says : "To understand the seriousness of sin, we must fathom three oceans—the ocean of human suffering, the ocean of the sufferings of the Lord Jesus Christ, the ocean of future suffering which awaits impenitent sinners."

"Now if anything is certain about sin it is this, it destroys the capacity by which alone its estimate can be rightly made. We must judge it from the standpoint of unshaken moral righteousness, from unsullied purity, and that exactly is what we have lost. If 'all have sinned,' then there is no scale, no measure, because we have all had our faculties disorganised, our senses dulled, and the true vision is denied us. . . . Secondly—Christ's challenge comes, 'Which of you convinceth Me of sin ?' Here is One that claims to have that essential requisite, a sinless judgment. . . . What is His estimate ? Nothing is more surprising perhaps than the awful warning He gives on the subject. Cut off hand and foot, pluck out the eye, etc.—and then the Cross and passion. And when it comes to action He does not flinch. He sees God is able to take no easier or shorter method. He who sees all justifies the view of sin that is taken by the Cross. Thirdly—those who draw nearest to the Lord in this world have the same estimate. Contrition, penitence, bitter tears of the saints, are simply unintelligible to the soul not in the same position ; the nearer they draw the more they increase in the severity of their judgment" (Canon Scott Holland).

Further, wherever God's Spirit is working mightily in the earth to-day, in bringing men to Himself, one of the inevitable results is a deep conviction of sin. Every account we read, alike of revivals in modern times and of revivals in the past, speaks clearly on this point.

What we have in type in Leviticus we have in reality in the Cross of Christ. The Cross was indeed an exhibition of God's love, the love of God the Father and of God the Son "who through the Eternal Spirit offered Himself " (Heb. ix. 14). But it was more than this, it was God's estimate of sin. "The Cross of Christ stands as God's estimate of what sin really is, something so deep and dreadful that it costs *that*." It was more even than this, it was the atoning sacrifice by which that sin could for ever be put away. It was because it was *necessary* that it satisfies. Though our intellect can never fathom the mystery of the atonement, our heart and conscience confess its power. "*Having made peace through the blood of His Cross*" (Col. i. 20)—what comfort these words have brought to troubled souls all down the ages. Those who know most of what it is to suffer under the Holy Spirit's conviction for sin know best how to value the Cross of Christ.

THE OFFERINGS. The first seven chapters of Leviticus are occupied with the description of the five kinds of offerings. It needs a great variety of types to convey any idea of the perfect completeness of Christ's sacrifice. The first point which requires our notice is this :—in each offering there are at least three distinct objects presented to us : there is the offering, the priest, and the offerer. A definite knowledge of the import of each of these is absolutely requisite if we would understand the offerings. Christ is the *offering*, "The offering of the body of Jesus Christ once for all" (Heb. x. 10). Christ is the *priest*, "We have a great High Priest, Jesus the Son of God" (Heb. vi. 14). Christ is the *offerer*, "Who gave Himself for us that He might redeem us from all iniquity" (Titus ii. 14).

The offerings are divided into two main classes—those offered as a sweet savour, of which the Burnt offering stands out most prominently ; and those offered as an expiation for sin, of which the Sin offering is the chief. The Burnt offering was a sweet savour offering for acceptance ; it was completely burnt upon the brazen altar in the court of the Tabernacle. It was a *whole* Burnt offering—nothing kept back. In it we see Christ's perfect life of obedience to His Father's will, Christ appearing for us, not as our Sin-Bearer, but as offering to God something which is most precious to Him, a life of unreserved surrender, the whole heart and mind and will, without blemish, wholly given to God without reserve. "He hath given Himself an offering and a sacrifice to God for a sweet smelling savour" (Eph. v. 2). It conveys the joy of sacrifice. "I delight to do Thy will, O My God."

In the Burnt offering, the surrender of life to God represents the fulfilment of man's duty to God. In the Meat offering— which was the adjunct of the Burnt offering—the gift of fine flour and oil represents the fulfilment of man's duty to his neighbour. Jesus as Man fulfilled both of these in His perfect human life on earth. In the fine flour, bruised, ground to powder, offered by fire, we see the bruising of Jesus day by day from those to whom He was ministering, for whom He daily gave Himself when He endured "such contradiction of sinners."

The Sin offering differed from the Burnt offering. It was offered distinctly in atonement for sin. The fat was consumed on the brazen altar to show that it was accepted, but all the rest was burnt without the camp to show the exceeding sinfulness of sin. The Lord Jesus became this Sin offering for us. "Now once in the end of the world hath He appeared to put away sin by the sacrifice of Himself" (Heb. ix. 26). We cannot conceive the anguish of that contact with sin to the sinless soul of our Redeemer, the hiding of God's Face when He was "made sin for us" (2 Cor. v. 21).

THE HIGH PRIEST. In the consecration of Aaron as High Priest, and in his priestly office and work throughout this book, we have a picture of our Great High Priest, and in the consecration of his sons and of the Levites we have a picture of the priesthood of all true believers in Jesus. We have a striking illustration of the truth that access to God must rest upon the blood of atonement in the account of Nadab and Abihu. Because they offered "strange fire" in their censers the fire of the Lord consumed them. The censers of the priests were to be lighted from the altar of burnt sacrifice (see Lev. xvi. 12 and Num. xvi. 46), only with this fire might they approach the Lord. In like manner it is on the ground of Christ's atonement that our prayers can arise to God as acceptable incense.

LAWS FOR DAILY LIFE. Many of the chapters of Leviticus are occupied with laws for the daily life of God's people. They show how great is God's concern for the well-being of His people in body and soul. "Ye shall be holy, for I the Lord your God am holy," is thrice repeated in this book. The words *clean, purify, holiness* occur constantly. No detail of daily life, whether it be in food, or clothing, or person, in family or national life, in agriculture or merchandise, is too small to be regulated by the will of God. "Whether therefore ye eat or drink, or whatsoever ye do, do all to the glory of God" (1 Cor. x. 31). "Having therefore these promises, dearly beloved, let us cleanse ourselves from all filthiness of the flesh and spirit, perfecting holiness in the fear of God" (2 Cor. vii. 1).

THE LEPER. In the type of the leper (chaps. xiii. and xiv.) we have the truth that sin excludes us from communion with

God. We read: "If the leprosy cover all the skin of him that hath the plague from his head even to his foot wheresoever the priest looketh . . . he shall pronounce him clean that hath the plague." Here we have the first condition for cleansing—the acknowledgment of need. Till we take the position of sinners there is no forgiveness for us. When the Publican cried "God be propitiated for me, *the sinner,*" he went down to his house justified.

For the cleansing of the leper the priest went to him outside the camp and carried out all the instructions of the law before the leper was fit to re-enter the camp. So Christ came all the way to us in our lost condition, and has cleansed us by His blood, and brought us nigh. The priest took two sparrows, and killing one he dipped the living bird and the cedar wood and scarlet and hyssop in its blood, and sprinkled the blood upon the leper and let the living bird loose. The two birds proclaim the double truth that Jesus Christ was "delivered for our offences and raised again for our justification." The upward flight of the living bird was the token that the leper was clean. How merciful God's provision is, the sparrows were within reach of the poorest. The simplest act of faith in a crucified Saviour procures the blessing of justification.

But the leper was not to rest content with ceremonial cleansing. Before he took his place within the camp he was to wash himself with water. The justified sinner is to separate himself from all known sin. Then the leper was to bring all the offerings of the law—still regulated in their value according to his circumstances, "Such as he is able to get." His head and hand and foot were to be sprinkled with the blood of the Trespass offering and then anointed with oil. For our sanctification as well as for our justification we need the precious blood of Christ, and then the anointing oil of the Spirit upon the blood.

THE DAY OF ATONEMENT. The deepest thought of the Book of Leviticus centres round the *Great Day of Atonement* (chap. xvi.). It was a day of humiliation. The sense of sin was to be deepened to its utmost intensity in the national mind. It occurred but once a year. "Christ was once offered to bear the sins of many" (Heb. ix. 28). There is no repetition of His sacrificial work. In the whole year of time there is but one atonement day. With his golden censer of incense and the blood of the bullock for a Sin offering the High Priest entered into the Holy of Holies and made atonement for himself and his family.

The Sin offering for the people consisted of two goats. The one on which the lot of the Lord fell was slain as a Sin offering, and the High Priest entered into the Holy of Holies, sprinkling its blood on the mercy-seat and before the mercy-seat seven times, as he had done with the blood of the bullock. The other goat was the scape-goat, and over its head Aaron confessed the sins of all the people, putting them upon the head of the goat, and sent it away by the hand of a "fit man" into the wilderness. "Behold the Lamb of God which taketh away the sin of the world"; "The Lord hath laid on Him the iniquity of us all" (John i. 29 ; Isa. liii. 6).

The two goats formed but one offering, two were needed to complete the type. The slain goat showed that perfect atonement had been made to God for sin, the living goat showed that perfect pardon was granted to the people. The sacrifice was altogether out of proportion to the need—two goats for the sins of the congregation for a whole year. It was *purposely* out of proportion to show that the whole system was temporary and typical. "For it is not possible that the blood of bulls and of goats should take away sins" (Heb. x. 4). No animal, no mere man, no angel could atone for sin. "God manifest in the flesh" alone could do it, and therefore He became Man that He might be able to suffer and die for sin in man's place. "God was in Christ reconciling the world unto Himself" (2 Cor. v. 19). It was as perfect God and perfect Man that He atoned for our sins (see Heb. i. 2, 3 and ii. 14).

The flesh of the Sin offering on the Day of Atonement was burnt outside the camp. "Wherefore Jesus also, that He might sanctify the people with His own blood, suffered without the gate. Let us go forth therefore unto Him without the camp, bearing His reproach" (Heb. xiii. 12, 13). The same Cross which has brought us inside the veil with regard to our access to God, has cast us outside the camp as regards our relation to the world.

The Book of Leviticus repeats even more emphatically than Genesis the meaning of the blood, it is the *life*. "The life of the flesh is in the blood : and I have given it to you upon the altar to make an atonement for your souls : for it is the blood that maketh atonement by reason of the life. . . . For as to the life of all flesh, the blood thereof is all one with the life thereof" (Lev. xvii. 11, 14, R.V.).

We need to realise the vital importance of the blood of Christ : it is the foundation of everything. A study of the following verses will show us something of the power of the blood :—

### THE PRECIOUS BLOOD OF CHRIST

1 Pet. i. 18, 19

*The Meaning of the Blood*, Lev. xvii. 11, 14.
*Redemption through the Blood*, 1 Pet. i. 18, 19.
*Forgiveness through the Blood*, Eph. i. 7.
*Justification through the Blood*, Rom. v. 9.
*Peace through the Blood*, Col. i. 20.
*Cleansing through the Blood*, 1 John i. 7.
*Loosing from Sin through the Blood*, Rev. i. 5, R.V.
*Sanctification through the Blood*, Heb. xiii. 12.
*Access through the Blood*, Heb. x. 19.
*Victory through the Blood*, Rev. xii. 11.
*Glory everlasting through the Blood*, Rev. vii. 14, 15.

### 4. NUMBERS

In the Book of Numbers we have the record of the failure of the Children of Israel to go in and possess the land. God's object in bringing them out of Egypt was to bring them into the Land of Promise (see Exod. iii. 8). In His tender care over them He did not lead them by the shortest route, "through the way of the land of the Philistines"; for God said, "Lest peradventure the people repent when they see war, and they return to Egypt" (Exod. xiii. 17). But when, having led them through the wilderness of Sinai to receive the law, He brought them to Kadesh Barnea, His time had come for them to go up and possess the land. But in Numbers xiii. and xiv. we have the record of their failure to enter in through unbelief of God's power and disobedience to His commands. Then began the long years of wandering in the wilderness, which were not part of God's plan for them, but the result of their disobedience.

What a picture this is of the life of many a child of God to-day. Redeemed out of the bondage of Satan, yet failing to enter into the fulness of the blessing of the Gospel of Christ. Do we not all know, either in the past or in the present, something of the wilderness life of failure and defeat? Yet even in their wandering the Lord did not forsake His people: He had compassion on them, He let them enjoy His provision and protection and guidance day by day.

PILGRIMAGE AND WARFARE. Numbers is the book of pilgrimage and warfare. In the early chapters we see God's complete arrangements for the journey. As we come to this fourth Book of Moses we find it again full of Christ. From almost every page there flashes forth some new beauty, if only we had space to consider it. We see the camp arranged in perfect order around the Tabernacle—a picture of Christ in the midst of His people.

THE CLOUD. We see the pillar of cloud and of fire resting on the Tabernacle over the Holy of Holies. It probably spread like a vast curtain over the whole encampment, by day a sheltering cloud from the sun, by night a column of fire to illuminate the whole encampment. The cloud regulated every movement of the Camp, its removal from the Tabernacle was the signal for the silver trumpets to sound the order to march. When the cloud rested the children of Israel rested, when it journeyed they journeyed, whether by day or by night, whether it abode two days or a month or a year. The cloud is a picture of the Lord's unfailing guidance. " He that followeth Me," Jesus said, " shall not walk in darkness, but shall have the light of life." We need to keep " looking unto Jesus," that we may not miss His leading.

THE SILVER TRUMPETS. Closely connected with the pillar of cloud was the sound of the silver trumpets. They were used as a signal for the journeying of the Camp, and for the calling of the assembly whether to war or in the day of gladness to keep the feasts. The sound of the silver trumpets could be heard to the utmost limits of the Camp, and when Israel heard the sound they were to obey. We need to listen to the voice of the Lord, whose words are as tried silver. " My sheep hear My voice, and I know them, and they follow Me."

The standards under which the tribes were ranged, the Ark of the Covenant going before, the substitution of the tribe of Levi in the place of the first-born to do the work of the Sanctuary, and their consecration, the coverings of the various vessels during the march, the law of the Nazarite,—all teach fresh lessons to those who have ears to hear.

The book opens with all the congregation appearing before Moses and Aaron to declare their pedigree (Num. i. 18). How many of us can do this spiritually? How many can respond to the test given by Peter: "Sanctify in your hearts Christ as Lord: being ready always to give answer to every man that asketh you a reason concerning the hope that is in you, yet with meekness and fear " (1 Pet. iii. 15, R.V.)? Let us pause and ask ourselves whether we have indeed known the great change which Christ taught us is absolutely necessary when He said, *"Ye must be born again."*

GOD'S LAWS FOR GIVING. The seventh chapter gives us the offerings of the princes. They each brought exactly the same, but instead of massing the offerings together each is repeated in detail. God delights to honour the gifts of His children. How carefully Jesus noted the gift of the poor widow who cast into the treasury all that she had, and He said that the anointing of His feet by Mary of Bethany should be told wheresoever the Gospel should be preached.

Surely in the light of Calvary our gifts should exceed the measure of the Israelites under the Law—but how far we come short! There are some who say, "The Jew gave a tithe, I give much more than a tenth of my income"; and yet if they really examined their accounts they would be surprised to find that they are giving less than a tenth. Besides, the tithe was only a small part of what the Israelites gave. The various other tributes probably brought the amount up to about one-fourth or even one-third of their incomes, and yet it was only *after* this had been paid that their free-will offerings began! If we as Christians were to give in like proportion, there would be no lack for our Foreign Missions or any other part of the work the Lord has entrusted to our care.

AARON. The Book of Numbers gives us fresh teaching about Aaron. When the Lord sent a plague among the people for their sin we see Aaron—the High Priest whom they had so recently maligned—with his censer of incense running quickly and standing between the dead and the living to make an atonement for the people (Num. xvi. 46-50). What a picture of One greater than Aaron—One whom they blasphemed and crucified—who having made a full atonement for the sin of the people, ever liveth to make intercession for us.

Immediately after this incident the representatives of each tribe were commanded by God to bring a rod and lay it up in the Tabernacle before the testimony, and the rod of the man whom God should choose, should blossom. The rods lay there through dark hours of the night, and in the morning the rod of Aaron alone brought forth buds, and bloomed flowers, and yielded almonds. The rulers' rods were symbols of mere natural power—Aaron's of spiritual power. Natural power may reform and civilise, the power of Jesus alone can change men's hearts and impart new life (chap. xvii.).[1]

The Priests and Levites were to have no inheritance in the land because the Lord Himself was their inheritance (chap. xviii.). They were no losers. All the best of the oil and all the best of the wine and of the wheat was theirs "by reason of the anointing." As we are the Lord's priests He Himself is likewise the portion of our inheritance, and we have all in Him and can say, "Yea, I have a goodly heritage."

The time came when Aaron must die (chap. xx.). Moses was commanded to take him up into Mount Hor and strip him of his priestly robes and put them upon Eleazar his son, and Aaron died there in the top of the Mount. Here the type falls short of the glorious Anti-type. "There ariseth another Priest who is made, not after the law of a carnal commandment, but after the power of an endless life" (Heb. vii. 15, 16). It was on account of the disobedience of Moses and Aaron in striking the rock that they were not allowed to enter the Promised Land. On the first occasion, in Exodus, the Rock was a type of our smitten Saviour. But only once was He smitten for us. On the second occasion they were commanded to *speak* to the Rock. The Hebrew word for rock in Exod. xvii. 6 signifies a low-lying bed-rock. The word in Numbers xx. 8 is a high and exalted rock.

THE WATER OF SEPARATION. In the nineteenth chapter of Numbers we have the account of the Water of Separation— God's beautiful provision for cleansing from the defilement contracted in daily life. The cleansing efficacy of the water consisted in the ashes of a red heifer, offered as a Sin offering, with which it was mingled. Thus it was a cleansing based upon atonement, a foreshadowing of the blood of Jesus Christ, which cleanseth (i.e. *goes on cleansing*) from all sin those who are walking in the light (1 John i. 7).

It was perhaps to this water that our Lord referred in His conversation with Nicodemus when He said, "Except a man be born of water, and of the Spirit, he cannot enter into the kingdom of God." Nicodemus's failure to understand the type called forth our Lord's reproof, "Art thou the teacher of Israel, and understandest not these things?" (John iii. 10, R.V.). How much of the teaching of the New Testament we Christians miss through our neglect of the study of the types.[2]

[1] See Urquhart's *New Biblical Guide*, vol. v. p. 217.
[2] *For Us Men*, p. 134. Sir Robert Anderson, K.C.B., LL.D.

Teaching by Types. Our Lord Himself used types in His teaching, as for instance the manna, the living water, and the light of the world. But the types of the latter part of the New Testament are mainly relating to His death and resurrection, and in the very nature of the case it is not likely that He should dwell much on these before the events took place. Indeed it is remarkable that He should have given us such clear types of His death as the water of separation in the passage now before us, and the one which closely follows of the brazen serpent, and finally in the Passover Supper, when He said, "This is My blood of the new testament, which is shed for many for the remission of sins." Of His resurrection He gave us the type of the Temple, which if destroyed He would raise again in three days, and of Jonah, "So shall the Son of Man be three days and three nights in the heart of the earth." His conversation with the two disciples on the way to Emmaus, after His resurrection, must have been full of the application of the types, and no doubt it formed the basis of this line of teaching by the New Testament writers.

The Brazen Serpent. In compassing the Land of Edom the Children of Israel came to the sandy stretch of land at the head of the Gulf of Akabah. Much discouraged because of the rugged way by which they had come, the people murmured bitterly against God. He sent fiery serpents among them (chap. xxi.). The thing near at hand was used to accomplish His will. Travellers tell us that this very district is still infested by poisonous snakes of large size, marked with fiery red spots and wavy stripes. When the people confessed their iniquity and entreated Moses to intercede, he was commanded by God to make a serpent of brass and to raise it upon a pole. "And it shall come to pass that every one that is bitten, when he looketh upon it—shall live."

Our Lord claimed this as a picture of the salvation which men were to find in Himself. It is plain that the power to save did not lie in the serpent of brass. Wherein did it lie? There is no answer to that question till we come to the Cross of Calvary. The Son of Man, who is also the Son of God, hung there for us. "There is life for a look at the Crucified One." The poison of sin is working death in man's experience to-day. The divinely appointed remedy was a serpent of brass lifted up, harmless, but bearing the image of that which wrought the woe. "For He hath made Him to be sin for us, who knew no sin : that we might be made the righteousness of God in Him" (2 Cor. v. 21).[1]

There is a point in the application which Christ made of this type to Himself which is often missed. It is this,—that regeneration, or the new birth, takes place as the result of faith in Christ's sacrifice for sin. The bitten Israelites were not merely *healed* by looking at the serpent, they received *life*. Bitten—they were as good as dead, death was already working in them ; and every one that looked—*lived*. So when Nicodemus was puzzling over Christ's words, "Ye must be born again," and querying how the new birth could take place, Jesus pointed him straight away to Calvary, and said, "*As* Moses lifted up the serpent in the wilderness, *even so* must the Son of Man be lifted up, that whosoever believeth on Him should not perish but have everlasting life" (John iii. 14, 15).

Every bitten Israelite that looked—*lived* ; every child of Adam—"dead in trespasses and sins"—who has looked to Jesus as his Saviour has received eternal life from Him. All down the ages, ever since the Gospel was first preached, there has been a multitude whom no man can number, of young and old, ignorant and learned, rich and poor, people of every clime and in every imaginable outward condition of life, who have all had this one circumstance, and many of them this one circumstance *only*, in common—that when they came as lost sinners to the Saviour the same result happened with each, they became "new creatures" in Christ Jesus.

PROPHECY. We close the study of the Book of Numbers with a reference to Balaam's prophecy. On the back of an Egyptian papyrus, now in the British Museum, is a note of a certain despatch sent in the third year of Menephtah by the Egyptian Government to the King of Tyre. The royal missive was entrusted to the care of Baal—, the son of Zippor. This old papyrus is a witness to the truth of the record before us. The name of the King of Moab, who dreaded the invasion of the Israelites, was in use in the district within a century or two of the time of which the Pentateuch speaks. The city of Pethor too, "by the river," has been identified as situated on the Euphrates.

The prophet from a far-off land who was called in to curse God's people could only bless them, and the words of his blessing form a prophecy which has remarkably described the Israelites ever since they were first uttered, over thirty

[1] See Urquhart's *New Biblical Guide*, vol. v. p. 226.

centuries ago. "*The people shall dwell alone, and shall not be reckoned among the nations*"—words which, among others, no doubt, Frederick the Great's chaplain had in his mind when the Emperor asked him to prove the truth of the Bible in one word, and he answered, "Israel." In these books of Moses many points were prophesied about Israel and the land which are true to-day. For instance :—

They should be driven out of their land (Lev. xxvi. 33),
 And their land should be desolate (Lev. xxvi. 33),
They should be scattered among the nations (Deut. iv. 27),
 And yet remain a separate people (Num. xxiii. 9).

The same has never been true of any other nation except Israel. Whenever we see a Jew, we have a witness to the truth of God's Word.

Again, Balaam looked down the ages and saw One who was to come. "I shall see Him, but not now ; I shall behold Him, but not nigh : there shall come a *Star* out of Jacob, and a Sceptre shall rise out of Israel . . . out of Jacob shall come He that shall have dominion" (Num. xxiv. 17, 19). "Where is He that is born King of the Jews ? for we have seen His Star in the east, and are come to worship Him" (Matt. ii. 2). Where is the King ? We have seen His Star. The Star and the Sceptre were foretold nearly 1500 years before they came to pass. And the wise men saw the star, shining in all its splendour, above all other stars in brightness, over the lowly spot where lay the Babe of Bethlehem. "I, Jesus, have sent Mine Angel to testify unto you these things in the Churches. I am the root and offspring of David, and the bright and morning Star" (Rev. xxii. 16).

## 5. DEUTERONOMY

MOSES. Of all the Old Testament characters Moses stands out as the greatest. He was prophet, legislator, historian, ruler, all in one; and in the world's history probably no name has ever stirred the heart of a nation as his has done. It is impossible to overrate the place Moses held in the Jewish nation. He laid the foundation of its literature, and no appeal has ever been made by the Jews from his laws, or from any word that he wrote. His Hebrew parentage and training, his learning in all the wisdom of the Egyptians, and his forty years of communion with God in the solitude of Horeb, combined to fit him both for his leadership of the people and his authorship of the books.

Nowhere does the character of Moses shine out with greater dignity than in the Book of Deuteronomy. We see him at the close of his long life with still unabated vigour, about to take leave of the people with whom he had borne patiently through all their provocations, with the one exception for which he was not allowed to enter the Promised Land. Yet there seems no bitterness against them in his heart for this ; instead, he rejoices in the prospect of their entrance into the land under the leadership of Joshua.

The word of the Lord came to Moses, "Get thee up into Mount Nebo, behold the land, and die " (Deut. xxxii. 49, 50), and with meekness he showed the same obedience in death as he had in life. "So Moses, the servant of the Lord, died there in the land of Moab, according to the word of the Lord " (xxxiv. 5). But a greater honour awaited God's faithful servant than even the honour of leading the chosen people into the land. A day came when he stood with Elijah beside the Saviour on the Mount of Transfiguration, within the Land, and communed with his Lord on that greatest of all themes—His decease which He should accomplish at Jerusalem.

In the Book of Deuteronomy Moses rehearses the wanderings and disobedience of the children of Israel, and recapitulates the Law. That Law had been given nearly forty years before at Mount Sinai, with special reference to the condition of the Israelites in the wilderness ; now it was given with special reference to their life in the land they were about to enter. In both instances the moral law was given greater prominence than the ceremonial law. The Ten Commandments were uttered by the voice of God to all the people from Mount Sinai. The instructions about the making of the Tabernacle were given to Moses, alone, in the Mount. Practical laws of purity and holiness in daily life were interwoven with the laws of the sacrifices as related in Leviticus and Numbers. In Deuteronomy, Moses addresses all the people, and the main point that he insists on is the duty of obedience.

OBEDIENCE. Obedience is the Key-note of the Book of Deuteronomy, as it is also the key-stone of blessing in the Christian life. This book brings out more than any other in the Bible the blessedness of obedience. "Oh that there were such an heart in them, that they would fear Me, and keep all My commandments always, that it might be well with them and with their children for ever!" (v. 29). This is God's yearning over His people amidst the terrors of Sinai. Again and again they were told that these laws and this demand of obedience are "for our good always" (vi. 24, etc.).

Moreover it is made clear that this obedience is not in order to purchase the favour of God, but it is demanded because they already enjoy His favour. They are not called to purchase their redemption by obedience, but to obey because they are already a redeemed people. Again and again they are told that the Lord chose them because He loved them, that He has redeemed them out of bondage with a mighty hand, and that therefore they are an holy people unto the Lord, a special people unto Himself, and that for this reason they are called to keep His laws with all their hearts and to serve Him with joyfulness.

What a message this contains for us to-day! How many are still thinking that they have to earn God's salvation by their obedience, instead of seeing that they must first accept His salvation as a free gift in order to enable them to obey. It is summed up for us in Titus ii. 13, 14: "Our Saviour Jesus Christ, who gave Himself for us, that He might redeem us from all iniquity, and purify unto Himself a peculiar people, zealous of good works." He redeems us from the bondage of sin and the world in order that He may bring us into a good land, a land of victory and of joy in the Lord. But how many of His redeemed children come short of this good land, through want of faith and want of obedience. "They entered not in because of unbelief."

If any such read these lines, God's message to you is one of hope. The Law cannot lead you into the Promised Land. Moses' act of sin was the actual thing which kept him out of it, but the fact that he could not bring the children of Israel in was *typical*. Moses was the embodiment of the Law, and the Law cannot bring us into the fulness of the blessing of the Gospel of Christ. That is reserved for Jesus, our Joshua, as we shall see in our next study.

SURRENDER. But as the first step towards this blessing we, who know that we have been redeemed by the precious blood of Christ, can yield ourselves absolutely to Him in an act of unreserved surrender, as Israel did in the plains of Moab. Only let it be as definite as Israel's surrender was, so that the Lord may be able to say to you as Moses said to Israel: "Thou hast avouched the Lord *this day* to be thy God, and to walk in His

ways, and to keep His statutes, and His commandments, and
His judgments, and to hearken to His voice : and the Lord hath
avouched thee *this day* to be His peculiar people, as He hath
promised thee, and that thou shouldest keep all His commandments . . . and that thou mayest be an holy people unto the
Lord thy God, as He hath spoken " (Deut. xxvi. 16-19).

The same act of surrender is pictured in the servant who
might have gone out free in the year of release, but chose rather
to serve his master for ever. Blessed are they who have thus
let the Lord bore their ear in token of surrender (Deut. xv.
12-17; Exod. xxi. 5, 6).

THE PROMISED MESSIAH. But the climax of the Book of
Deuteronomy is when the majesty of the coming Messiah bursts
upon the vision of Moses. " The Lord thy God will raise up unto
thee a Prophet from the midst of thee, of thy brethren, like unto
me ; unto Him ye shall hearken " (chap. xviii. 15). Here, again,
the necessity for the Incarnation is brought out, as it is in each
part of Christ's threefold office as Prophet, Priest, and King.
Even under the old dispensation each office had to be filled by a
brother—one of the same flesh and blood.

*As Priest* God said : " Take Aaron, *thy brother*, that he may
minister unto Me in the Priest's office " (Exod. xxviii. 1). And
of Jesus we read : " In all things it behoved Him to be made
like unto His brethren, that He might be a merciful and faithful
High Priest " (Heb. ii. 17).

*As King.* If, when they came into the land, they should
desire a king, the command was : " One from among *thy brethren*
shalt thou set king over thee ; thou mayest not set a stranger
over thee, which is not thy brother " (Deut. xvii. 15).

" *A Prophet* from the midst of thee, *of thy brethren*, like unto
me."

In many points, even in his outward history, Moses was a
type of Christ. In his deliverance from violent death in infancy,
in his years of silent training, in his willingness to leave the
palace of a king to deliver his people from bondage, in his meekness, in his faithfulness, in his finishing the work God gave him
to do (Exod. xl. 33 ; John xvii. 4, xix. 30). In his work as a
mediator between God and the people, in his communion with
God face to face ; in all these he was a picture of the *Son of
Man* who was to come.

But in how much the picture fell short ! " Moses was faithful in all God's house as a servant, but Christ as a Son over His
own house." Moses sinned under provocation. Christ was with-

out sin. Moses was not able to bear the people alone. Christ
has borne the burden of our sins in His own body on the tree, and
invites us to cast the burden of all our cares upon Himself. Moses
was not able to die for the sin of the people. "Christ died for
our sins, according to the Scriptures." Moses was not able to
bring the People into the Promised Land ; Christ is able to bring
us in, and to give us an inheritance among all them that are
sanctified by faith that is in Him. In all these things He is
" declared to be the *Son of God* with power " (Rom. i. 4).

Moses' word was law, because it was God's word. He said,
expressly : " Ye shall not add unto the word which I command
you, neither shall ye diminish ought from it, that ye may keep
the commandments of the Lord your God which I command
you " (Deut. iv. 2). If the word of God spoken by the servant
was authoritative, how can we question the word spoken by the
Son ? " I will raise them up a Prophet from among their
brethren like unto thee, and will put My words in His mouth ;
and He shall speak unto them all that I command Him. And
it shall come to pass, that whosoever will not hearken unto My
words, which He shall speak in My name, I will require it of
him " (Deut. xviii. 18, 19).

How exactly was this fulfilled by Christ ! He said : " He
that rejecteth Me, and receiveth not My words, hath One that
judgeth him : the word that I have spoken, the same shall judge
him in the last day. For I have not spoken of Myself ; but the
Father which sent Me, He gave me a commandment, what I should
say, and what I should speak " (John xii. 48-50). Our only
safe course is to believe Christ's words absolutely. The problem
before us to-day is not one simply of the authorship of certain
books of the Bible, but of the reliability of Christ's testimony.
We have already seen (page 2) that each time our Lord
answered the tempter it was with the words, " It is written,"
and the passages quoted were from the Book of Deuteronomy.

This book is quoted, altogether, ninety times in the New
Testament. In Deuteronomy xxxi. 9, 24-25, the authorship is
distinctly ascribed to Moses, and the whole book gives us to
understand that it was written by him. Moses bore witness
to Christ and said, " Unto Him shall ye hearken." Christ bore
witness to Moses, and said, " If ye had believed Moses ye would
have believed Me, for *he wrote of Me.*"

Peter had been an eye-witness of the glory of Jesus in the
Mount when He talked with Moses and Elias. He had heard
God's voice from heaven proclaim, " This is My beloved Son,
hear Him." Well might Peter call the attention of the people

to the fact that He whom they had denied and put to death was the Prophet whom Moses had foretold, and whom they were to hear in all things (Acts iv.).   Well might the woman of Samaria say, "Come, see a Man which told me all things that ever I did : is not this the Christ ? "   Well may we too recognise Him and cry with Thomas, " My Lord and my God."

We see Christ again in Deuteronomy vi. 4, 5.   The Rev. John Wilkinson, in his book *Israel My Glory*, points out that in the original Hebrew this passage brings out the truth of the Trinity.   "Hear, O Israel : the Lord our God is one Lord." The literal translation of this would be : " The Lord our Gods the Lord is One."   Here the name of God is mentioned three times, and the word translated *one* (*echad*) expresses a *compound* unity, as in the expressions " *one* cluster of grapes," " the con- gregation was assembled as *one* man," and again, " All the men of Israel were gathered against the city, knit together as *one* man."   The Hebrew word *one* (*yacheed*), which expresses *absolute* unity, is never once used to express the unity of the Godhead. The next verse calls upon man's threefold nature to love his triune God.   " Thou shalt love the Lord thy God with all thine heart, and with all thy soul, and with all thy might."

There are other passages in Deuteronomy which speak to us of our Saviour.   The Ten Commandments are repeated (v. 6), and this reminds us of His summing them up into two—" to love God with all our heart, and our neighbour as ourselves."

CITIES OF REFUGE.   The Cities of Refuge (iv. 41 and xix. 1), and the Rock (xxxiv. 4, 15, 18, 20), remind us of Christ Jesus our Hiding-place.   God commanded that when His people came into possession of the land six Cities of Refuge should be appointed, to which he who slew a man, through ignorance or unintentionally, might flee from the avenger of blood who, according to Eastern custom, would pursue and kill the man-slayer.   These six cities were so placed, three on each side of Jordan, that some one of them was always within reach.   So has the Saviour placed Himself within the reach of all, even of such as are in the utmost peril of vengeance.   High roads led to each city, and their gates were always open.   Jewish tradition declares that there were posts at the cross roads with " Refuge !   Refuge ! " upon them, pointing out the way, and that runners, learned in the law of God, were stationed to guide the fugitives to the place of safety. If this were so, they would be a fit picture of the evangelist, whose feet should be swift to lead souls to Christ, and whose lips should be filled with God's truth.

In the City of Refuge the manslayer was tried by the judges, and if found innocent he was allowed to dwell in the city as a refugee until the death of the High Priest. But with the accession of a new High Priest he might return to his own city and take possession of his property. This was God's provision to maintain His land guiltless of innocent blood.

But while we have in the Cities of Refuge a picture of the sinner finding salvation in Christ, there is a yet fuller application in reference to God's people Israel. Israel was the manslayer who shed innocent blood on Calvary. As we read in Acts: "Ye killed the Prince of Life. . . . Now, brethren, I wot that *through ignorance* ye did it, as did also your rulers." Israel has been a fugitive ever since, his possession is forfeited and to all appearances lost. But the High Priest dwells within the veil in the heavenly sanctuary, and one day He will come forth, the Heavenly Priest, and Israel shall receive forgiveness and be restored to his heritage.

The law concerning a man hanged upon a tree takes us to Calvary. The margin says: "He that is hanged *is the curse of God.*" "Christ hath redeemed us from the curse of the Law, being made a curse for us" (Gal. iii. 13). As we read the terrible curses of the Law in chapters xxvii. and xxviii., how it should deepen our gratitude to Him who bore the curse and fulfilled the Law for us.

THE URIM AND THUMMIM. "Of Levi He said, Let thy Thummim and thy Urim be with thy Holy One" (Deut. xxxiii. 8). These were placed in the breastplate of the High Priest, and he was to bear them before the Lord when he sought to know His will on solemn occasions. It is vain to speculate what these were; it is enough to know that the judgment of the Urim was always a true judgment (Num. xxvii. 21). In Hebrew the words mean "Light and Perfection." Our Lord Jesus Christ is *the true Light;* He has promised to give light to all who follow Him. He alone is *the Perfect One.* In Christ Jesus, our High Priest, are "hid all the treasures of wisdom and knowledge."

Moses was not able to bear the burden of the people, but we have seen that Christ is able. There are several verses in Deuteronomy which speak of the Lord's power to bear us. "The Lord thy God bare thee, as a man doth bear his son" (i. 31); "As an eagle beareth them on her wings (xxxii. 11); "The beloved of the Lord shall dwell in safety by Him; and the Lord shall cover him all the day long, and he shall dwell between His shoulders" (xxxiii. 12). These verses remind us of the Good Shepherd carrying the sheep; but those who come to God through Him, know what it is to hide as His little ones in the bosom of the Father. "The eternal God is thy refuge, and underneath are the everlasting arms" (xxxiii. 27). Therefore "As thy day so shall thy strength be."

# III. CHRIST IN THE HISTORICAL BOOKS

## 1. JOSHUA

WE now come to a new Leader and a new command to arise and go in to possess a new land. Moses was not able to bring the Children of Israel into the Land of Promise. Moses was the embodiment of the Law. The Law cannot bring us into the fulness of the blessing of the Gospel of Christ. That Jesus Christ alone can do, and through this book Joshua is a type of Him. The very name has the same meaning. Joshua means "Jehovah is Salvation." "And thou shalt call His name Jesus—Saviour; for He shall save His people from their sins."

God gave His people a threefold encouragement to go forward and possess the land :—

*First*—The Gift of the land. "Every place that the sole of your foot shall tread upon, that have I given unto you."

*Second*—The Command. "Arise and go. Have not I commanded thee?"

*Third*—The Promise of His presence. "As I was with Moses so will I be with thee."

And the Lord commanded them to observe to do according to all the law which Moses commanded, and to meditate therein day and night.

THE LAND. The entrance of the Children of Israel into the Land of Canaan is full of teaching for the Christian. It is true that in one sense it is a picture of the Better Country to which we look forward as our eternal Home. But in many respects it is far more truly a picture of our present inheritance in Christ Jesus, a good land we are called upon to enter here in this life.

It is a land of *Rest* from the wanderings of the wilderness life. A land with "great and goodly cities, which thou buildedst not, and houses full of all good things, which thou filledst not" (Deut. vi. 10, 11).

It is a land of *Plenty*. "A land of wheat, and barley, and

43

vines, and fig-trees, and pomegranates; a land of oil-olive and honey; a land wherein thou shalt eat bread without scarceness, thou shalt not lack anything in it; a land whose stones are iron, and out of whose hills thou mayest dig brass" (Deut. viii. 8, 9).

It is a land of *Living Water.* "A land of brooks of water, of fountains, and depths that spring out of valleys and hills" (Deut. viii. 7).

It is a land of *Promised Victory.* "There shall no man be able to stand before you" (Deut. xi. 25).

Surely this is a picture of our present inheritance in Christ Jesus; it is He who can give such rest to our souls that we are able to say, "We which have believed do enter into rest." He who did not spare His own Son has promised with Him to "freely give us all things." Christ has promised to give the Living Water, the Holy Spirit, to those who come to Him and drink. And He has promised continual victory to those who commit themselves to His leadership. A victorious life, full of the Holy Ghost and of power, is God's purpose for every Christian, and is experienced through continual abiding in Christ. He promises us—not absence of tribulation, but in Him peace; not freedom from temptation and conflict, but through Him victory; not immunity from toil, but in Him rest. "Let us therefore fear, lest, a promise being left us of entering into His rest, any of you should seem to come short of it" (Heb. iv. 1).

In the purpose of God, those who have been redeemed by the precious blood of Christ are already not only "accepted in the Beloved," but also "complete in Him"; but it is necessary for us by faith to enter into possession of what is already ours in Christ.

WARFARE. The Epistle to the Ephesians is the New Testament counterpart of the Book of Joshua. It tells of the Christian's inheritance in Christ, the good land, the "heavenly places," to which He has already raised up by His grace those who trust in Him. It is the epistle most full of deep spiritual experience, yet nowhere have we a fuller description of the armour the Christian needs. It is the highest kind of warfare, "against principalities, against powers, . . . against spiritual wickedness in heavenly places" (Eph. vi. 12, margin).

Israel's enemies are a type of ours. Egypt was a type of the world. In the Amalekites in the wilderness—those descendants of Esau who sold his birthright for a mess of pottage, a people near of kin to Israel—we have a picture of the flesh, or self. But in the Canaanites we have a picture of a still more deadly foe. From contemporary records as well as

from Scripture, these nations seem to have been the very personi-
fication of evil.   Highly civilised, versed in arts and full of intellectual culture, they were nevertheless hopelessly corrupt.   In
God's command to Israel to destroy them utterly (Deut. xx. 16-18)
we recognise at once His plan of dealing in judgment with
nations after having given them full time to repent (see Gen.
xv. 16), and we have also His care for the moral well-being
of His people.   "God has a right to choose, without being
questioned, the best method of chastening a guilty people,
whether by flood, fire, brimstone, earthquake, famine, pestilence,
or war.   Study carefully these 'Acts of God' in the Bible and
in our own time" (H. S. Richardson).

THE WILES OF THE DEVIL.   Israel's warfare with the Canaanites is a picture of our conflict with Satan.   "Put on the whole
armour of God, that ye may be able to stand against the wiles of
the Devil.   For we wrestle not against flesh and blood."   The
word "wrestle" implies a hand-to-hand conflict, and it is just
this that the Church is experiencing in our own time.   From
all lands to-day we hear the same testimony—those who know
most of the power of the Holy Spirit are experiencing most of
personal conflict with the Devil.   It would seem that he knows
that "his time is short," and that he is therefore putting forth
all his power, and they alone can overcome who have learnt the
threefold secret of Rev. xii. 11 :  "They overcame him (the
Devil) (1) by the blood of the Lamb, (2) by the word of their
testimony, (3) by not loving their lives unto the death," *i.e.*
taking their place on the Cross as crucified with Christ.

The verse before us speaks of "the wiles of the Devil."   He
comes not only as a roaring lion, but as a serpent, as an angel of
light, and the climax of his wiliness is the invention of the lie of
his non-existence.   He is willing to deny his own personality
even, if by so doing he can blind men and women to his power.

THE RED SEA AND JORDAN.   In "The Faith Chapter"—
Heb. xi.—there is a gap of forty years between the crossing of the
Red Sea and the taking of Jericho.   The interval is filled with
unbelief and disobedience, and even the act of faith—the Crossing
of Jordan—which brought the Children of Israel into the land is
omitted ; for had there been no wandering there had been no
Jordan : they would have marched straight up from Kadesh-
Barnea without having to cross the river.

The two crossings are coupled together in Psalm cxiv. 5 :
"What ailed thee, O thou sea, that thou fleddest ? thou Jordan,

that thou wast driven back?" There is a close connection between them. Going down into the bed of the sea and into the bed of the river alike signified death. Both show our participation in the death of Christ. The Red Sea crossing includes it all in God's purpose, though not always so in our experience. There are some Christians who, like Paul, enter into the deep meaning of Christ's death and receive the baptism of the Spirit almost immediately after their conversion. It was Israel's wandering that made the second crossing necessary.

And so it often is with Christians now. Through want of clear teaching, it may be, about God's purpose of blessing, or through personal unfaithfulness, how many wander in a wilderness experience for years after their conversion, and need some definite act like the crossing of Jordan to bring them into "the Lord's delightsome land" of peace and rest and victory? They have seen Christ crucified for them as the ground of their salvation, but they need to see themselves crucified with Christ. The history of the Israelites crossing Jordan makes this so beautifully simple that it cannot fail to be a help to any soul seeking to know the fuller meaning of Christ's death.

The channel of the river has several sets of banks, cut out by the stream in its varying fulness, and at this time it was overflowing all its banks. For a great multitude —including women and children and cattle—to have crossed it at such a time was an absolute impossibility. But as soon as the feet of the Priests, bearing the Ark of the Covenant, touched the brimming flood, the waters divided, and the priests stood firm on dry ground in the midst of Jordan until all the people were clean passed over. And Joshua set up twelve stones in the midst of Jordan, where the feet of the priests stood, and he commanded a man from each tribe to take a stone out of the midst of Jordan, twelve stones, and he set them up in Gilgal on the other side of Jordan as a memorial, " that all the people of the earth might know the hand of the Lord, that it is mighty; that ye might fear the Lord our God for ever" (Josh. iv. 24).

BURIED AND RISEN WITH CHRIST. The Ark was a type of Christ : He has gone down into death for us. " Therefore we are buried with Him by baptism into death : that like as Christ was raised up from the dead by the glory of the Father, even so we also should walk in newness of life." The twelve stones buried for ever under the waters of death show us our place as crucified with Christ. The twelve stones set up on the other side show us our place as risen with Him. " Likewise reckon ye also your·

selves to be dead indeed unto sin, but alive unto God through Jesus Christ our Lord" (Rom. vi. 11). God's word to us is: "Ye are dead, and your life is hid with Christ in God." To believe this is as great an impossibility as for Israel to cross Jordan; but as we take Him at His word, and reckon the self-life to be dead with Christ, He makes it true in our experience, and enables us to live the risen life in Christ Jesus.

This is only the beginning of a new life of victory, the acceptance of our position, as risen with Christ, which makes victory possible. It is what Paul meant when he said: "I am crucified with Christ: nevertheless I live; yet not I, but Christ liveth in me: and the life which I now live in the flesh I live by the faith of the Son of God, who loved me, and gave Himself for me" (Gal. ii. 20).

The next step for the Children of Israel was the renewing at Gilgal of the Covenant with God by the neglected rite of circumcision, separating themselves unto the Lord. God's separated people were then immediately called to keep the neglected Feast of the Passover. And they ate of the old corn of the land, the manna ceasing from that time. In the slain Lamb and the Bread of Life we have another picture of Christ.

THE CAPTAIN OF THE LORD'S HOST. Not only in type do we see Christ in the Book of Joshua. There came a day when the Lord Himself shone through in all His glory. "And it came to pass, when Joshua was by Jericho, that he lifted up his eyes and looked, and, behold, there stood a man over against him, with his sword drawn in his hand: and Joshua said, Art Thou for us, or for our adversaries? He queried whether his mysterious Guest had come as an ally or as an enemy; but the Lord said: "Nay, but as Captain of the Host of the Lord am I now come. And Joshua fell on his face to the earth, and did worship, and said unto Him, What saith my Lord unto His servant? And the Captain of the Lord's Host said unto Joshua, Loose thy shoe from off thy foot; for the place whereon thou standest is holy. And Joshua did so. . . . And the Lord said unto Joshua, See, I have given into thy hand Jericho."

The Burning Bush was a picture of the Incarnation, but how much more vivid was this foreshadowing in the form of a man. God says, "I have given Him for a Leader and Commander to the people." Ofttimes to-day some servant of the Lord is hard pressed with responsibility at the thought of some great undertaking, when if he would but lift up his eyes and look he would see One mighty to save, who has come to take entire control.

VICTORY. "By faith the walls of Jericho fell down." That is the simple record in the New Testament of the taking of the city. "The weapons of our warfare are not carnal, but mighty through God to the pulling down of strongholds." Those who are living in the Spirit have ceased to fight with carnal weapons; they have learned to wield the sword of the Spirit which is the Word of God, and quench the fiery darts of the wicked by the shield of faith. The saint wins his victories beforehand on his knees, and then stands still and sees the salvation of the Lord. "Shout; for the Lord hath given you the city." This book may also be compared to the Book of Acts, where, through the Spirit, Christ leads His Church to victory, and heathen strongholds yield to the preaching of the Gospel and to prayer.

"By faith Rahab perished not with them that believed not, when she had received the spies in peace." The token for her salvation was the scarlet cord with which she had let down the spies, tied in her window. It was like the token of the blood on the door-posts in the Passover. In former days in the Royal Navy every rope and cord was marked with a scarlet thread running right through its entire length, so that wherever you cut the rope you found the scarlet cord. The scarlet line of redemption through the precious blood of Christ runs through the Bible from Genesis to Revelation.

INDEPENDENT EVIDENCE. Each step in the record of the conquest of Canaan is the vivid story of an eye-witness, if only there were space to dwell upon all the details. The points of vantage, the configuration of the land, the fertility dependent on laborious cultivation, the picture given of a densely populated country, with walled and garrisoned cities and chariots of iron, of its occupation by various independent nations,—all is exactly the Canaan of Joshua's day as given in the contemporaneous records of the Egyptian hieroglyphics and the Tel-el-Amarna tablets, and therefore proves that the Book of Joshua is—as it claims to be (Deut. vi. 25)—a contemporary document and not of late date. "No mark of late date is discoverable in the names of the cities" (Col. Conder). Jerusalem is mentioned in this book, and it has been objected that this city was not called Jerusalem until the reign of David. "But letters were found at Tel-el-Amarna in Egypt, from the king of Jerusalem, which were written about the very time when Joshua was invading Canaan.  In these letters the name Jerusalem appears as it does in the Scripture" (Urquhart). These tablets also constantly refer to the *Habiri*, who have been identified with the Hebrews.  There are frequent appeals from all parts of Canaan to Egypt for help against this powerful foe.  One letter says, "The hostility of the Hebrews waxes mighty against the land, and against the gods"; proving their monotheism.

The victory at Jericho was followed by the defeat before Ai. The way to Ai led up a steep rocky defile, so it was natural that the spies who were sent to view the country said, "Let about two or three thousand men go up and smite Ai; make not all the people *to labour thither*, for they are but few."  The result of this attack was defeat and ignominious retreat.  The thought of God's honour was uppermost in Joshua's mind. "What wilt Thou do unto Thy great Name?  And the Lord said, Get thee up; wherefore liest thou thus upon thy face? *Israel hath sinned* . . . therefore they could not stand before their enemies."  All the spoil of Jericho was to be devoted to the Lord (chap. vi. 19; Deut. vii. 25, 26), but some one had taken of the "devoted thing" (R.V.).  Early in the morning all Israel had to appear before the Lord, tribe by tribe, and family by family, and man by man, till the guilt was brought home to Achan, and he confessed his sin.  "I have sinned . . . I saw . . . I coveted . . . I took . . . I hid."  And the stolen treasure was found, and judgment was executed on Achan and all his house.

The defeat before Ai was caused by hidden sin.  There is a very solemn lesson here—that sin always means defeat.  All may look right outwardly, but God is not deceived.  Absolute obedience is the condition of victory in the land.  "If ye then be risen with Christ, seek those things which are above, where Christ sitteth on the right hand of God."  After the sin of Achan had been judged the Lord said, "Fear not; take all the people of war with thee, and arise, go up to Ai."  After sin has been confessed and put away God gives victory.  We may have had some great victory, like Jericho, and then fail in some little Ai of daily life.  He will give victory in the very place where we have been shamefully defeated.  But we need all the power of God for every battle, and our position is one of absolute dependence on Him.

EBAL AND GERIZIM.  Next, we have the carrying out of God's command, through Moses, that the tribes should stand on Ebal and Gerizim, six on one mount and six on the other, and pronounce the blessings and the curses of the Law. It has been objected that people could not hear each other at such a distance; but the acoustic properties of the valley are remarkable, and Canon Tristram tested it on the spot, two of his party stationing themselves on opposite sides of the valley and reciting the Ten Commandments in turn with perfect ease. Ebal is to the north of the valley, Gerizim to the south. The priests standing with the Ark would no doubt be facing the east. The Ark did so wherever the Tabernacle was pitched. Thus Mount Ebal would be on the left hand northwards, Gerizim on the right hand southwards—the same position as regards blessing and cursing as in the parable of the Sheep and the Goats. In the Tabernacle the sacrifices were slain "on the north side of the altar before the Lord." The altar of sacrifice was likewise on Mount Ebal to the north, the atonement was made in the place over which the cloud of Divine wrath was resting. We cannot but see Divine plan in the perfect harmony of all these details.

Then follows the stratagem of the Gibeonites, who with their mouldy loaves and ragged garments led the Children of Israel to believe they had come from a far country, and therefore entered into a covenant with them. It was because Israel asked not counsel of the Lord, but took of their victuals, that they fell into the snare. Here again we are taught the need of absolute dependence upon the Lord in the life of faith. He is willing to guide us in every detail of our lives, but we must seek to know His will, and not judge by the sight of our eyes or lean upon our own understanding.

Having entered into league with the Gibeonites, Israel was bound to respond to their appeal for help when five other nations rose up against them. God overruled this circumstance to deliver the five kings into the hands of His people. As these nations worshipped the sun and moon, there was a special reason for the miracle which God wrought on that day in showing them His power in controlling the hosts of heaven. We do not know how that miracle was wrought, it is enough for us to believe that He who made the universe could control its action. The ancient annals of Greece, Egypt, and China each confirm the record of a certain "long day" such as God's Book tells us of.[1]

POSSESSION. The first half of Joshua is mainly occupied with the Key-note of *Victory*, the second half with the Key-note

[1] For authorities see *The Scripture of Truth*, by Sidney Collett, p. 287.

of *Possession*. Though "all things are ours" in Christ, it remains for us to take possession of them experimentally by faith. The promise was that every place that the sole of their foot should tread should be theirs. And in the thirteenth chapter of this book the Lord said unto Joshua, "There remaineth yet very much land to be possessed." There was a slackness on the part of Israel to possess the land which the Lord had given them (xviii. 3).

Then follows an account of the division of the land. The inheritance of the two-and-a-half tribes beyond Jordan, and the inheritance of Caleb. That old warrior claimed the mountain of the Anakims, with its cities great and fenced, which God had promised him forty years before. He said: "As my strength was then, even so is my strength now, for war . . . if so be that the Lord will be with me, then I shall be able to drive them out, as the Lord said." Caleb promised his daughter Achsah to whomsoever would take the city of Kirjath-sepher. Othniel his nephew took it and won the prize. Achsah said to her father, "Give me a blessing: for thou hast given me a South land; give me also springs of water. And he gave her the upper springs and the nether springs." Our Heavenly Father waits to bless us in like manner, and "to give the Holy Spirit to them that ask Him."

FAILURE. Next we read of the inheritance of Judah, and then of Ephraim and Manasseh. We read that the children of Manasseh could not drive out the Canaanites, but put them under tribute and let them dwell in the land (Josh. xvii. 12, 13 ; see also xiii. 13 and xv. 63). When we come to study the Book of Judges we shall see what trouble came through Israel not obeying God in driving out the Canaanites. The process of degeneration had begun even in the time of Joshua. Though the children of Joseph failed they were also ambitious, and came to Joshua with the plea that they were a great people and their lot was not enough for them. Then Joshua bade them go up into the wood country and take the land of the giants. But the children of Joseph feared to go because the inhabitants had chariots of iron. Joshua's answer was a wise one: he bade them prove their greatness by driving out the Canaanites, which they were well able to do "though they have iron chariots, and though they be strong."

Then we read of the Tabernacle being set up at Shiloh, and the congregation of Israel were assembled there, as the central place of sacrifice. Then the seven remaining tribes received their portion, and Joshua his own special portion, and the six Cities of Refuge were fixed. The Levites held their cities upon a different tenure from the other tribes, for the Lord Himself was the portion of their inheritance.

CONCLUSION. The book closes with Joshua's exhortation to the people. He reminds them that it is God who has fought for them. He exhorts them to keep all that is written in the Law of Moses, and to serve the Lord with all their heart. He invites them to choose this day whom they will serve, but adds his own resolution, " As for me and my house, we will serve the Lord." Joshua's last act was to write these words in the book of the Law of God, and to set up a great stone as a witness to the renewal of the Covenant. He died at the age of a hundred and ten years, leaving a character without blemish. After the account of his death we have the ominous words : " And Israel served the Lord all the days of Joshua, and all the days of the elders that outlived Joshua, and which had known all the works of the Lord, that He had done for Israel."

Our Joshua never dies. It is He who brings us into the good land, and it is only as we abide under His leadership that we shall possess it and overcome all our enemies.

## 2. JUDGES

We now come to one of the darkest periods in the history of God's people. "There is something startling in the swiftness with which the Israelites degenerated. Caleb's nephew, Othniel, was raised up for their deliverance " (Moorehead). This teaches the great lesson that no position of spiritual blessing is sufficient to ensure a life of holiness without a close walk of faith and obedience.

The book opens with a note of victory. Judah went up against the Canaanites and overcame them in various places. But even this record of victory has an exception—they "could not drive out the inhabitants of the valley, because they had chariots of iron." This surely was a want of faith ; for the promise by Joshua had been, "Thou shalt drive out the Canaanites, though they have iron chariots, and though they be strong " (Joshua xvii. 18).

We have in the words of one of the kings—Adoni-bezek— an incidental testimony to the justice of God's judgment upon the Canaanites ; even this heathen king acknowledged it. The remainder of the first chapter is a record of failure. We read of one tribe after another that "they did not wholly drive out the Canaanites, they would dwell in the land." "When Israel was strong, they put them under tribute, and did not utterly drive them out."

SUMMARY. Judges ii. 11-23 gives us a summary of the whole book. "The Children of Israel did evil in the sight of the Lord, and served Baal and Ashtaroth, and forsook the Lord God of their fathers. And the anger of the Lord was hot against Israel, and He delivered them into the hand of the spoilers, and sold them into the hands of their enemies round about. Nevertheless the Lord raised up judges, which delivered them out of the hand of their enemies; for it repented the Lord because of their groanings. And it came to pass, when the judge was dead, that they corrupted themselves more than their fathers, in following other gods to serve them, and ceased not from their own doings and from their stubborn way. And the Lord said that because they had broken His covenant, and failed to obey Him in driving out the Canaanites, that hence-forth He would cease to drive them out before them, and would leave them in the land to prove Israel, whether they would keep His way or not."

ISRAEL'S SEVENFOLD DECLENSION. In the history that follows (chap. iii. to xvi.) we have this record of failure and deliverance seven times repeated. Israel fell into idolatry, and God raised up some one of the surrounding nations to carry out His punishment. Israel repented under the chastening, and cried to the Lord, and the Lord sent a deliverer. God allowed the very sins His people indulged in to be their punishment. He allowed the Canaanites and other surrounding nations to oppress them and bring them into bondage. "He that committeth sin is the servant of sin." If we give quarter to any known sin, and allow it to dwell with us, it is likely to become our master.

Jabin, King of Canaan, and Sisera, his captain, "mightily oppressed the Children of Israel twenty years" (chap. iv. 2, 3). "Midian prevailed against Israel." They were so utterly broken under this oppression that they took refuge in the dens and caves of the mountains (chap. vi. 2). When they cried to the Lord, He did not at once send a deliverer, but sent a prophet to deepen their sense of conviction. "The anger of the Lord was hot against Israel, and He sold them into the hands of the Philistines, and into the hands of the children of

Ammon, and they vexed and oppressed the Children of Israel eighteen years" (chap. x. 7, 8). Again when they cried unto the Lord He reminded them that they had turned to serve other gods, and He said, "Go and cry unto the gods which ye have chosen, and let them deliver you in the time of your tribulation." This rebuke once more deepened the sense of sin, and humbled Israel to cry, "We have sinned: do Thou unto us whatsoever seemeth good to Thee; deliver us only, we pray Thee, this day. And they put away the strange gods from among them, and served the Lord: and His soul was grieved for the misery of Israel" (chap. x. 10-16).

A SAVIOUR. What a picture of man's continued sin and failure, and God's continued patience and grace! We read of seven distinct departures from God, and of seven distinct deliverances by the hands of Othniel, Ehud, Shamgar, Deborah and Barak, Gideon, Jephthah, Samson. In these deliverers or saviours of Israel we can see a foreshadowing of the Great Deliverer who was to come. The Lord's promise in Isaiah is: "He shall send them a Saviour and a Great One" (Isa. xix. 20). God had mercy upon man in his sin and hard bondage, and sent the Lord Jesus to be our Saviour.

*A Saviour.* Luke ii. 11: "Unto you is born . . . *a* Saviour, which is Christ the Lord."

*The Saviour.* John iv. 42: "This is indeed the Christ, *the* Saviour of the world."

*My Saviour.* Luke i. 47: "My spirit hath rejoiced in God *my* Saviour."

It is not enough to know Him as *a* Saviour, or even as *the* Saviour of the world. We need each one for ourselves to be able to say, "He is *my* Saviour."

DOWNWARD STEPS. Israel sinned in not driving out the Canaanites, but allowing them to dwell amongst them. Compromise instead of obedience. The next step was that they intermarried with them (iii. 6), and the next that they were drawn into their idolatries (ver. 7). The result was that all the land became corrupt. The Book of Judges contains the blackest picture of the condition of God's people. Chapters xvii. to xxi. do not follow the rest of the book in chronological order, but give us an illustration of the gross wickedness of the people during this period. In the Song of Deborah we have another glimpse of the lawless state of the country: "The highways were unoccupied, and the travellers walked through byways. The inhabitants of the villages ceased" (chap. v. 6, 7). Later in the book, four times the statement is repeated, "In those days there was no king in Israel"; and twice the words, "Every man did that which was right in his own eyes." The Key-note of the book is *Anarchy*.

GOD'S LAW. All this terrible state of things came about through disregard of God's Law. That they possessed the Law as given by Moses is evident from frequent allusions to things contained in those books. God Himself referred to them in a manner that implied that they were known to Israel. He reminded them of the conditions of His Covenant (chap. ii. 1-3). He told Gideon to order the fearful and faint-hearted to depart from the army of Israel, according to the command in Deut. xx. 8. It was a wise provision, for faint-heartedness was terribly infectious, then as now. He told the parents of Samson to carry out in his case the vow of the Nazarite. The reference to the offerings, the trumpet by which Ehud summoned the Children of Israel to battle, and the trumpets of Gideon,— Jotham's reference to the oil of consecration, and the oil of the lamp, and to the wine of the drink-offering,—are all evidences that Israel possessed the Law of God as given by Moses, and that in times of revival that Law was honoured. But the tendency during the whole period was to disregard the Law, and the result was idolatry, wickedness, and utter lawlessness in the land. This is always the result where the people of any country are deprived of God's Word. It accounts for the gross darkness of the Middle Ages, and of those countries in which Roman Catholicism is shutting up the Bible to-day.

THE BIBLE OUR CHART. In these days we sometimes hear it said that if we have Christ we do not need the Bible. But what do we know of Christ apart from the revelation God has given us in the Bible? Other writings establish the bare fact of His historical identity, but they reveal nothing of His person, teaching, and work. If we had not learned of Christ through the written Word, what should we know of Him revealed within? That the conscience and reason of man are not a sufficient guide we have abundant evidence in the Book of Judges, for we are twice told, *not* that every man violated his conscience, but that every man did that which was *right* in his own eyes; and we see to what awful excesses of sin such a course led.

The writer of the book was in all probability Samuel, for

it is written after the establishment of the monarchy (ch. xix. 1, xxi. 25), and prior to the capture of Jerusalem (ch. i. 21), which was captured by David (2 Sam. v. 6-8), and therefore written during the reign of Saul; and the most probable author during that reign was Samuel. In the words "In those days there was no king in Israel," the writer was referring to the outward kingship, with its reign of law and order.

But the words have a deeper meaning for us: they give us a picture of the lawless state of the heart where the Lord Jesus is not reigning as King, and when we are doing what is right in our own eyes. The Bible contains the laws of the Kingdom, and where this is disregarded, disloyalty is sure to follow. "Wherewithal shall a young man cleanse his way? By taking heed thereto according to Thy Word." The neglect of God's Law accounted for the uncleanness of the land in the days of the Judges. "Whatsoever any man says or does which is contrary to the Scriptures, though under profession of the immediate guidance of the Spirit, must be reckoned and accounted a mere delusion. . . . There can be no appeal from them to any other authority whatsoever" (*Book of Discipline of the Society of Friends*).

For the safe guiding of our barque on the sea of life we need to have on board the Chart of the Scriptures, the Compass of the Holy Spirit, and the Captain of our Salvation, the Lord Jesus Christ. It would be folly for the seaman to reason: "I do not need a chart because I have a compass," or *vice versa*. As invariably as the compass points to the North, so does the Holy Spirit glorify Christ. The Scriptures also testify of Him. These two witnesses agree together, for the Holy Spirit takes of the things of Christ, as revealed in the written Word, and makes them life to our souls.

IDOLATRY. The sin of Israel was idolatry. Idolatry is the worship of a false god, a god of man's imagination and creation. When people imagine a god for themselves which is not the God revealed to us in the Bible—or a Christ who is not the Christ of the New Testament, but of their own imagination—they are guilty of idolatry.

Again, an idol is anything which usurps God's place in our hearts. It may be in itself a sinful thing, or a questionable thing, or an innocent thing, or even a sacred thing, but if it takes the *first* place in our hearts it is an idol. When Gideon made the ephod of gold, very likely his first intention was good. He had refused to be made a king, saying, "The Lord shall rule over you "; and by the ephod, which was evidently not intended to be worn, he may have wished to indicate that the victory was from the Lord. But Israel worshipped it, and it became a snare to Gideon and his house.

The desire to be rich was probably one of the reasons why the Israelites made friends with the Canaanites, and God tells us that "covetousness is idolatry."

GOD'S WITNESSES. Even in this dark period, as in every age, God did not leave Himself without a witness, and we may see in the deliverers whom He raised up, not only a general type of Christ, but much teaching for the Christian, showing us that through the power of Christ we also may become witnesses for Him. Judges is a practical commentary on the truth that "God has chosen the weak things of the world to confound the things that are mighty . . . that no flesh should glory in His presence."

*Deborah.* God used Ehud, the left-handed man, to deliver Israel, and Shamgar with his ox-goad. He used a woman to inspire the failing courage of Barak, and to censure the men who did not help in the hour of need. Deborah said to Barak: "Hath not the Lord God of Israel commanded, Go and draw to Mount Tabor, and I will deliver Sisera into thine hand?" (chap. iv. 6, 7). When Barak made his obedience conditioned by her going with him, she told him that the journey would not be to his honour, "for the Lord shall sell Sisera into the hand of a woman."

*Gideon.* The account of Gideon is specially encouraging. He was a man conscious of his own nothingness. "Oh, my Lord, wherewith shall I save Israel? behold, my family is poor in Manasseh, and I am the least in my father's house." "I have sent thee, I will be with thee. Go in this thy might, thou mighty man of valour." The "Lord looked upon him" and encouraged his faith by various signs of His mighty power. That look and that command made a hero of Gideon. He began at home, and at the bidding of the Lord threw down the altar of Baal in his father's house. "His natural shrinking came out in the fact that he did it by night; his God-given courage in the fact that, though shrinking, he got it done."

Then the Lord had to reduce Gideon's army so that it might be clearly seen that the victory was His; and with the three hundred eager men, who would not stop to quench their thirst by a long draught, He delivered Israel.

Every detail of Gideon's life is full of teaching. He was

allowed to overhear the dream of one of the enemy, and the enemy's own interpretation of it, to strengthen his faith. A cake of barley bread falls into the camp of Midian and overthrows a tent. Barley bread was the poorest of all foods, thus carrying out the lesson that it was man's weakness cast upon God's almightiness that gained the victory that day.

*Samson.* In Samson we have the greatest contrast to Gideon. He was too weak to rule himself. A man of splendid possibilities, who squandered them through tampering with the world and breaking his Nazarite vow. When the Christian tries to make the best of both worlds, his testimony for God loses its power.

THE ANGEL OF THE COVENANT. In this dark period of the Judges, the Angel of the Covenant, the Son of God Himself, appeared three times to His people. In the first instance (Judges ii. 1) He came up from Gilgal—where He had appeared to Joshua as Captain of the Lord's Host—to Bochim, and there He spoke as none but Jehovah could speak, reminding them of His power and goodness, and reproving them for their disobedience. At His words "the Children of Israel lifted up their voices and wept. And they sacrificed there unto the Lord."

About a hundred and fifty years later, He appeared to Gideon to call him to his great work of delivering Israel. Gideon brought a burnt offering and a meat offering, and the Angel of the Lord commanded him to lay them upon the rock— the rock itself a type of Christ as well as the offering—and He touched the offering with His staff, and fire rose up out of the rock and consumed the offering as a token that it was accepted.

About thirty years after this event the Lord appeared in like manner to the wife of Manoah, and again to her and her husband together. Manoah likewise brought a burnt offering and a meat offering, and offered it upon a rock, "and the Angel of the Lord did wondrously"; for the fire went up to heaven from off the altar, and the Angel of the Lord ascended in the flame of the altar. When Manoah had asked His name, the Angel of the Lord said, "Why askest thou after My Name, seeing it is secret?" or "Wonderful," R.V.; the very Name given later on through Isaiah to the Messiah that was to be born. Thus we are brought face to face with the Babe of Bethlehem in the Person of the Angel of Jehovah.

### 3. Ruth

Out from the darkness we have been studying, "in the days when the judges ruled," there shines forth the sweet story of Ruth. In the midst of war and lawlessness and idolatry there were still those, both rich and poor, who feared God and lived virtuous and simple lives to His praise.

The family of Elimelech were evidently among these, though they took the backsliding step of going down into the Land of Moab for succour. The name Elimelech means "My God is King"; and if his faith had been strong enough to depend upon his King, much trouble might have been spared. "There was a famine in the land," even in Bethlehem, "the House of Bread," and they went to Moab in search of food, and, as often happens, "they continued there." Trouble upon trouble followed this downward step. Elimelech died, his two sons married Moabitish women, and then the sons died also.

After about ten years Naomi heard "that the Lord had visited His people in giving them bread," and she arose to return to her own land. And then follows the memorable choice of Ruth to cleave unto her mother-in-law in following her to an unknown land, and to what seemed a life of privation and toil. When Naomi saw that she was "stedfastly minded" to go with her, she left speaking to her.

There must have been something very beautiful in Naomi's life thus to win the devotion and love of Ruth, first to herself and then to her God; and it has been well to keep her name, which means "Pleasant," instead of substituting her suggestion of Mara.

They arrived at Bethlehem at the beginning of barley harvest, and proved it to be the House of Bread once more. The calm poetry of those harvest fields of Bethlehem, the eager gleaner among the maidens, the reapers, the lord of the harvest, —have all lived in golden sunshine in our imagination from our childhood.

"Her hap was to light on a part of the field belonging to Boaz." Behind our lives there is a guiding Hand which causes even insignificant things to be fraught with mighty issues.

In Boaz, the kinsman of Elimelech, "a mighty man of wealth," we have another beautiful character. The simplicity of his life, the courtesy of his behaviour to all with whom he came in contact, his generosity, his regard for the Law, above all his constant reference of every event to God, stand out in striking contrast against the dark background of his time.

THE GOËL. It was to this man that Naomi bade Ruth appeal to fulfil the kinsman's part. The word used is Goël, the redeemer, the one whose right and duty it was according to the Law to redeem the inheritance of the deceased relative, and marry his widow (see Lev. xxv. 25-31, 47-55; Deut. xxv. 5-10). As these rights belonged to the next of kin, Goël came to mean the nearest kinsman. To fulfil these rights was his bounden duty according to the Law of God, and it was the fulfilment of this law that Naomi sought to bring about.

The reply of Boaz was: "It is true that I am a goël (redeemer), but there is also a goël nearer of kin than I. If he will redeem thee, well, let him redeem thee; but if he is not willing to redeem thee, then will I redeem thee, as the Lord liveth."

Then follows the quiet rest of faith on the part of Naomi and her daughter, and the dignified carrying out of the Law in the presence of the elders in the gate of the city, on the part of Boaz.

The next of kin was willing to purchase the land that belonged to Naomi, but he was not willing for what that purchase involved, to take Ruth to be his wife, lest he should mar his own inheritance. This left Boaz free to carry out his gracious purpose; and he bought the inheritance of Elimelech, and he purchased Ruth the Moabitess to be his wife, "to raise up the name of the dead upon his inheritance."

THE ROYAL LINE. "So Boaz took Ruth, and she became his wife; and she bare a son. And Naomi took the child, and laid it in her bosom, and became nurse unto it. And the women her neighbours gave it a name, saying, There is a son born to Naomi; and they called his name Obed: he is the father of Jesse, the father of David."

This story shows how unselfish devotion to God and to duty is rewarded. Orpah, who was content with the outward profession of affection, and returned to her people and her gods, forfeited her place in Israel. The kinsman who failed to fulfil his duty because of his own interests has not even his name recorded in God's Book. Ruth, on the other hand, who gave up all to follow Naomi and Naomi's God, and Boaz, who unhesitatingly fulfilled the kinsman's part, have their names handed down to all time as worthy of praise, and as the ancestors, not only of David, but of David's greater Son.

THE PRECISION OF PROPHECY. One of the most marvellous

proofs of the truth of the Bible is to be found in the prophecies concerning the birth of the Messiah. Every time prophecy predicts a fresh branch of the family as being the chosen one, a fresh risk, humanly speaking, is involved. But because God inspired the prophecies, the choice is made with unerring precision. Of Noah's sons, Shem is chosen; of Abraham's sons, Isaac; of Jacob's twelve sons, Judah is selected; and the promise is renewed to David. Again, Messiah must have a birthplace. Of three known continents Asia is chosen, and of its many countries the Land of Promise. Of its three districts, Judæa; and of its thousands of villages, Bethlehem is selected. "The prophet puts his finger on one obscure village on the map of the world; but he speaks infallibly, for the Omniscient God was behind his utterance" (Dr. Pierson).

THE KINSMAN REDEEMER. But the Key-note of the book of Ruth is *The Kinsman Redeemer*. In him we see Christ, who has purchased the Church to be His Bride. "Thirty times in this short book the word 'kinsman' is found, or 'redeemer,' 'near kinsman,' 'next of kin,' 'kindred,'—like words, all having reference to like things. . . . How plainly this book is intended to teach the doctrine concerning Redemption will be seen by examining chapter iv. 4-10. Here the word 'redemption' occurs five times in three verses; and in the tenth verse, Boaz declares that in redeeming the property he also purchases the widow of Mahlon to be his own wife. Nothing can explain the extreme minuteness of detail here except a typical design on the part of the inspiring Spirit. . . . Our Lord Jesus had to become one with man in order to have the right to redeem. He is therefore our fellow-man; but if He had been involved in man's fall and identified with man's sin, He could not have acted as Redeemer. No sinner can redeem himself, much less can he redeem his brother (Ps. xlix. 7). He is therefore, as the God-man, our Boaz ('Ability'); by that kinship and strength or ability, He is able to save to the uttermost all that come unto God by Him" (Pierson). "The Church which He hath purchased with His own blood" (Acts xx. 28). "Christ also loved the Church, and gave Himself for it; that He might present it to Himself a glorious Church, not having spot, or wrinkle, or any such thing."

THE CHRISTIAN LIFE. For the individual believer the book is full of teaching. First, the definite choice has to be made, the trust placed under the wings of the Lord God of Israel.

Then the diligent gleaning in the field, the beating out of the corn and the feeding upon it, which represents the diligent feeding of our souls upon the Word. The soul thus fed has food to pass on to others (Ruth ii. 18). The work in the harvest field is also a picture of the wider service of the ingathering of souls in God's great harvest field of the world, and we may well ask ourselves evening by evening, "Where hast thou gleaned to-day ? "

UNION WITH CHRIST. Though the union of Ruth with Boaz is typical of the Church as a whole, yet there is for the individual believer the blessed experience of union with Christ set forth under so many figures, such as the abiding of the branch in the Vine. If there has been in our lives any of the failure Israel experienced in Judges, a turning unto our own way, the remedy for us is to seek a closer union with Christ. Lest we be discouraged, God has placed the Book of Joshua and the Book of Ruth on each side of the Book of Judges, as if to show us that the Victory of Faith and the Rest of Faith is the experience we are to look for as followers of an Almighty Saviour.

### 4. THE SIX BOOKS OF KINGS

In the Hebrew these six books are only three, each pair forming but one book.

Samuel and Kings form a consecutive history and the Key-note of both is *Kingdom*.

Chronicles is the story of 2 Samuel and 1 and 2 Kings told over again from a different standpoint. Its Key-note is *Theocracy*. It deals only with the Kingdom of Judah, and relates the history as it touches the Temple and the worship of God. It was possibly written by Ezra.

The special privilege of the Children of Israel was to have God for their King, and to be chosen by Him to be a peculiar people unto Himself, to show forth His praise in the world.

During the period of the Judges Israel had rejected God from being their King. This rejection reached a climax in Samuel's day, when "they asked for a King like all the nations." When God's children are afraid of being different from the world around them they lose their power of testimony for Him. God gave them Saul—*a King after their own heart*. When Saul broke God's covenant through disobedience, God gave them David—"*a King after His own heart.*" David was a

type of the one perfect King.   Solomon likewise was a type of
Him.   But after Solomon God's power departed from the kings
and became vested in the prophets.   Elijah sent word to Ahab,
"Behold, Elijah is here!   And Ahab went to meet Elijah."
As Moody said, "Who was king now?"   Moses was a prophet.
Samuel was a prophet, as well as being the last of the Judges,
and also priest.   But the great line of prophets began with
Elijah, and they represented God to His people through all the
years of the decline and fall of the monarchy.

## 5. 1 SAMUEL

The lawless state of God's people, described in the Book of
Judges, is continued in the early part of 1 Samuel, and seems
to reach its height when the Ark of the Lord was in the hands
of the Philistines, and the priests were given over to wickedness.   We have a solemn lesson of the result of failure in
parental discipline, even on the part of good parents.   Of the
sons of Eli we read: "The sin of the young men was very
great before the Lord," and "Eli restrained them not."   In
the same way the sons of even the righteous Samuel "walked
not in his ways, but turned aside after lucre, and took bribes,
and perverted judgment," until the people of Israel made their
behaviour the excuse to demand a king.   David also seems to
have shown an inability to rule his own house, as is evident in
the rebellion of both Absalom and Adonijah.   Of Adonijah we
read: "And his father had not displeased him at any time in
saying, Why hast thou done so?"   David, evidently, had not
acted the father's part in chastening his son.

Samuel, Saul, and David stand out as the three central
figures of 1 and 2 Samuel.

SAMUEL'S NAME.   Samuel himself was a picture of our
Saviour.   The meaning of his name was one of the perplexities
of Hebrew scholarship till the year 1899, when the Twelfth
Congress of Orientalists held its meeting at Rome, and Professor Jastrow, of Philadelphia, showed that, in the Assyrian,
which is closely allied to the Hebrew tongue, the word *sumu*
means *son*, and he translated Samuel as "son (or offspring) of
God."   Hannah, in the depth and sincerity of her surrender,
gave up her first-born son to God utterly.

He was "God's son" from the moment of his birth.
"Therefore I have given him to the Lord" (not "lent" as in

A.V.). The word, common to the Babylonian and Hebrew tongues *before their separation*, becomes a witness to the antiquity of the book. It disappeared from the language of the Israelites so completely that no Jewish student of the Bible, ancient or modern, was able to explain it. But it is evident that it was in common use in Hannah's day; for she wanted *every one* to know that he was altogether the Lord's own, and she must have chosen a word, therefore, which every one could understand.

The name "God's son" takes us a step further. The resemblance between Hannah's Song and that of Mary, the mother of Jesus, has always been marked. Mary's Song is not a repetition of Hannah's, yet both see the same vision. It is a vision of the earth's full salvation, and of the Lord's Christ. "The adversaries of the Lord," sings Hannah, "shall be broken to pieces; out of heaven shall He thunder upon them: the Lord shall judge the ends of the earth; and He shall give strength unto His King, and exalt the horn of His anointed" —that is of His Messiah (1 Sam. ii. 10). "He hath showed strength with His arm," responds Mary: "He hath scattered the proud in the imagination of their hearts. . . . He hath holpen His servant Israel, in remembrance of His mercy; as He spake to our fathers, to Abraham, and to his seed for ever" (Luke i. 51-55).[1]

Hannah's Song, and the name she gave her child, are alike a prophecy of Christ. She has the honour of being the first to use the name "*Messiah*."

"THE LORD OF HOSTS." Another and most majestic Divine title occurs for the first time in the first chapter of this book, and that is "The Lord of Hosts." The Rev. A. Craig Robinson bases upon this fact the following argument: "The Divine title 'Lord of Hosts' never occurs in the Pentateuch; it occurs for the first time in 1 Samuel i. 3. After this it occurs very frequently, especially in the prophets—281 times in all. If the Pentateuch was written by a multitude of writers in the later age, when this title for Jehovah was so much in vogue, how is it that not one of them has in the Pentateuch used this expression *even once*?"[2]

That Jehovah of Hosts was a title of Christ we see from comparing Isa. vi. 1-3 with John xii. 41, and Isa. viii. 13, 14 with 1 Peter ii. 5-8.

---

[1] See *The Biblical Guide*, by Rev. John Urquhart, vol. vi. p. 140 *et seq.*
[2] *The Divine Title "Lord of Hosts": a Problem for the Critics.* Marshall Bros., 10 Paternoster Row. Price 4d.

Samuel was a type of Christ in combining the offices of prophet, priest, and ruler. The Schools of the Prophets founded by him are a foreshadowing of the Lord's service in pouring out His Spirit upon apostles, evangelists, and teachers.

Above all, Samuel was a picture of Christ in his life of prayer and intercession. From the time that God "called Samuel"—the story we have loved from our childhood—his life was one of continual communion. Samuel had access to the ear of God, and his own ear was open to God's voice. He and Moses are God's chosen examples of intercessors. "Though Moses and Samuel stood before Me, yet My mind could not be toward this people" (Jer. xv. 1). Samuel said to the rebellious nation, "God forbid that I should sin against the Lord in ceasing to pray for you." "Jesus . . . ever liveth to make intercession for them."

A FRIEND. In Jonathan we have another picture of Christ, showing the love and friendship of our Heavenly Friend. "There is a Friend that sticketh closer than a brother." ·He, the King's Son, was not ashamed to own the shepherd lad his friend, and Jesus is not ashamed to call us brethren. "The soul of Jonathan was knit with the soul of David, and he loved him as his own soul." Jesus, "having loved His own which were in the world, loved them to the uttermost" (John xiii. 1, R.V. margin).

Jonathan made an everlasting covenant with David (xviii. 3, xx. 15, 16, xxiii. 18): "He stripped himself of the robe that was on him, and gave it to David, and his garments, even to his sword, and to his bow, and to his girdle." So Christ stripped Himself of His glory, and He has covered us with the robe of His righteousness, and has armed and girded us for the fight. Jonathan strengthened David's hands in God (xxiii. 16), and the Lord says to us, "My strength is made perfect in weakness." The picture falls short, as all pictures do, of the glorious reality. Jonathan, at the risk of his own life (xx. 33), sought to reconcile his father to David. Christ laid down His life as ''the propitiation for our sins'' (1 John ii. 2). He is our Mediator, our Advocate with the Father, and has made us sharers of His throne in glory.

THE SHEPHERD KING. Both as Shepherd and as King, David is a type of our Saviour. In 1 Samuel we have the account of David's long season of preparation for the Kingdom.

The little town of Bethlehem is the birthplace alike of

David and of his greater Son.  The quiet years of toil with his father's flock remind us of the years spent at Nazareth and in the carpenter's shop.  Many of the Psalms recall David's watch over the flock: "When I consider Thy heavens, the work of Thy fingers, the moon and the stars, which Thou hast ordained; What is man, that Thou art mindful of him! and the son of man, that Thou visitest him?" (Ps. viii. 3, 4). "The heavens declare the glory of God; and the firmament showeth His handywork" (Ps. xix. 1).  On the same plains round Bethlehem the shepherds kept watch over their flocks by night, while the star which guided the wise men shone over their heads, when, lo, the angel of the Lord brought them the good tidings of great joy, of the birth, in the city of David, of a Saviour which is Christ the Lord.  "And suddenly there was with the angel a multitude of the heavenly host praising God, and saying, Glory to God in the Highest, and on earth peace, good will toward men."  Those who have watched the sunrise from those plains where David must often have watched it, tell us that no words can describe its magnificence.  "In them hath He set a tabernacle for the sun ; which is as a bridegroom coming out of his chamber, and rejoiceth as a strong man to run a race" (Ps. xix. 4, 5).

PSALM XXIII.  In the Shepherd Psalm, David surely describes his own care of the sheep.  How often he had led them by still waters, and caused them to lie down in green pastures, and many a time he must have had to lead them down one of the gorges of the wilderness of Judæa.[1]  This wilderness is fifty miles long, and ten miles broad, with many valleys just such as are described by the word *gay* in this Psalm.  There are eight different words for *valley* in Hebrew, but *gay* signifies a deep, rocky gorge, some of them only two or three feet wide at the bottom, almost as dark as night even in the daytime, because of the steep, rocky sides rising 800 feet high on each side.  Here the hyenas stalk the sheep if they get separated from the shepherd.  But with his club the shepherd does battle both with wild beast and with wilder Bedaween, and reassures the sheep with the touch of his staff in the dark valley.  More than once David had risked his life, and left the rest of the flock, to rescue one lamb from the mouth of the lion or the bear.  The good shepherd has always to take his life in his hand and be ready to lay it down.  With what confidence David says, "Jehovah is my Shepherd, I shall not

[1] See *Palestine Explored.*  Rev. Jas. Neil, M.A.

want." And the Son of David responds, "I am the Good Shepherd: the Good Shepherd giveth His life for the sheep." He leaves the ninety and nine in the wilderness and goes after the one that was lost until He finds it.

The Eastern sheep-fold is an enclosure, open to heaven, with a small place of shelter at the back, and enclosed with a rough, stone wall. At one corner there is a tiny doorway, but every shepherd is himself the door. He sleeps in the doorway to guard the sheep at night. He stands in the doorway as they come home in the evening, and examines every sheep before it goes in. He has a bowl of water for the thirsty sheep, and a bowl of oil for the wounded ones; he anoints with oil those whose heads have been bruised against the rocks. The imagery of the twenty-third Psalm does not change in the middle, as some have thought, to that of an indoor banquet; the imagery of the shepherd's care is sustained throughout.[1]

The Shepherd and the King were blended in David and in David's Son. A true king must always have the heart of a shepherd. When David saw the Angel of the Lord about to destroy Jerusalem, he cried: "I it is that have sinned, and done evil indeed; but as for these sheep, what have they done? Let Thine hand be on me . . . but not on Thy people" (1 Chron. xxi. 17).

"I will set up one Shepherd over them, and He shall feed them, even My Servant David; and He shall be their Shepherd" (Ezek. xxxiv. 23). He is:—

The Good Shepherd in death.        John x. 11.    See Ps. xxii.
The Great Shepherd in resurrection. Heb. xiii. 20.   „   Ps. xxiii.
The Chief Shepherd in glory.       1 Peter v. 4.    „   Ps. xxiv.

### 6. 2 SAMUEL

David was three times anointed: first in his father's house, then over Judah, and lastly over all Israel. God has anointed Jesus of Nazareth with the oil of gladness. He is King of kings and Lord of lords, but as David—though anointed king—was in exile while Saul reigned over the people, so Christ is rejected by the world, and the "Prince of this world" is reigning in the hearts of men.

A day came when the men of Judah gathered to David and anointed him king in Hebron. "The Spirit clothed Amasai and he said, Thine are we, David, and on thy side" (2 Sam. ii. 4; 1 Chron. xii. 18). It is a joyful day in the experience of the

[1] *The Song of our Syrian Guest.*

believer when he yields the full allegiance of his heart to the
Lord Jesus Christ, and says, "Thine am I, and on Thy side";
when he can look up into His face and say, "Thou art my
King" (Ps. xliv. 4).

"Now there was long war between the house of Saul and
the house of David: but David waxed stronger and stronger,
and the house of Saul waxed weaker and weaker" (2 Sam. iii. 1),
until at last Abner said to the elders of Israel: "Ye sought for
David in times past to be king over you. *Now then do it*: for
the Lord hath spoken of David, saying, By the hand of My
servant David I will save My people Israel out of the hand
of the Philistines, and out of the hand of all their enemies."
"Then came all the tribes of Israel to David unto Hebron, and
spake, saying, Behold, we are thy bone and thy flesh. . . .
And they anointed David king over Israel" (v. 1-3). "One
from among thy brethren shalt thou set king over thee : thou
mayest not set a stranger over thee, which is not thy brother"
(Deut. xvii. 15). "The king is near of kin to us" (2 Sam. xix.
42). "In all things made like unto His brethren" (Heb. ii. 17).
Here we see all Israel united under their rightful king. A
picture of a heart which is wholly true in its allegiance to the
King of kings.

God's promise to Israel was that He would save them from
all their enemies by the hand of David. And this was literally
fulfilled from the day that he slew Goliath all through his reign.
We never read of his being defeated. So Christ has vanquished
our great enemy, Satan. He has come "that we, being delivered
out of the hand of our enemies, might serve Him without fear."
"He must reign till He hath put all enemies under His feet."
"Of the increase of His government and peace there shall be
no end" (Isa. ix. 7).

"And David took the stronghold of Zion." This is like the
central citadel of our will. When that is surrendered to the
Lord His reign is established.

In the story of Mephibosheth we have a beautiful picture of
the grace of our King, in bringing us nigh and making us "as
one of the King's sons," "to eat bread at His table continually."
He brings us into His banqueting-house and bids us partake,
saying, "Eat, O friends ; drink, yea, drink abundantly, O beloved." He Himself is the heavenly food, for He says, "The
bread that I give is My flesh," and "My flesh is meat indeed."

DAVID'S SIN. But any type of our blessed Saviour falls
short somewhere. And David, as a type, is no exception. We

come next to the record of David's awful sin.  How can such a sinner be described as "a man after God's own heart"?    All through the life of David there is one characteristic which marks him out from other men, and in special contrast to Saul, and that is his continual trust and confidence in God, his acknowledgment of God's rule, his surrender to God's will. The great desire of his heart was to build God's House, yet when God sets him aside because he has been a man of war, he acquiesces with perfect grace in the Divine will.   When Nathan brings home to his conscience the great sin of his life—absolute monarch that he is—he acknowledges it at once, and the depth of his penitence is such as only a heart that knows God can feel.  For all time the fifty-first Psalm stands out as the expression of the deepest contrition of a repentant soul.  In that Psalm, David speaks of a broken heart as the only sacrifice he has to offer, a sacrifice which God will not despise.  And the high and Holy One that inhabiteth eternity goes further in His wondrous condescension and says, by the mouth of Isaiah, "I dwell in the high and holy place, with him also that is of a contrite and humble spirit, to revive the spirit of the humble, and to revive the heart of the contrite ones" (Isa. lvii. 15).

The Bible does not cloak sin, least of all in God's own children.  It does not spare God's saints.  There were steps leading up to David's sin—his multiplying wives, his tarrying still at Jerusalem when he should have been at the war.   It is always the case that there is backsliding of heart, before it is seen in outward act.  David sinned grievously, but his repentance was immediate, deep, and sincere.  God, indeed, blotted out his transgressions, according to the multitude of His tender mercies, but he did not remove the consequences of the sin: He chastened David through sore trials in his own family.

A REBEL.   In the flight of Absalom after the murder of his brother we have a picture of a rebel soul far off from God. In David we have a picture of God's sorrow over sinners. "The King wept very sore. . . . And David mourned for his son every day. . . . And the soul of David longed to go forth unto Absalom."   In the word of the wise woman of Tekoa, "God deviseth means, that he that is banished be not an outcast from Him" (2 Sam. xiv. 14, R.V.), we have an echo of God's words : "Deliver him from going down to the pit, I have found a ransom," or "atonement" (Job. xxxiii. 24, margin).

Even when Absalom was in rebellion the King commanded,

"Deal gently, for my sake, with the young man, even with Absalom." In this we see the forbearance of God with sinners. And when he heard of his death he cried: "O my son Absalom! my son, my son Absalom! would God I had died for thee, O Absalom, my son, my son!" David would fain have died for the rebel, but he could not. How this carries our thoughts on to One who was not only willing but able to lay down His life, the Just for the unjust, to bring us to God.

LOVE'S ALLEGIANCE. In David's exile we have again a picture of the rejected Saviour. The eastern walls of Jerusalem are bounded by a deep ravine—the torrent-bed of the Kidron. When the rebellion of Absalom drove David from his own city, we can imagine him coming forth by an eastern gate—probably what answered to the modern gate of St. Stephen—and following the winding path down the rocky side of the valley. The King did not go alone. A band of faithful servants went with him; and a little in advance, six hundred Philistines from the city of Gath, under their leader, Ittai, the Gittite. David had probably won the hearts of these men during his tarriance in the Philistine city of Ziklag, some thirty years before, and now they were ready to stand by him in time of trouble. When David came up with this band at the bottom of the ravine, he tried to dissuade Ittai from following him. He besought him as a stranger, and as one who had but recently joined his service, not to attach himself to a doubtful cause, and he bade him return with his blessing. But Ittai was firm, his place, whether in life or in death, was by the master he loved. Touched by such devoted allegiance, David allowed Ittai to pass over the torrent-bed with all his men, and with the little ones that were with him—no doubt the families of the band. With the voice of weeping all the exiles passed over, and climbed the grassy slopes of the Mount of Olives on the other side. David set captains of thousands over the people that were with him—a third part under the hand of Ittai the Gittite. The devotion of his followers comes out at every turn. When they found that their King intended to go forth with them into the battle, they would on no account allow it, but restrained him with the words: "Thou shalt not go forth; for if the half of us die they will not care for us; *but thou art worth ten thousand of us!*"

A thousand years have passed. Again a rejected King goes forth from the Jerusalem gate, and down the pathway into the dark valley, and up the slopes of Olivet. Instead of the strong band that went with David, there are but eleven men to go with

David's Son, and of the chosen three not one remains awake to share His agony. "I have trodden the wine-press alone, and of the people there was none with Me." The enthusiasm of David's followers led them to restrain him from going into the battle. But when the soldiers came to take the Lord of Glory, His little body-guard all forsook Him and fled, and He who is *the chiefest among ten thousand*, and altogether lovely, laid down His life for rebels and deserters.

Nearly two thousand years have passed since then. "Our Lord is still rejected and by the world disowned." There is still the golden opportunity to-day of making His heart glad by such a devotion as Ittai's. We are His blood-bought possession. It is His purpose that we should share His glory throughout eternity. And He claims our heart's love now.

Hushai the Archite and Zadok and Abiathar were to represent the King at the very centre of rebellion—"in the world, but not of it"; ambassadors in an enemy's country. In Shimei, who cursed David in his rejection, we have a picture of those who reviled Jesus, wagging their heads and mocking Him.

"I will smite the King only," was Ahithophel's advice to Absalom, "and I will bring back all the people unto thee." "Smite the Shepherd, and the sheep shall be scattered." Jesus, our Shepherd, was "stricken, smitten of God" for us. And the King passed over Jordan, that river of death.

THE RETURN OF THE KING. We have a vivid picture of the return of David to the city of Zion. The people clamoured for the return of the King. "Now, therefore, why speak ye not a word of bringing the King back?" The King heard of this and sent an encouraging message to the elders. "And the heart of all the men of Judah was bowed to the King, even as the heart of one man; so that they sent this word unto the King, Return thou, and all thy servants."

"Amen. Even so, come, Lord Jesus." According to Eastern custom, the men of Judah went right over Jordan to meet their King, and bring him back, and the crowd of rejoicing subjects increased as they drew near the city. One day the cry will go forth, "Behold, the Bridegroom cometh; go ye out to meet Him." Then "the dead in Christ shall rise first," and the saints that are alive on the earth shall be caught up to meet Him in the air. Our King has set this certainty of hope before us, and calls us to live in the joyful expectation of it. This should lead to faithfulness in service—"Behold, I come quickly; and My reward is with Me, to give every man according as his work shall be" (Rev. xxii. 12)—and to holiness of life (Titus ii. 11-14).

A GOSPEL FOR THE HOPELESS. The "Mighty Men" of David's kingdom were those who came to him in the time of his exile, when he was fleeing from Saul. They were escaped outlaws and criminals, but under David's leadership they became brave, self-controlled, magnanimous men, like their captain. "Every one that was in distress, and every one that was in debt, and every one that was discontented, gathered themselves unto him; and he became a captain over them : and there was with him about four hundred men" (1 Sam. xxii. 2). "This Man receiveth sinners." It is a glorious Gospel that is committed to our trust ! It is the Gospel for the outcast, for the refuse of society. It is the gospel of hope for the worst and the lowest. The transforming power of the Cross of Christ is seen in changed lives wherever the Gospel is preached.

## 7. 1 KINGS

We need the magnificent reign of Solomon, the Prince of Peace, to complete the picture of Christ as King. The Lord said to David : "Behold, a son shall be born to thee, who shall be a man of rest ; and I will give him rest from all his enemies round about ; for his name shall be Peaceable, and I will give peace and quietness in Israel in his days." Solomon's peaceable kingdom was the result of the victories David had obtained. It is because Christ has fought and conquered our enemies that we can enjoy the peace of His glorious reign in our hearts. The Kingdom of God is "righteousness, and peace, and joy in the Holy Ghost" (1 Chron. xxii. 9, margin ; Rom. xiv. 17).

THE TEMPLE. The glory of Solomon's reign was the building of the Temple. He seems to have been raised up specially for this purpose, for David says : "He hath chosen Solomon my son to sit upon the throne of the kingdom of the Lord over Israel. And He said unto me, Solomon thy son, he shall build My house and My courts. . . . Take heed now, for the Lord hath chosen thee to build an house for the sanctuary : be strong, and do it" (1 Chron. xxviii. 5-10). But for the account of the Temple we will wait till we come to the Book of Chronicles.

"SOLOMON IN ALL HIS GLORY." The wisdom of Solomon is a foreshadowing of the wisdom of Christ, in "whom are hid all the treasures of wisdom and knowledge."

Psalm lxxii. is "a Psalm for Solomon." It describes the glory of his kingdom, but it finds its perfect fulfilment only in the reign of One greater than Solomon, who shall indeed one day "have dominion from sea to sea, and from the river unto the ends of the earth." But though the millennial fulfilment of this Psalm is yet to come, it has a fulfilment already in those hearts where the King is reigning in righteousness. Solomon said to Hiram, King of Tyre, "The Lord my God hath given me rest on every side, so that there is neither adversary nor evil occurrent" (1 Kings v. 4). The magnificence of his kingdom is described in 1 Kings iv. 21-34 : "And Solomon reigned over all the kingdoms, from the river unto the land of the Philistines, and unto the border of Egypt: they brought presents, and served Solomon all the days of his life. . . . And he had peace on all sides round about him. And Judah and Israel dwelt safely, every man under his vine and under his fig-tree."

THE QUEEN OF SHEBA. Our Lord Himself draws the contrast between the Queen of Sheba, who "came from the uttermost parts of the earth to hear the wisdom of Solomon," and the men of His generation, who were so indifferent though "a Greater than Solomon" was among them. Following the same line of thought, the visit of this Queen is a beautiful picture of a soul coming to the Saviour and finding full satisfaction in Him. She came from afar off, and we "who sometimes were afar off are made nigh by the blood of Christ." She brought all her hard questions to Solomon, and communed with him of all that was in her heart. We may bring all our difficulties to the Lord, and we shall find, as she did, that "there is not anything hid from the King" which He cannot solve for us. We too shall find that He is "made unto us wisdom." And when she had seen all his wisdom, and riches, and the appointments of his kingdom, and his marvellous buildings, there was no more spirit in her. And she said : "It was a true report that I heard in mine own land of thy acts, and of thy wisdom. Howbeit I believed not the words, until I came, and mine eyes had seen it ; and, behold, the half was not told me : thy wisdom and prosperity exceedeth the fame that I heard. Happy are thy men, happy are these thy servants, which stand continually before thee, and that hear thy wisdom. Blessed be the Lord thy God, which delighted in thee, to set thee on the throne of Israel : because the Lord loved Israel for ever, therefore made He thee king, to do judgment and justice " (ch. x.).

"A True Report." The Gospel message is the " report " which drew us from the far country of alienation to seek the King.   And when we have really come near, and our eyes have seen Him in His beauty, we too can say the half " was not told me."   We find that His service is, indeed, a happy service, and that God has indeed proved His love in giving us such a King, not as the Queen of Sheba knew Solomon, in a passing visit, but to be our King for ever.   "And King Solomon gave unto the Queen of Sheba all her desire, whatsoever she asked, beside that which Solomon gave her of his royal bounty."   And so our King gives to us " according to His riches in glory."

Failure.   Again we see failure written over every human life.   Solomon failed in exactly those things against which the Law of God has warned the future kings of His people (Deut. xvii. 16, 17) : " He shall not multiply horses to himself, nor cause the people to return to Egypt, to the end that he should multiply horses. . . . Neither shall he greatly multiply to himself silver and gold."   " Neither shall he multiply wives to himself, that his heart turn not away."   Solomon did all three. And, moreover, the multitude of his wives were taken from the heathen nations, whom God had expressly commanded them not to marry, lest they should turn away the heart of His people to other gods.   This is exactly what came to pass.   " When Solomon was old, his wives turned away his heart after other gods : and his heart was not perfect with the Lord his God, as was the heart of David his father " (1 Kings xi. 4).

Disaster.   On this account God stirred up enemies to Solomon, and his reign ended in disaster, and at his death his kingdom was rent asunder, and only Judah and Benjamin were left to his son Rehoboam, while all Israel made Jeroboam, his servant, king.   "And to his (Solomon's) son will I give one tribe (that is the tribe of Benjamin, which remained steadfast to the kingdom of Judah), that David My servant may have a light alway before Me in Jerusalem, the city which I have chosen for Myself to put My name there" (1 Kings xi. 36). "To give any one a lamp in a place came to mean to establish his house and line in that place.   It must be borne in mind that the city of Jerusalem, and all its northern suburbs, stood in the territory of Benjamin.   Had this tribe joined the ten in their revolt against the throne of Solomon, the royal city could not have remained, as God had promised it should, the dwelling-place of the kings of David's line; that is, in the highly figurative language of Bible lands, their lamp in the Holy City would have been put out."[1]

THE KINGDOM DIVIDED. Then follows the history of the divided kingdom—a picture of the divided heart and of the impossibility of serving two masters. The kings of Israel followed the example of "Jeroboam, the son of Nebat, who made Israel to sin," by setting up the worship of the golden calves, and all their kings were given to idolatry. The history of the Kingdom of Israel is an almost unbroken story of wickedness, king after king coming to the throne through the murder of his predecessor.

2 Kings xvii. gives us the account of the Captivity of Israel, and goes fully into the reason of this punishment. They had descended to the very level of the nations whom God had bade His people drive out of the land—exactly what He had predicted as the result of their disobedience had come to pass. They forsook the Lord, and served the gods of the heathen, and walked in their ways, and wrought according to their wicked-ness, and therefore God permitted the King of Assyria to carry Israel away captive into Assyria, according to His warning, given by Moses in Deut. xxix. 24-28. "And the Lord rejected all the seed of Israel, and afflicted them, and delivered them into the hand of spoilers, until He had cast them out of His sight" (2 Kings xvii. 20).

THE PROPHETS. Long before the outward semblance of royalty had disappeared, God had transferred the power from the kings to the prophets. Out of the darkness of this evil time two figures stand forth as His witnesses, showing us that through all the failure God was quietly working onwards towards His eternal Kingdom of Righteousness.

Elijah and Elisha, in the contrast of their characters and of their mission, remind us of John the Baptist and of our Saviour. Our Lord Himself referred to John the Baptist as fulfilling the prophecy that Elijah must first come before the coming of the Son of Man. "Elias verily *has* come," He said. Elijah, the rugged prophet of the wilderness, clad in his mantle and leathern girdle—the ordinary dress of the Fellaheen, which every prophet wore—suddenly bursts upon the scene in the

[1] *Palestine Explored.* Rev. Jas. Neil. Nisbet and Co.

court of Ahab, and pronounces the judgment of the Lord. "As the Lord liveth, before whom I stand, there shall not be night-mist,[1] nor rain these years, but according to my word." The secret of his power lay in those few words "before whom I stand." He knew what it was to have power with God, and therefore he had power with man. He reminds us of John, clad in the same manner, at the court of Herod, denouncing as fearlessly the sins of that king.

On Mount Carmel it was "at the time of the offering of the evening sacrifice" that God sent the fire from heaven. We have several instances of deliverance coming at the time of the morning or evening sacrifice, reminding us of the power of the Cross which those sacrifices foreshadowed.

THE FORERUNNER. When God was about to send the rain in answer to Elijah's prayer, Elijah sent Ahab the message, "Prepare thy chariot, and get thee down, that the rain stop thee not." And then it appears that Elijah acted the part of *sais* to Ahab. The modern *sais* of Egypt is the "runner" attached to the household of kings and nobles. The same custom was in vogue in Israel, for Samuel warned the people that the king they so eagerly desired would exact this oppressive custom of his subjects: "He will take your sons, and appoint them for himself, for his chariots, and to be his horsemen; and some shall run before his chariots." "These facts lend great force to the act of Elijah, who, in an ecstasy of joy and zeal at the triumph of Jehovah, and desirous to 'honour the King' who for a brief moment had honoured God, when the hand of the Lord came upon him, girded up his loins, and ran before Ahab to the entrance of Jezreel—that is, for a distance of some twenty miles or more across the great plain of Esdraelon the man of God acted as the *sais* or runner of the King, clearing the way for his chariot and announcing his arrival!"[2] Does not this office of outrunner explain the figure of Hebrews vi. 20: "whither Jesus entered for us as a forerunner"? He who, in His condescension, has said that in heaven "He will gird Himself and make (His people) sit down to meat, and will come forth and serve them," is pictured here as having entered in only a brief moment earlier to announce their arrival and to be prepared to receive them there.

ELISHA. Elisha's was a ministry of blessing and healing.

[1] "The *matar* or 'rain' falls at all hours during winter, while the *tal* or 'night mist' falls in the night in summer and autumn" (Neil).

[2] *Palestine Explored*, p. 28. Rev. J. Neil.

In this he was a type of Christ. We have, moreover, in the life and miracles of Elisha a series of most beautiful lessons on Christian life and service. "Ploughing one day with his father's oxen and servants, in the open country, he saw the outlawed prophet of Gilead coming towards him. Passing by, he cast his mantle upon him. Elisha knew what the sign meant. He was a wealthy man. The call was to follow Elijah as a servant, pour water on his hands, perhaps to die with him. There was no time to think, the decision had to be made in a moment. The call of God in his heart was at once responded to. Obtaining leave to say farewell to his parents, he kills the oxen, smashes up the implements, and shows to all his companions that he has no more to do with his former life. God is calling each one of us, let us follow at whatever cost" (W. H. Wilson).

## 8. 2 KINGS

POWER FOR SERVICE. The blessing that Elisha craved in asking for a double portion of the spirit of his master, when Elijah was about to be taken from him, was not to be twice as great, but to have the portion of the first-born son. The first-born son inherited a double portion of his father's property, twice as much as each of the other sons. Elisha asked to have the prophetic office, and with it the power of the Spirit to enable him to fulfil it. In this last scene we sometimes almost wonder whether we are in the Old Testament or the New. We have an ascending master, a waiting disciple, a descending power. "Ye shall receive power, after that the Holy Ghost is come upon you: and ye shall be witnesses unto Me." No Christian is exempt from the call to be a witness. Christ wants witnesses everywhere, and we cannot do it without His power. "Thou hast asked an hard thing."

There are two conditions: (1) Absolute surrender. In his first call Elisha showed this thoroughness. He shows it now. Unhindered by the discouragement of others, and even by the seeming discouragement of his master, he pressed on from point to point, having counted the cost. It is a serious thing to follow Christ; He always bids us count the cost. At last it meant Jordan itself, death to the self-life. The baptism of the Spirit always means a baptism into the death of Christ. (2) The second condition was faith. "If thou *see* me when I shall be taken from thee, it shall be so." He kept his eye fixed on his master. "And Elisha saw it." The result was, he rent his own clothes—no more dependence on self—and took up the mantle of Elijah, for that was to be his only power now. He put it to the test at once, and was able to do the same works as Elijah had done. "The works that I do shall ye do also." And the prophets found it out, and a life of blessing and service to others was the outcome (Rev. E. W. Moore).

SALT. The healing of the waters of Jericho at their source, by casting in salt from a new dish, touched the people of Elisha's day, and is full of significance for us. It shows the power of the Gospel to change men's lives at their source. Christ brought this life-giving power in His perfect manhood. But we may recognise the "new vessel" also in every renewed heart which brings the power of the Gospel to other lives. Christians are to be "the salt of the earth." Dr. Thomson tells us there seems no reason to doubt the identity of the fountain which tradition points out as the scene of the miracle. The water is abundant, transparent, sweet and cool, and abounds in fish, and on the margin of this delightful brook grow a great number of bushes.

DITCHES. The miracle by which water was brought to relieve the need of the hosts of Israel, Judah, and Edom, who had combined to put down the rebellion of Moab, also contains a lesson on the manner of the Spirit's coming. When the hand of the Lord came upon Elisha, he said: "Make this valley full of ditches." It was a valley to begin with, a low place, a place of humility. God's rivers choose the valleys to flow in. Water always seeks the lowest level. But ditches had to be cut, the humbling work carried still further. If we would be the means of blessing to others, we must allow the Lord to cut His channels deep in our hearts. "For thus saith the Lord, Ye shall not see wind, neither shall ye see rain; yet that valley shall be filled with water, that ye may drink, and your beasts." No sound, but the waters came. So it is with the Spirit:—

> He came sweet influence to impart,
>   A gracious, willing Guest,
> While He can find one humble heart
>   Wherein to rest.

"And it came to pass in the morning, *when the meat offering was offered*, that, behold, there came water by the way of Edom, and the country was filled with water." Again we are reminded that it was Calvary that procured the blessing of Pentecost.

A Pot of Oil. In the multiplication of the widow's pot of oil we have another illustration of the work of the Spirit. Again, it is a lesson of emptying. The poor widow had nothing in the house wherewith to discharge her debt, save a pot of oil. We also owe a debt we cannot pay. We are debtors to live after the Spirit, we are debtors to love one another, we are debtors to carry the Gospel both to the Greek and to the Barbarian, both to the wise and to the unwise. Nothing of our carnal nature can avail to discharge the debt. The oil—the Holy Spirit—will alone avail. But as in faith we begin, at God's bidding, to pour it out into the empty vessels around us, we shall find that His supply is an inexhaustible one, and that the only limit is the measure of our expectation. "Go and pay thy debt, and live of the rest." The power of the Spirit is enough both for life and for service.

Soul-Winning. In the raising of the Shunammite's son we have a lesson for the messenger of the Gospel. Gehazi had the outward symbol of office without the power. When he laid the prophet's staff upon the dead child nothing happened. But with Elisha was the secret of the Lord. "He went in, and shut the door upon them twain, and prayed unto the Lord. And he went up, and lay upon the child, and put his mouth upon his mouth, and his eyes upon his eyes, and his hands upon his hands; and he stretched himself upon the child, and the flesh of the child waxed warm." We see in the action of Elisha the secret of dependence upon God, of power in prayer, of personal influence. It gives us a picture of how much it costs to win souls; he seemed to give his very life, as Paul was ready to do when he said, "We were willing to have imparted unto you, not the Gospel of God only, but also our own souls, because ye were dear unto us" (1 Thess. ii. 8).

Influence. In the healing of the deadly pottage we have a picture of how a Christian may cleanse the moral atmosphere around him, or purify the conversation, by the introduction of an element that is positively good.

In the multiplying of the barley loaves we have a foreshadowing of a greater miracle by the shores of the Sea of Galilee.

Naaman. And now we come to the healing of Naaman the Syrian, and in it we see the whole Gospel in miniature. Naaman, a great man, honourable, gracious, exalted, a

victorious captain, a mighty man of valour—BUT *he was a leper.*
There is that "*but*" in every life that has not come to Jesus
Christ for cleansing. "If I wash thee not, thou hast no part
with Me." The leprosy of sin, be the outward show of it ever
so slight, incurs God's declaration "utterly unclean." "If any
man keep the whole law, and yet offend in one point, he is
guilty of all." God says, "There is no difference : for all have
sinned, and come short of the glory of God." Nine steps of
humbling brought Naaman low enough to receive the blessing.
He accepted the testimony of a little captive maid. He found
it was not the great King of Israel who was to cleanse him.
He found that the cleansing could not be bought, even with
£7500. He had to go to the house of a poor prophet. The
prophet did not even come out to work the miracle, but sent a
message. He was to wash in the despised little river of Jordan.
He had to be guided by the good advice of his servants. He
had to obey. He had to become as a little child. "*And he
was clean !*"

Before his cleansing Naaman said "I thought." Now he
could say "*I know.*" In some such manner God has to remove,
one by one, all our preconceived notions of how we will be
saved, and bring us to Calvary. We may hear the message
of salvation from a very humble source. No good deeds or
fancied merits of our own can purchase it. No earthly rivers
of reformation or culture can remove the guilt of sin. There
is only one thing in all the universe that can do it : "The
blood of Jesus Christ His Son cleanseth us from all sin."

THE LOST AXE-HEAD. John M'Neil of Australia[1] has drawn
a lesson for us from the lost axe-head. We may lose that
sharp axe-head, the power of the Spirit for service, by disobedience, by want of separation, by neglect of the Bible, by
neglect of communion, by lack of faith. If you have lost
it, go back and look for it. You will find it where you lost
it : just there and nowhere else. Have you found the spot
where obedience failed ? Yield, and obey just there. Do not
continue at work chopping with the axe-handle. Many do this ;
there is much effort but no results—no chips fly off at the
stroke. If we have enjoyed and have lost the fulness of the
Spirit, let us confess, betake ourselves to the open fountain,
and obey, and He will put away our sin, and give us afresh
of His fulness. For His sake, for the sake of souls, for our own
sake, we must not try to live and labour without being filled.

[1] *The Spirit-filled Life.* Marshall Brothers.

CHARIOTS OF FIRE. Elisha lived in the calm sense of God's immediate presence. This was the secret of his power. When he and his servant were surrounded in the city of Dothan with the army of Syria, "a great host," and the servant said, "Alas, Master! how shall we do?" Elisha said, "Fear not; for they that be with us are more than they that be with them. And Elisha prayed, and said, Lord I pray Thee, open his eyes, that he may see And the Lord opened the eyes of the young man; and he saw: and, behold, the mountain was full of horses and chariots of fire round about Elisha." If we lived continually in the sense of God's protecting presence what calm power there would be in our lives!

WITNESSING. The four lepers who carried the good tidings of the plentiful supply in the deserted camp of the Syrians to the starving people of Samaria, are an example for us as Christians. If we have discovered the riches of Christ for ourselves, "we do not well to hold our peace." We should make the same resolve they did: "Now therefore come, that we may go and tell the King's household."

LOYALTY. "Is thine heart right?" said Jehu to Jehonadab the son of Rechab, "Is thine heart right, as my heart is with thy heart?" And Jehonadab answered, "It is." "If it be, give me thine hand. And he gave him his hand; and he took him up with him into his chariot." Our King sees us toiling along life's journey, and He puts to us this question: "Is thy heart right towards Me? Lovest thou Me more than these?" If we can reply, "It is. Thou knowest that I love Thee," our King, as it were, stretches out His hand and draws us up and seats us with Himself in heavenly places, and makes us to ride in His chariot of power. We have the same thought in the Book of Chronicles: "The eyes of the Lord run to and fro throughout the whole earth, to show Himself strong on the behalf of those whose heart is perfect toward Him."

The history of Judah is so bound up with the history of the Temple that it will be better for us to study it as a whole, in the Book of Chronicles. Those books, as we have already seen, are written from the Temple standpoint.

## 9. 1 CHRONICLES

These books cover the same period as 1 and 2 Kings, but they deal exclusively with the Kingdom of Judah and with the

House of David. They impress the importance of the worship of God upon the people, and the interest centres round the Temple.

GENEALOGIES. The first nine chapters of the book are taken up with genealogies. Unpromising as these chapters appear, much may be learnt from them. Perhaps the chief lesson is that of God's selection.

Chapter x. gives an account of Saul's miserable end, and chapter xi. opens with the anointing of David king over Judah in Hebron.

BRINGING THE ARK TO ZION. One of the first acts of David was to fetch the Ark of the Lord from the house of Abinadab, at Jabesh Gilead, to bring it to Zion. For twenty years the Ark with its mercy-seat, God's appointed meeting-place with His people, was neglected and almost forgotten—a true picture of a heart out of communion with God. God ordained that the Ark should always be carried on the shoulders of the Levites, but they seem to have thought they could improve on God's plan, and the result of disobedience was death. God blessed the house of Obed-edom during the three months the Ark remained there, and David was encouraged to bring it to Mount Zion, to the tent he had prepared for it.

David had now learnt the lesson of obedience, for he says : " None ought to carry the Ark of God but the Levites, for them hath the Lord chosen to carry the Ark of God and to minister unto Him for ever. And David gathered all Israel together to Jerusalem, to bring up the Ark of the Lord unto his place." For he desired to impress the whole nation with the importance of the event. The priests and Levites and singers, with their instruments of music, were each appointed to their several places. And David was clothed with a robe of fine linen and " danced before the Lord with all his might " (2 Sam. vi. 14). It is a common sight to-day, in " the changeless East," in any procession, to see a man dancing with strange attitudes to do honour to the bridegroom, or other hero of the day, and the more grotesque his attitudes the more honour is done. The man dances backwards, and with his dress girded to give free play to his limbs, as the common peasants gird themselves for active work. Thus, no doubt, David danced to do honour to God's Ark.[1] Michal, the daughter of Saul, looked out at a window and saw him dancing and playing, and she despised him in her heart. The enthusiasm of God's people is still a

[1] *Pictured Palestine*, pp. 166 and 228. Rev. James Neil.

matter of ridicule with the world, but would there were a little more of it in these days when people are more readily enthusiastic about anything else than His service! The Son of David showed such enthusiasm in the cleansing of the Temple that His disciples applied to Him the words, "The zeal of Thine House hath eaten Me up."

Sacrifices were offered as the Ark left the house of Obededom; and, again, when it was set in the tent on Mount Zion, they offered burnt sacrifices and peace offerings. The bringing of the Ark to Zion was typical of restored communion. In the presence of the Ark, with its blood-stained mercy-seat, the peace offerings could be offered. The peace offering included a meal of which the offerer partook before God. Reconciled and accepted, he was now God's guest and was privileged to eat bread in His presence. The joy which accompanied the bringing back of the Ark, and the feeding of the people with bread and meat and wine, are symbolic of the joy of restored communion and feeding upon Christ.

GOD'S PROMISE TO DAVID. The great desire of David's heart was to build a temple for the Lord. God set this on one side because David had "shed much blood upon the earth," but He promised that a son should be born unto him, who should be "a man of rest," and should build Him a house, and God would establish his throne for ever.

David accepted God's decision without a murmur, and poured forth a song of praise for the condescension of His promise. In the promised Son we see "a Greater than Solomon." "Thou shalt call His name Jesus. He shall be great, and shall be called the Son of the Highest; and the Lord God shall give unto Him the throne of His father David: and He shall reign over the house of Jacob for ever; and of His kingdom there shall be no end" (Luke i. 31-33).

The preservation of Israel as a nation is guaranteed till the end of time, "as long as the sun and the moon endure" (Jer. xxxi. 35-37). David's throne is secured as permanently, with the added sign, "and as the faithful witness in the sky" the rainbow (Ps. lxxxix. 3, 4, 27-37). David's Son shall sit upon David's throne in Jerusalem. Christ Jesus "is the *only Person alive now* as known to be of David's seed, and as possessing a right to David's throne." [1]

MOUNT MORIAH. The next event in the history of the

[1] *Israel, My Glory*, p. 82. Rev. John Wilkinson.

Temple was brought about through David's sin in numbering the people. His sin in this was no doubt twofold. First, pride at the greatness of his kingdom ; second, no mention is made of the tribute money having been paid, as commanded by the Law of Moses, at the time of the census. "When thou takest the sum of the Children of Israel after their number, then shall they give every man a ransom for his soul unto the Lord, when thou numberest them ; that there be no plague among them, when thou numberest them" (Exod. xxx. 12). The half shekel of silver, given by every man when he was numbered, was the token that the people belonged to the Lord : it was an acknowledgment of His right to their lives. This was evidently omitted in David's reign, and the plague came upon the people. The plague was stayed at the threshing-floor of Ornan the Jebusite, on Mount Moriah, and David bought the threshing-floor from Ornan for fifty shekels of silver "and built there an altar unto the Lord, and offered burnt offerings and peace offerings, and called upon the Lord ; and He answered him from heaven by fire upon the altar of burnt offering" (1 Chron. xxi. 26). Thus the Temple, as well as the Tabernacle, rested upon the foundation of the silver of redemption money. Mount Moriah was also the place of Abraham's sacrifice. All these circumstances are more than coincidences ; they fall into their place in God's great plan of redemption.

David also bought the *makoam* (translated "place") of the threshing-floor from Ornan for six hundred shekels of gold. These *makoams* were sacred places, the "places" of the Canaanites (Deut. xii. 2, 3), similar to the *bamoth* or "high places" so frequently mentioned in Scripture. They abound in Palestine to-day, and are called by the same word in the Arabic, *mukam*, "place," and are very valuable, often bringing in great gain to their owners through those who come to worship there. This might account for David having to pay such a high price for the *makoam* as recorded in Chronicles, though he only paid fifty shekels of silver for the threshing-floor as recorded in Kings. They appear to have been two separate transactions. Ornan the Jebusite was one of the Canaanitish inhabitants of the land. The place was evidently a *makoam* as long back as the time when Abraham was told to offer Isaac on what was probably the same spot, for the word occurs four times in the brief narrative, applied to the summit of Moriah, afterwards to be Jehovah's great *makoam*, where He would "record His Name" and place His temple. For Jehovah also would have His *makoam*. "Offer not thy burnt offering in every *makoam* thou seest: but in the *makoam* that Jehovah shall choose in one of thy tribes, there thou shalt offer thy burnt offerings " (Deut. xii. 13, 14).[1]

"In 2 Sam. xxiv. 24 we read that David bought the oxen and threshing-floor of Araunah for fifty shekels of silver. From 1 Chron. xxi. 25 we learn that David gave six hundred shekels of gold for the place. It is extraordinary that any honest and intelligent mind could find a difficulty here. Fifty shekels of silver were presumably a fair price, though to us it seems very little, for the oxen and for the temporary use of the threshing-floor, for the purpose of the sacrifice. And this was all that the king had in view at the moment. The English reader must not base anything on the force of the English words 'buy' and 'bought' in 2 Sam. xxiv. 24. The narrative in Chronicles suggests that it was the Lord's 'answering by fire' that led the king to go on to the purchase of the 'place.' But does any one imagine that the fee simple of 'the place'—the entire site of the Temple—was worth only fifty shekels? David went on to purchase the entire homestead out and out; and the price he paid for it was six hundred shekels of gold. And this is what the 'Chronicler' records." [2]

DAVID'S PREPARATION. "Solomon my son is young and tender," said David, "and the house that is to be builded for the Lord must be exceeding magnifical, of fame and of glory throughout all countries."

"So David prepared abundantly before his death," and the princes and the people brought their offerings. "Then the people rejoiced, for that they offered willingly, because with perfect heart they offered willingly to the Lord : and David the king also rejoiced with great joy." It is a marvellous thought that it brings joy to the heart of our King when we offer willingly to His service, whether it be ourselves or our dear ones, or our substance that we give. David's thanksgiving shows the right attitude of heart, the recognition that all indeed belongs to God. "Who am I, and what is my people, that we should be able to offer so willingly after this sort? for all things come of Thee, and of Thine own have we given Thee" (1 Chron. xxix. 14).

---

[1] *Pictured Palestine*, chap. v.   Rev. James Neil.
[2] *The Bible and Modern Criticism*, p. 161.   Sir Robt. Anderson.

## 10. 2 CHRONICLES

THE BUILDING OF THE TEMPLE.  Solomon sent to Hiram, King of Tyre, for his help in building the Temple, in supplying both materials and workmen skilled in all manner of cunning work.

To raise the surrounding ground to a level with the threshing-floor on the summit, Solomon constructed a stupendous foundation platform—raised high above the valley beneath—of great hewed stones of white marble, polished and costly. When our Lord said that there should not be left one stone upon another that should not be thrown down, He was not speaking of the foundations underneath, but of the stones composing the Temple of Herod, built upon it.  The foundation was built into the solid rock, a picture of the Rock of Ages, the foundation of God which standeth sure and which nothing can shake.  That the whole of the Temple—like the Tabernacle—in its ministry, its furniture, and its services, is typical of Christ and His great work of man's redemption, must be admitted by all who accept the inspiration of the Epistle to the Hebrews, which so clearly links together the Old and New Covenants, and shows them to be essentially one in their teaching.

We read of the heavenly City: " I saw no Temple therein : for the Lord God Almighty and the Lamb are the Temple of it."  And because it represents His work in redemption, His redeemed people also are included in the type.  It is the consummation of God's work through all the ages, Himself and all His people united in glory.  Some of the foundation stones are from twenty to thirty feet in length, and fitted so closely together that even a pen-knife cannot be inserted between them.  On some of these the Palestine Exploration Society found the quarry-marks in vermilion, to show where the stones were to be placed, for we read that "the house, when it was in building, was built of stone made ready before it was brought thither : so that there was neither hammer, nor axe, nor any tool of iron, heard in the house while it was in building " (1 Kings vi. 7).  All true believers in all ages are the living stones of that heavenly Temple, and God is preparing them in His quarry down here, amid the noise and tumult of earth, each for its place in His Temple above.  Rugged and shapeless are the stones to begin with, no wonder that the blows of the hammer fall heavily, that the chisel is sharp, and the polishing severe before the stones are ready.   But "oh for more mouldings of the Hand that works a change so vast ! "

Every part of the Temple must be full of spiritual teaching, for David told Solomon that God had given him the pattern of it by the Spirit.   It was a building of surpassing magnificence, and shone a mass of burnished gold beneath the splendour of that Eastern sky.

THE TEMPLE FILLED WITH GLORY.   When the work of the house of the Lord was finished, Solomon assembled all the elders of Israel to bring up the Ark of the Lord out of Zion the city of David.   Then " the house was filled with a cloud, even the house of the Lord ; so that the priests could not stand to minister by reason of the cloud : for the glory of the Lord had filled the house of the Lord."

What a picture is here of the Holy Spirit coming to fill the heart which has been prepared for His coming, the heart cleansed by the precious blood of Christ and surrendered to him, and thus made fit to become a temple of the Holy Ghost (1 Cor. vi. 19).

SOLOMON'S PRAYER.   Then follows Solomon's prayer at the dedication of the Temple—a prayer which well repays careful study.   It is based on the promises of God, as all prayer should be.   He speaks of every man knowing the plague of his own heart, and then goes on to the deeper thought that only God knows the hearts of all the children of men (1 Kings viii. 38, 39). In confessing our sin to God, what a rest it is to know that He knows all the worst about us, better even than we know it ourselves.   "If our heart condemn us, God is greater than our heart, and knoweth all things."   He can discriminate when we cannot, whether the condemnation we feel is the conviction of His Spirit, or only the false accusation of the enemy.   And as we wait upon Him, if all is well He will give us His peace. "Beloved, if our heart condemn us not, then have we confidence toward God " (1 John iii. 20, 21).

In his prayer Solomon mentions six varied vicissitudes of human life, and asks that if the people repent and pray, looking towards that house which he had built, that God would hear in His dwelling-place and give His answer.   This Solomon proposed to Jehovah as a covenant, and God replied with fire as the seal of His sanction.   To understand this it must be remembered that, throughout the East to this day, all worshippers pray looking towards their sanctuary, whether it be the Mohammedans towards Mecca, or those who pray to the saints at the

various *makoams*.  Solomon desires from God that that which
was falsely believed of all the idol temples around might be
true in the case of Jehovah's Temple.  But more than this,—
the Temple in every part of it was a type of the person and
work of the Lord Christ and of His relations with His people ;
everywhere it sets forth Christ—in the sacrifices, in the Passover, in the High Priest, in everything.  Therefore, though
Solomon could not have known it, in the spirit of prophecy he
is asking that those who look to Jesus, in drawing near to the
Father, may be answered.  It was only to say in symbol what
the Master says in set words, "Whatsoever ye shall ask the
Father in My name He will give it you."

In our study of 1 and 2 Kings we saw the disaster in which
Solomon's reign closed, and the division of the kingdom.

Even as early as in the reign of his son Rehoboam,
"Shishak king of Egypt came up against Jerusalem, and took
away the treasures of the house of the Lord" (2 Chron. xii. 9).
How soon was this beautiful Temple desolated !  Later, even
some of the kings robbed it to ward off an enemy.

BRIGHT SPOTS.  During the long time of departure from
God which followed, we find here and there a king who stood
forth for God and for His worship.

To Asa God sent a message by Azariah the prophet, the son
of Oded, and when Asa heard his words "he took courage, and
put away all the abominable idols out of all the land of Judah
and Benjamin."  And he removed his mother from being queen
because she had made an idol in a grove, and he made a
covenant with the Lord, and enriched the house of God with
gold and silver.

Jehoshaphat, his son, sent Levites throughout all the cities
of Judah to teach the book of the Law of the Lord—a proof
that Israel possessed the Law at this time.  The account of
Jehoshaphat's victory over the Ammonites and Moabites is one
of the greatest encouragements to a simple reliance on God in
the face of insurmountable difficulties.  " Be not afraid . . .
the battle is not yours, but God's. . . . Ye shall not need to
fight in this battle : set yourselves, stand ye still, and see the
salvation of the Lord."  "And when they began to sing and
to praise, the Lord set ambushments," and their enemies were
scattered.

FAILURE.  Then followed the evil reigns of Jehoshaphat's
son, Jehoram, and his grandson, Ahaziah.  After Ahaziah had

been slain by Jehu, his wicked mother, Athaliah, "destroyed all the seed royal of the house of Judah." But Joash, the little son of Ahaziah, was saved, and he was hidden in the Temple six years. Then Jehoiada the priest brought him out and made him king, and Athaliah was slain. Under the influence of Jehoiada, Joash repaired the Temple which Athaliah had broken up to bestow the dedicated things upon Baalim. But after the death of Jehoiada Joash lapsed into idolatry, and, at the instigation of the princes of Judah he slew Zechariah, the son of Jehoiada, who was sent to rebuke him.

His grandson, Uzziah, sinned against the Lord in burning incense in the Temple, and in punishment for this he became a leper till the day of his death.

Uzziah's great-grandson, Hezekiah, "opened the doors of the house of the Lord and repaired them." And he cleansed the Temple, and commanded the priests and Levites to sanctify themselves, and he offered sacrifices and kept the Passover, "so there was great joy in Jerusalem : for since the time of Solomon, son of David, king of Israel, there was not like it in Jerusalem."

Hezekiah's great-grandson, Josiah, carried out similar reforms. He purged Jerusalem from its idolatries, and repaired the house of the Lord. It was during this work of repair that Hilkiah, the priest, found in the Temple the book of the Law of the Lord given by Moses, and sent it by Shaphan the scribe to the king, and Shaphan read it before the king. When Josiah heard the words of the Law he rent his clothes in grief over this neglected Law which they had failed to keep. He sent to inquire of the Lord ; and Huldah, the prophetess, told him of the evil that should come on Jerusalem and the inhabitants ; but because Josiah had humbled himself the evil should not come in his day.

The young king stood by a pillar in the Temple and made a covenant with the Lord, and he kept the Passover. "And there was no Passover like to that kept in Israel, from the days of Samuel the prophet ; neither did all the kings of Israel keep such a Passover as Josiah kept" (2 Chron. xxxv. 18).

CAPTIVITY. But troublous times followed this good reign. God sent His messengers to the people, but they mocked and despised them, "until the wrath of the Lord rose against His people, till there was no remedy. Therefore He brought upon them the king of the Chaldees, who slew their young men with the sword in the house of the sanctuary, and carried the vessels

of the house of the Lord to Babylon, and burnt the house of
the Lord, and brake down the walls of Jerusalem, and burnt
all the palaces. And them that had escaped the sword carried
he away to Babylon; where they were servants to him and to
his sons until the reign of the kingdom of Persia."

## 11. Ezra

The decree of Cyrus is one of the most remarkable proofs that
God's Spirit speaks to those outside the covenant of His grace.
Seventy years before, Jeremiah had prophesied the return of the
Children of Israel from Babylon at this time.   Isaiah, a hundred
and seventy years before, foretold that one who did not know
God, but whom He called by name—Cyrus—was to perform all
God's will in the restoration of His people.   The Hebrew text
reads *Koresh* for this name, instead of *Kuresh*, which latter would
be the exact form for Cyrus.   But the Hebrew points (vowel
signs) were not inspired—not occurring in the ancient MSS.;
the word, therefore, could be read either way, and no doubt is
to be read *Kuresh*, when it exactly represents Cyrus.   A marvellous prophecy, naming him long before he was born.   It may
well be that Daniel drew the attention of the great Persian
conqueror to these prophecies, and that Cyrus learned much
from him about the religion of the one true God.

God's Spirit was at work also among His people, stirring
many of them up to take this opportunity to return  to
Jerusalem and build the Temple.   It was only the bitter
persecution they had met with in Egypt that led them to come
out from that land, leaving not a soul behind.   In Babylon,
on the other hand, they had prospered, and it was only those
"whose spirit God had raised" who were willing to go back
under the leadership of Zerubbabel and Joshua the priest.
They numbered in all nearly 50,000; a very small remnant
compared to the numbers in the old days of Israel's prosperity,
and also compared to the number who remained behind in
Babylon.

RESTORATION.   The Key-note of this book is *Restoration*;
for in this faithful remnant we have a picture of restoration
from backsliding, of individual faithfulness, and of a true effort
after a closer walk with God.   The worldliness and unbelief that
we see all around us in the Church to-day need be no hindrance
to a faithful walk, on our part, with the God who is still calling
us to come out and be separate unto Himself.

The restored remnant seem to have begun at the core, and to have worked from within outwards. They did not begin with building up the walls, nor even with building the Temple, but "they builded the altar of the God of Israel, to offer burnt offerings thereon, as it is written in the Law of Moses, the man of God, and they kept the feast of Tabernacles." At the very heart of this book we see Christ and His great atoning work in these burnt offerings. The restored people are pointed forwards to Him that was to come. And every soul that returns from its backsliding to-day must begin afresh at the foot of the Cross.

The next step was laying the foundation of the Temple amidst praise and thanksgiving. But some of the old men who remembered the glory of the former house wept with a loud voice, so that the people could not distinguish between the shouts of joy and of weeping. As the restored soul rests back upon the one foundation—Christ Jesus—there is mingled the sadness over wasted days with the joy of restored communion.

SEPARATION. We next come to a very practical lesson for the Church of Christ to-day, on the need of separation for service. The adversaries of the Jews were the semi-heathen Samaritans (chap. iv. 1, 9, 10) whom Shalmaneser, King of Assyria, had transplanted to the cities of Samaria, in the place of the captives whom he had carried into Assyria at the time of the captivity of the ten tribes. We have a full account of this in 2 Kings xvii. There we read, also, that the King of Assyria sent back one of the captive priests to teach these people what he called "the manner of the God of the land." The result was that these people "feared the Lord *and* served their own gods"; and this mixed worship was perpetuated among their children.

These adversaries showed their hostility first by offering to help build the Temple. That is how the world often begins its hostility to the Church to-day; and we need to take the firm stand these restored Israelites took, and not compromise God's work by accepting such offers of help, or placing unbelievers in prominent positions in our Churches and Sunday Schools. There is a growing tendency in these days to seek to bring about union with the Church of Rome, and meanwhile to join with them in work, through blindness in recognising that they are as truly "adversaries" as were those to whom Zerubbabel refused any share of the building.

The true nature of these men soon came out. They harassed the people of Judah in their work, and at last succeeded in stopping them. But the Lord sent the prophets Haggai and Zechariah, who so encouraged the leaders, that they began to build again in spite of the opposition. Then Tatnai the Governor asked them, "Who gave you a decree to build this house?" Not believing their answer he sent to Darius the king to inquire. The decree of Cyrus was found at Achmetha, or Ecbatana, the summer palace of the king; and, encouraged in every way by Darius, the building went forward to its completion.

THE SAMARITAN PENTATEUCH. The Samaritans were fiercely hostile to the Jews at this time, as we have seen, and their hostility was no less during the days of Ezra and Nehemiah, eighty years, and a hundred years, later. In view of this hostility it is certain that the Samaritans would not have accepted any additions or alterations in the Pentateuch made by Ezra, for, as we have already seen, they had been taught by a Jewish teacher, sent by the King of Assyria, "the way of the God of the land," which they could only have learnt from the writings of Moses as they then were. They had had these writings—or the teaching drawn from them—in their possession a hundred and seventy years before Ezra's day, and would never have allowed any additions to be made to them by this their great enemy, or, indeed, by any of the Jews, whom they so scorned and hated. The enmity, we know, was continued down to the time of our Lord, and yet the Samaritans, to this day, possess the whole Pentateuch, which is virtually the same as the Pentateuch of our Hebrew Bible. We seem, then, driven to the conclusion that they must have received their Pentateuch before their enmity with the Jews commenced, which it did eighty years before Ezra's arrival at Jerusalem. The existence of the Samaritan Pentateuch—written as it is in the ancient Phœnician style of writing—is a very substantial witness to its antiquity (Dr. Rouse). We have also abundant evidence in this book that the Israelites likewise possessed the Law of Moses, the man of God, before the days of Ezra. The altar and burnt offerings and feast of Tabernacles of Zerubbabel's day add their testimony to the fact.

As soon as the Temple was finished the people kept the dedication of it with joy, and among their offerings were "twelve he goats according to the number of the twelve tribes of Israel" (Ezra vi. 16). This is one of the proofs that among the remnant which returned were some of the ten tribes of Israel, as well as of the two tribes of Judah and Benjamin; as also in the next remnant, which returned under Ezra, when "twelve bullocks for all Israel" were offered (viii. 35). Besides this, before the captivity of Israel, large numbers of those ten tribes "fell away to Judah" on account of the idolatry of Israel (see 2 Chron. xi. 14-17 and xxxi. 6). The returned captives were properly representative of the entire nation, and so are the Jewish people throughout the world to-day, though a number of the ten tribes are no doubt to be found in the Nestorians of Persia.[1]   "The sharp contrast between Judah and Israel was given up in a strange land.  To the ten tribes in the penitent sorrow of the exile the name of Jerusalem was again a dearly loved and cherished one."[2]

After the dedication of the Temple the returned exiles kept the Passover. We do not often read of the keeping of this feast. In times of backsliding Israel neglected to keep the feasts of the Lord ; the joy went out of their lives. But whenever we do read of the keeping of the Passover it carries our thoughts back to the Redemption in Egypt and forward to the Redemption wrought out for us on Calvary.

EZRA. Between the dedication of the Temple and the return of the next remnant under Ezra there is a gap of sixty years in the history of this book. Then God raised up a great reformer in Ezra. He was by birth a priest. But in Babylon there was no temple and no altar, so Ezra gave himself instead to the study of God's Law. He was a ready scribe in the Law of Moses, because he had "prepared his heart to seek the Law of the Lord, and to do it, and to teach in Israel statutes and judgments." God's Law was burnt in upon his own soul, and lived out in his life, before he taught it to others. This enabled him to speak with the intensity of conviction.

It was a high tribute to Ezra's character and ability that Artaxerxes the king gave him a letter authorising all the people of Israel, who were willing, to go with him, and commanding that he should be supplied with all that was needful for the house of God, and authorising him to set magistrates and judges to judge the people, and instructing him to teach them the Law of God.

Ezra attributes all his success, the favour of the king, the preparation of the people, the safety of the journey, to the good hand of his God upon him. He was in all things under the hand of the Lord. Only a few thousand gathered with him at the river Ahava, and there, with fasting and prayer, they committed

[1] *Israel My Glory*, p. 101.   Rev. John Wilkinson.
[2] *Commentary on Esther*, p. 50.   Dr. Cassel.

their way unto the Lord, for Ezra was "ashamed" to ask for a guard of soldiers.   No doubt the remembrance of God's deliverance of His people under Esther, which had occurred during the interval of the sixty years, made Ezra doubly sure of His protection now.

A MAN IN DEAD EARNEST.   This interval had been once more a period of backsliding among the Jews at Jerusalem. They had again intermarried with the idolatrous nations around. The only reason for Israel's existence as a nation was to be a holy people, separated unto the Lord ; and when Ezra heard how utterly Israel had failed he was overcome with grief and "sat down astonied until the evening sacrifice."   Again, at that sacred hour relief came.   He poured out his soul in a deep agony of prayer to God, associating himself with his people in confession of sin.   His prayer, coming from his very heart, touched the hearts of the people, and, assembling in great numbers, men, women, and children, they caught the fire of his spirit and "wept very sore."   But this contrition did not end with weeping. They took sides with God against themselves, and promised to stand by Ezra in his work of reformation.   It needed all Ezra's courage to carry it through, and no doubt the authority of the king's letter was part of God's provision for His servant.   Out of the whole population there were a hundred and twelve cases of these mixed marriages, and the Law of Moses was applied to them all.

## 12. NEHEMIAH

An interval of about twelve years had passed since the reforms of Ezra, when Nehemiah obtained leave of King Artaxerxes, to whom he bore the office of cup-bearer, to go up to Jerusalem. His spirit had been stirred by the news of the desolate condition of the city with its broken walls.   Nehemiah found it even as he had heard, and he gathered the elders together and told them of the good hand of his God upon him, and they said, "Let us rise up and build.   So they strengthened their hands for this good work."

The Key-note of this book again is *Restoration*.   It is practically a continuation of the Book of Ezra.   In that we saw the Temple rebuilt ; in this the walls.   The restoration began at the heart of things and spread outwards.   When the heart is right with God, and established as His dwelling-place, the outward work of His service in the world can go forward.   This whole book is full of lessons for the servant of Christ. It begins with Nehemiah's confession to God, in which he humbles himself on account of the condition of his people. Both beforehand in Shushan, and on the spot in Jerusalem, he makes himself acquainted with the details of the need. Throughout we find him a man of prayer. But he is not only that, he is a born statesman, and brings his natural powers into God's service. He sees the power of co-operation, and he inspires a feeble people to accomplish a great work.

HEARTY SERVICE. In building the wall of Jerusalem, Nehemiah began at the Sheep Gate, and portioned out a complete circuit of the city. Frequently we read that "every man built over against his own house" (see iii. 10, 23, 28, 29). Priests and rulers, goldsmiths and apothecaries, and merchants, worked side by side, brothers working together, and Shullum, the ruler of half Jerusalem, helped by his daughters. Several of the builders seem, cautiously, first to have undertaken one bit, and then having accomplished that, as their enthusiasm grew, to have volunteered for another. Such was Meremoth, the son of Urijah (ver. 4, 21), and Meshullam, the son of Berechiah, who repaired a piece of the wall, besides that over against his own chamber (ver. 4, 30), and Nehemiah, the son of Azbuk, whose work is described in three pieces (ver. 16). "Baruch, the son of Zabbai, *earnestly* repaired the other piece, from the turning of the wall unto the door of the house of Eliashib the high priest" (ver. 20). We are told who set up the various gates, with the locks and the bars thereof. No detail of work done for His glory is overlooked by God, and He delights to place on record the humblest service.

ADVERSARIES. But the descendants of the Samaritans, who had harassed Zerubbabel, were indefatigable in their efforts to hinder Nehemiah. First they mocked them : " What do these feeble Jews ? that which they build, if a fox go up, he shall even break down their stone wall." " Hear, O our God ; for we are despised," was Nehemiah's prayer. " So built we the wall ; and all the wall was joined together unto the half thereof : for *the people had a mind to work* " (iv. 1-6).

Mockery having failed, the enemy conspired to fight against Jerusalem. But Nehemiah says : " We made our prayer unto our God, and set a watch day and night."

Watch, as if on that alone
Hung the issue of the day ;
Pray, that grace may be sent down :
Watch and pray.

Nehemiah armed the builders, and gave orders that in what place they heard the sound of the trumpet they were to resort thither to defend the city.

Then the enemy tried stratagem, and four times sent a message to Nehemiah, asking him to meet them in the plain of Ono. Four times he sent the same reply, "I am doing a great work : why should the work cease, whilst I leave it, and come down to you ?" If we have a good answer there is no need to vary it. Then they accused them of rebellion, and sought to weaken their hands and make them afraid, but Nehemiah replied to Tobiah : "There are no such things done as thou sayest, but thou feignest them out of thine own heart." And as a last resort, one bade him take refuge in the Temple, "for they will come to slay thee." "Should such a man as I flee ?" was Nehemiah's steadfast reply. "So the wall was finished in fifty and two days " (vi. 15).

Our soul's enemies still use wiles and threats and plots, similar to all of these, if by any means they can hinder or discourage us from doing God's work ; and we need, like Nehemiah, to remember *Who* has commissioned us, and making our prayer unto Him, to disregard all suggestions that would weaken our hands.

Our Great High Priest. The register of those who first came from Babylon under Zerubbabel is again repeated here. And there were some of the priests who sought their register in the genealogy, but it could not be found, "therefore were they, as polluted, put from the priesthood. And the Tirshatha (Governor) said unto them, that they should not eat of the most holy things, till there stood up a priest with Urim and Thummim " (vii. 63-65).[1] We have here one of those instances in the Old Testament when the Face of Christ suddenly shines upon us in the most unexpected and unlikely places. Merely a register and a few priests who could not find their place in it. But it makes our hearts thrill with the consciousness that we have a great High Priest—even Jesus—who has the Urim

---

[1] Urim and Thummim, " Lights and Perfections." In Hebrew, when two nouns occur together in this form, one is to be understood as an adjective, making it especially emphatic. Thus, this should be translated "perfect light," for the plural form here is the Hebrew "plural of majesty." See also page 41.

and Thummim, who is the "Perfect Light," to whom all hearts are open, who can settle the question unhesitatingly as to our right to communion with God, answering to the eating of the most holy things, and as to our worthiness to act as His priests in blessing to others. Unclean, unworthy, polluted as we know we are, He has, by His own blood, entered in once for all into the holy place, having obtained eternal redemption for us (Heb. ix. 12, R.V.). And if we trust in His one sacrifice for sins for ever, we also may draw nigh and have communion with Him, not once a year, or once a month, or once a week, merely, but day by day.

Christ is a great High Priest—not by genealogy from Aaron, but "after the order of Melchizedek," who was "without genealogy" (Heb. vii. 3, R.V.). Melchizedek's genealogy was, no doubt, omitted to fit him all the more to be a type of Him who had no earthly father. God has called all believers in Christ to be Priests unto Him, and our right of priesthood depends upon whether we have been born again and have our names written, not in an earthly register, but in the Lamb's Book of Life. He has, moreover, provided for our fitness in the present tenses of John's Epistle. First, "The blood cleanseth," so that there need never be any cloud between our souls and God. Second, "The anointing abideth," so that there need never be any lack of the supply of His Spirit for service.

EZRA'S PREACHING. The immediate result of the work of restoration was a great hunger for God's Word. The people gathered themselves together as one man unto Ezra before the Water Gate, and begged him to bring forth the Book of the Law of Moses. Here Ezra, perhaps an old man now, comes forward again, and we see him and Nehemiah uniting in God's service. We are given a striking picture of Ezra's preaching. Already we have seen him as a reformer, and as a man of prayer, and now all his skill in the Law of the Lord comes out as he stands on that pulpit of wood—"made for the purpose"—with thirteen of the leaders of the people standing beside him, and all the people thronging round. He opened the roll of the book, and having prayed, read the Law distinctly, and gave the sense, and caused the people to understand it. Hour after hour, and subsequently day after day, they listened, men and women and children, "all that could understand."

Such preaching stirred Jerusalem as Savonarola's preaching stirred Florence. The people wept as they found how far short they had come of God's will. But Ezra and Nehemiah and the Levites stilled the people, and told them not to weep, and from the context and what follows we gather that their weeping was turned into joy through yielding to God's will and accepting its claim upon their lives. "And the people went their way . . . to make great mirth, because they had understood the words that were declared unto them" (viii. 12). "Great peace have they that love Thy Law."

The Children of Israel sealed themselves under a solemn covenant to keep the Law, specially with regard to marriages with the heathen, to keeping the Sabbath, and to maintaining the worship of God.

The dedication of the walls was a joyful occasion, for "God had made them rejoice with great joy : the wives also and the children rejoiced ; so that the joy of Jerusalem was heard even afar off" (xii. 43).

BACKSLIDING ONCE MORE. Once more twelve years have rolled away, and Nehemiah, who had been back at the Court of Shushan for a time, returned to Jerusalem, to find all the terms of the covenant broken and the Law disregarded. With a firm hand he dealt with all these abuses. Again the Law of Moses was brought out, and it was found written that the Ammonite and the Moabite should not come into the congregation of God for ever. Yet Eliashib, the priest, because he was allied unto Tobiah the Ammonite, had actually given over a chamber in the Temple to this enemy of the Lord. Nehemiah turned him out immediately. We need in these days to be careful that we do not let the ties of relationship weaken the straightforwardness of our testimony for the Lord.

Again Nehemiah contended with the rulers because he found that the service of the House of the Lord was neglected. Next he found a wholesale disregard of the Sabbath. The utter disregard of God's Day is one of the evidences of the backslidden condition of the Church in our own time. It is rapidly growing upon our land, and, together with disobedience to parents, is a sign of the perilous times of these last days, when "Men shall be lovers of their own selves . . . *lovers of pleasure more than lovers of God*" (2 Tim. iii. 1-4).

"THE SPEECH OF ASHDOD." Lastly, Nehemiah found that, again, the Jews had married among the heathen, with the result that their children spoke half in the speech of Ashdod, and half in the Jews' language. God has distinctly commanded that Christians shall marry "only in the Lord," and that they shall " not be unequally yoked together with unbelievers." When they disobey God's distinct command in this, and marry those who are not Christians, it always brings sorrow. How often the argument is used that the Christian husband or wife will be able to win the loved one to the Lord's side, but it is not to be expected that God will grant His blessing upon an act of disobedience, and the result that usually follows is that the Christian is drawn, it may be almost imperceptibly, to love the things of the world, and is found—together with the children of such a marriage—speaking " half in the speech of Ashdod," and unable to speak as a citizen of the heavenly city. The spirit of compromise with the world mars the testimony for Christ of many a home which ought to be a witness for Him.

In all these breaches of the Law Nehemiah " contended with the Jews "; whether they were nobles or rulers or the common people, he dealt with them in the most summary manner, and did not rest till all was put right. This was no want of love on his part, for he was willing to spend and be spent for his people. It is an evidence of true love to deal faithfully with false teaching and wrong-doing of any kind. The Church of Christ would be in a purer state to-day if her leaders had had the courage to deal with disregard of God's Law in the same spirit as Nehemiah dealt with it.

## 13. ESTHER

The Book of Esther is designed to show God's providential care of His people. Though the name of God is not mentioned, the hand of God, ruling and over-ruling the events for the preservation of His people, can be seen throughout.[1] In the Talmud the question is asked : " Where do we get Esther from the Law ? " The answer is Deuteronomy xxxi. 18, " And I will surely hide My face, or presence." God was hiding His face from His people on account of their sins; they had deliberately chosen to continue in the land of their captivity among the heathen, instead of availing themselves of the opportunity of returning to Jerusalem with Zerubbabel. The events in this book occur during the sixty years between the return of that first remnant and of the second under Ezra.

PRAYER. Though there is also no actual mention of prayer to God, it is distinctly implied in the mourning and fasting

[1] Dr. Bullinger points out that some Hebrew scholars have found the name Jehovah four times repeated in acrostic form in the Book of Esther.

among the Jews when they heard the royal decree for their destruction (iv. 1-3); and again, when Esther ordered a three days' fast among her people before she ventured to go before the king (iv. 16). The Feast of Purim, instituted by Esther and Mordecai, witnesses still, not only to the truth of the narrative, but to a nation's gratitude and a memorial throughout all generations of their deliverance. "Their fastings and *their cry*" are also mentioned, and to whom could they cry but unto God? (ix. 17-32).

THE GOLDEN SCEPTRE. The king holding out the golden sceptre has been an encouragement to many a saint of God in bringing their petitions to the King of kings.

> Thou art coming to a King;
> Large petitions with thee bring;
> For His grace and power are such,
> None can ever ask too much.

We need never fear that our King will refuse us an audience, or that we shall incur His anger by drawing nigh; but there are seasons when He seems in a special manner to hold out the golden sceptre, and to give us more abundant access to Him in prayer.

SATAN. Behind the personal enmity of Haman was the deeper malignity of Satan, seeking to make void the promises of God through the destruction of the whole Jewish race; for Xerxes was king over all the Jews in Palestine as well as over those in Persia and Babylon. Satan knew that the great Deliverer who was to arise of the House of David was to destroy his power, and we may trace his hand behind such events of history as Saul throwing his javelin at the youthful David, and Queen Athaliah's attempt to destroy all the seed royal. But God turned aside the blow in the one case, and nourished the infant Joash in the Temple courts in the other. The same enmity of the devil prompted Herod to slay the babes of Bethlehem, but God delivered His Son by sending Him into Egypt. The great enemy succeeded in bruising His heel when he gathered together Herod and Pontius Pilate, with the Gentiles and the people of Israel, against the Holy Child Jesus; but God raised Him from the dead.

HISTORIC ACCURACY. There is hardly a book in the Bible upon the trustworthiness of which there has been made so determined an attack as the Book of Esther. But the writings of Herodotus and the discoveries at Xerxes' palace of Shushan by the Frenchman Dieulafoy, together bring out the truthfulness of every detail of the story.[1] The relative position of the different parts of the palace and gardens fit in exactly with the account in this book. The vain and capricious character of Ahasuerus—the Xerxes of history—his extravagant feast, the Persian names of the courtiers, the golden couches, the sceptre, the seal, the scribes, the posts, are all matters of history, if space permitted to examine them in detail. In the account of the king's feast (chap. i. 6) the hangings of the court are described as "white, green, and blue." The word translated "green" is really an old Persian word meaning "fine cotton." So it should read "hangings of fine purple and white cotton." These, Xenophon tells us, were the royal colours of Persia. The pillars of marble have been found in the court of the garden, and it is clear that the pavement was a mosaic, as described in verse 6.

SALVATION. There have been various attempts to trace elaborate types in the Book of Esther, but the simple fact stands out that here was one who was willing to lay down her life for her people. It is here that we find Christ in the Book of Esther. A picture of Him who was not only willing, but who actually did lay down His life for us, and through whose intercession salvation is assured to us.

OPPORTUNITY. But the great practical lesson for us in this book is the all-importance of using God-given opportunities. The power of life and death lies in these opportunities both to ourselves and to others. Mordecai was so sure of God's working that he sent Esther this message: "If thou altogether holdest thy peace at this time, then shall there enlargement and deliverance arise to the Jews from another place; but thou and thy father's house shall be destroyed: and *who knoweth whether thou art come* to the kingdom for such a time as this?" (iv. 14). We may be tempted to think that our opportunities are so insignificant, our circle of influence so small, that they are of little importance; if we were a great queen, like Esther, it would be a different matter. But "who knoweth whether *thou* art come to the kingdom for such a time as this?" *Thou,*

---

[1] "M. Dieulafoy has set up the *bîthân* (*apadana*, the great banqueting-hall or throne-room) in the museum of the Louvre, where one can now see the remains of the marble pillars, and of the marble pavement, of the hall of the feast" (*New Biblical Guide*, vol. vii. p. 359. Rev. John Urquhart).

whoever thou art, and whatever thy circumstances, thou art
called to "reign in life by One, Jesus Christ." See to it that
thou dost not miss thy opportunity. God has a purpose for
each one of our lives. He has placed us where He can best use
us for His glory. If we fail just there, it may be that He will
work out His purpose in some other way ; but we shall suffer
untold loss. Like Esther, we must be ready to take our life in
our hand and risk everything in His service.

# IV. CHRIST IN THE POETICAL BOOKS

## 1. JOB

IN whatever aspect we look at it, the Book of Job is perhaps the most wonderful poem that has ever been written. Tennyson called it "the greatest poem whether of ancient or modern literature." Luther regarded it as "more magnificent and sublime than any other book of Scripture."

The scene is laid in patriarchal times, and it is said to be the oldest book in existence. That Job was a real person is settled by Scripture itself. Through the prophet Ezekiel God says of the land: "Though these three men, Noah, Daniel, and Job, were in it, they should deliver but their own souls" (Ezek xiv. 14, 20).

The book is wonderful in the beauty of its language, in the wide sweep of knowledge it displays, in its scientific accuracy. It is wonderful in that it deals with the mystery of pain, and with the riddle of all times, "Why do the righteous suffer?" It lifts the veil of the spirit world, and teaches us both the extent and the limit of the power of Satan. It is wonderful in clearly revealing the fact of the resurrection, and, above all, in foreshadowing the mystery of redemption.

The language of the book is sublime in its simplicity. The pathos of Job's description of his sufferings has found an echo in countless souls who have been brought into God's crucible. As Elihu describes the gathering storm we can see the clouds rolling up, the flashing of the lightning, and hear the roar of the thunder. Out of the midst of the storm God speaks.

GOD'S BOOK. Though the object of the Bible is not to teach science, its language is always abreast of the latest discoveries. This is nowhere more noticeable than in the Book of Job.

"He hangeth the earth upon nothing" (chap. xxvi. 7). What could more accurately describe the poise of our world in space?

"Canst thou bind the sweet influences of the Pleiades?" (xxxviii. 31). Alcyone, the brightest of these seven stars, is actually, so far as is known, the pivot around which our whole solar system revolves. How mighty and at once how sweet must be its influence to hold these worlds in place at such a distance and to swing them round so smoothly!

"The morning-stars sang together" (xxxviii. 7). Only modern science has discovered that the rays of light are vocal, and that if our ears were more finely tuned we should hear them (see Ps. xix. 1-3).

"By what way is the light parted?" (xxxviii. 24). Could language more exact be employed even after the discoveries of the spectrum analysis?

Had Bildad been taught the chemical absorption of chlorophyll by plants from light, he could have used no exacter term than this, "He is green (or is full of juice) before the sun" (viii. 16).[1]

THE MYSTERY OF SUFFERING. The Book of Job deals with the mystery of human suffering, especially the suffering of the righteous. Job's friends erred in thinking that all suffering is God's special judgment upon some special sin. "Who ever perished, being innocent?" (iv. 7) was the burden of all their consolation. They reckoned that Job's sin against God must be exceptionally great to account for such exceptional suffering. In this connection it is important to remember Job's attitude towards God. He was one who, having access to Him through the blood of sacrifice (i. 5), was walking with Him in integrity of heart and conformity of life.

God's own testimony of him was, "There is none like him in the earth, a perfect and an upright man, one that feareth God, and escheweth evil" (i. 8). "Of all men he was the one most fitted to be entrusted with the service of suffering, being chosen as a pattern of the ways of God in the ages to come, for all His children in the service of trial."[2] Job knew that his heart was true to God, and he could not accept the accusations of his friends. He shows them that their conclusion is false, and that the wicked often prosper in the world. "They gather the vintage of the wicked" (xxiv. 6). One of the elements of danger in a course of sin is that it is so often

---

[1] See *Bible Teachings in Nature* (Hugh Macmillan); *God's Living Oracles* (Dr. Pierson); and the writings of Canon Tristram.

[2] *The Story of Job*, by Mrs. Penn-Lewis. A book full of helpful teaching on this subject.

successful. The young man who wins his first stake in gambling is in far greater peril than the one who loses.

CHASTISEMENT. Elihu, who had been listening to the argument of Job and his friends, sums up their discussion in two terse sentences: "Against Job was his wrath kindled, because he justified himself rather than God. Also against his three friends was his wrath kindled, because they had found no answer, and yet had condemned Job" (xxxii. 2, 3). Elihu was a true messenger from God to Job, and brought out His gracious purpose in the chastisement of His children. Elihu's words prepare the way for God's own revelation of Himself which followed. *Chastisement* is the Key-note of this book.

SPECTATORS OF THE CONFLICT. But God has a deeper purpose in the suffering of His children than even their personal perfection. We have the clue in the words of Paul: "To the intent that now, unto the principalities and powers in heavenly places, might be known by the Church the manifold wisdom of God" (Eph. iii. 10). An unseen cloud of witnesses is eagerly watching the conflict carried on in the arena of this little world. God is unfolding to the angels of light and to the hosts of darkness "the eternal purposes" of His grace in His dealings with His redeemed children on the earth. The adversary had challenged the integrity of Job in the council of heaven, and God's honour is in question. How little did Job realise the issues which hung upon his steadfastness when he said, "The Lord gave, and the Lord hath taken away; blessed be the Name of the Lord"; and again, "Though He slay me, yet will I trust in Him." How little the Church to-day realises the issues which hang upon her faithfulness, or God would find among those *who trust Him* a larger number of saints *whom He could trust*.

THE ADVERSARY. Both the extent and the limit of Satan's power are brought out in this book. He had power to bring up the hordes of hostile Sabeans and Chaldeans to carry off the oxen and the asses and the camels. He had power to manipulate the lightning to consume the sheep, to summon the wind to slay Job's children, and to smite Job himself with a terrible disease; for is he not the Prince of the power of the air, the spirit that now worketh in the children of disobedience? And did he not bring against Paul a thorn in the flesh, the messenger of Satan to buffet him? But, on the other hand, he had no power at all, except in so far as God permitted him to break through the protecting hedge with which He had surrounded His servant (i. 10). What comfort there is here for the child of God : no calamity can touch him except as his Father permits it ; and He who has "shut up the sea with doors, and said, Hitherto shalt thou come, but no further ; and here shall thy proud waves be stayed" (xxxviii. 8-11), will never suffer us to be tempted above that we are able, or allow the furnace to be hotter than we can bear.

We have in the Book of Job not merely the theory of suffering, but a living example of one of God's children placed in the crucible, and the effect of it upon his life. Because God *trusted* Job He assigned to him the ministry of suffering. Because He *loved* him He chastened him. Even in the midst of his anguish Job recognised that it is only the gold that is worth putting in the fire. Job, in his prosperity and uprightness and benevolence, was in danger of becoming self-confident, and not recognising that he had only held his power and position in trust for God. But as God dealt with him we see him broken (xvi. 12, 14, xvii. 11) and melted (xxiii. 10) and softened, so that he could say, "The hand of God hath touched me" (xix. 21); "God maketh my heart soft" (xxiii. 16).

"Now mine Eye seeth Thee." But it was the vision of God Himself that completed the work and brought Job into the very dust. He had protested that he was prepared to reason with God over His strange dealings with him. But when God took him at his word and said, "Shall he that contendeth with the Almighty instruct Him?" Job replied, "Behold, I am vile (or contemptibly mean); I will lay mine hand upon my mouth." God continued to deal with him until Job was brought to the very end of himself, and cried out, "I have uttered that I understood not ; things too wonderful for me, which I knew not. I have heard of Thee by the hearing of the ear; but now mine eye seeth Thee : *wherefore* I abhor myself, and repent in dust and ashes" (xlii. 1-6).

God's "Afterward." God's chastened, softened servant is now ready to intercede at God's command for the friends who had so aggravated his woe. Before his own misery is relieved he offers the appointed sacrifice which they have brought, and prays for them. As he does so God turns the captivity of Job, and his prosperity returns to him, doubled in every particular. Twice as many sheep and camels and oxen and asses fell to Job's portion as before—but only the same number of children, seven sons and three daughters. We have here the most beautiful intimation of the certainty of resurrection. Job's prayers had evidently been answered, and his sacrifices accepted, on his children's behalf, and the fact that he was only given the same number as before was God's assurance that those who had been taken were safe in His keeping, "where the wicked cease from troubling, and the weary are at rest" (iii. 17).

"MY REDEEMER LIVETH." Job's vision of the future life had been obscure at first, for we find him asking the question, "If a man die, shall he live again?" (xiv. 14). But with his affliction his faith grows, and he answers his own question in the glorious words: "I know that my Redeemer liveth, and that He shall stand at the latter day upon the dust: and though after my skin worms destroy this body, yet in my flesh shall I see God: Whom I shall see for myself and on my side. Mine eyes shall behold Him and not a stranger" (literal translation). However dimly Job himself may have understood the Spirit-given words, what a vision of the future life we have here, what a prophecy of the coming Saviour, sounding forth in the earliest ages! Job sees Him as the Goël, the Kinsman Redeemer—not a stranger; the One who, because He is the next of kin, has the right to redeem.

Again and again in this book we have the foreshadowing of the Saviour. We see Him in the accepted sacrifices which Job offered for his children as the book opens, and for his friends as it closes.

We see Him in Job's question, "How shall man be just before God?" A question answered only in Him who has justified us "by His blood" (Rom. v. 9).

ONE MEDIATOR. We see Him in the "Daysman," the "Umpire," Job longs for between him and God. "For He is not a man, as I am, that I should answer Him, and we should come together in judgment. Neither is there any Daysman betwixt us, that might *lay His hand upon us both*" (ix. 32, 33). The need of the human heart has only been met in "God our Saviour," the "one Mediator between God and men—Himself, Man—Christ Jesus, who gave Himself a ransom for all" (1 Tim. ii. 4-6, R.V.).

A RANSOM. Yet once more we see Christ again in the words of Elihu, "Then He is gracious unto him, and saith, Deliver him from going down to the pit; I have found a ransom" (margin, "atonement"). The ransom prophesied by Elihu and the ransom proclaimed by Paul are one. "Job had seen his Redeemer as the living One who would vindicate him in the day of His coming, but let him now see Him as the ransom, the One who would be gracious to him, and deliver him from going down into the pit—not on the ground of Job's integrity, but on the ground of His own shed blood as the price paid for the redemption of fallen man."[1]

The next verse gives the result of this ransom. "His flesh shall be fresher than a child's: he shall pray unto God, and He shall be favourable unto him; and he shall see His face with joy." Cleansing and communion resting on the ground of full atonement.

Yet once again we see the Cross dimly foreshadowed in Job's sufferings. His sufferings were through the enmity of Satan. "The suffering upright man pointed the way to the suffering sinless man—the Man of Sorrows." Job was wounded by his friends. He was "the song and by-word" of base men. "They spare not to spit in my face. . . . My soul is poured out upon me . . . my bones are pierced in me. He hath cast me into the mire, and I am become like dust and ashes. I cry unto Thee, and Thou dost not answer me" (chap. xxx.).

How closely all this answers to the description of the suffering Saviour. But while Job complained and justified himself, the sinless Lamb of God was dumb before His shearers, and poured out His soul a sacrifice for our sins.


## 2. PSALMS

The Book of Psalms—or *Praises*, as it is called in the Hebrew—has undoubtedly found more response in the human heart in all ages than any other book in the Bible. It is the book of the inner life, of private devotion. It expresses the doubts and fears, the joys and sorrows, the sufferings and aspirations of the soul at all times.

Notwithstanding its tone of sadness, it is a book of praise. With only one exception (Ps. lxxxviii.) all the Psalms which begin in despondency end in trust as the eyes of the Psalmist are lifted above his circumstances to his God. Its Key-note is *Worship*, and it has been used in the worship of God, by

[1] *The Story of Job.* Mrs. Penn-Lewis.

Hebrews and Christians alike, down to our own day.  It is the book of worship, not only in the Temple, for whose service many of the Psalms were composed, but the worship of the Creator under the starry heavens, or in the caves of the mountain fastnesses where David was hiding from his enemies.

Psalms is the book of nature.  Nowhere do we breathe the pure air of God's creation more freely, or see the marvels of His handiwork more clearly, than in the Psalms.  It is the book for all who are in distress, the prisoners, the sailors, the exiles, the persecuted, the sick and suffering, the poor and needy.  It shows the relative duties of life, the duty of kings and rulers, of ministers, and citizens, and brethren.  It is the book for the sinner, telling him of God's forgiveness ; the book for the saint, leading him into deeper communion.  It is the book of God's Law, showing it to be the most perfect work of His creation, and the blessing which rests upon keeping it with the whole heart.

"When I consider Thy heavens, the work of Thy fingers, the moon and the stars, which Thou hast ordained ; what is man, that Thou art mindful of him ? and the son of man, that Thou visitest him ?" (Psalm viii. 3, 4).  The wonder of modern astronomy is here !  When our place among infinities was discovered it raised the infidel cry, Was it conceivable that God would concern Himself about the salvation of the inhabitants of such a mere speck in His creation ?  It was the very cry of the Psalmist, anticipating the inexpressible wonders which the science of his day had not yet revealed, but revealing the still greater wonder of God's redeeming love.

In Ecclesiastes i. 7 we read : "All the rivers run into the sea, yet the sea is not full ; unto the place from whence the rivers come, thither they return again."  What an accurate description of the facts of the absorption and condensation of water from the sea into clouds and then into rain, by which the equilibrium of sea and land is maintained.  We have a similar description in Ps. civ. 8, 9, where we read of the waters going *up* by the mountains as well as *down* by the valleys.  The facts are still further explained in Ps. cxxxv. 7 : "He causeth the vapours to ascend from the ends of the earth : He maketh lightnings for the rain : He bringeth the wind out of His treasuries."  The watery vapour is rising from the ocean's breast in such volume as no pumps ever imagined by man could produce.  In the upper sky the cold air condenses the watery vapour and holds it in clouds.  If left there the waters will fall again upon the sea, but the verse tells us how this is averted. God has made preparation. "He bringeth the wind out of His treasuries." The clouds are borne in silent majesty to the mountains. How are these clouds to become rain? "He prepareth lightnings for the rain." The shock precipitates the rain upon the waiting earth. Lord Kelvin has said, "I believe there never is rain without lightning." And thus the Psalmist, inspired by God, described in simple but accurate language what science is to-day revealing.[1]

THE WRITERS. At the head of the list of the writers of the Psalms stands David, the poet-king, the sweet singer of Israel, the one who arranged the service of song in the sanctuary. Seventy-three of the Psalms are ascribed to him, fifty are anonymous, and it is thought that some of these are likewise his. Moses is declared to be the author of the ninetieth. We know he was a poet, and the majestic character of the Psalm is in keeping with his writings. The internal evidences corroborate the heading. It is emphatically a wilderness and pilgrim song. To Solomon two are ascribed (lxxii. and cxxvii.). Some are believed to have been written during and on the return from the Captivity. It is generally believed that David arranged those Psalms which were existing in his time, and probably Ezra collected and arranged the book as we now have it.

The Psalms are divided into *Five Books*, as shown in the Revised Version.

Each book ends with a doxology, the last with five Hallelujah Psalms. Thus the structure of the Book of Psalms is very beautiful, and this not only as a whole but each Psalm is arranged on a definite plan, so that the various parts of which it is composed either alternate with one another or are introverted, with sometimes a combination of both arrangements in the same Psalm.[2]

Several of the Psalms are written in acrostic form, following the letters of the Hebrew alphabet (ix. and x., xxv., xxxiv., xxxvii., cxi., cxii., cxix., cxlv.). This is specially the case with Psalm cxix., each verse of which, in the entire twenty-two parts, begins with its own acrostic letter.

Fifteen of the Psalms (from cxx. to cxxxiv.) are Songs of Degrees, Pilgrim Psalms, probably sung by the caravan pilgrims as they went up to Jerusalem to keep the feasts.

[1] This description is abridged from *Roger's Reasons*, by Rev. J. Urquhart.
[2] *A Key to the Psalms*, by Rev. Thomas Boys, edited by Rev. E. W. Bullinger.

"IN THE PSALMS CONCERNING ME." We can never exhaust the treasures of the Book of Psalms. Spurgeon wrote seven large volumes, containing two and a third million of words, on this one book, and it has probably been more commented on than any other book in the Bible. Seeing that it is impossible to give any adequate idea of its teaching in so short a space as this, it will be well to confine our attention to one aspect, and that the special aspect of the whole of these Bible Studies, what we can learn about Christ in the book.

We see Him in the frequent mention of the Good Shepherd (Ps. xxiii., lxxvii. 20, lxxviii. 70-72, lxxx. 1, xcv. 7, c. 3, cxix. 176); of the Rock of Ages (Ps. xxvii. 5, xl. 2, xxviii. 1, xxxi. 2, 3, lxxi. 3, xlii. 9, lxi. 2, lxii. 2, 6, 7, lxxviii. 20, lxxxix. 26, xciv. 22, xcv. 1); of the Light (xxvii. 1, cxviii. 27, xliii. 3). In the redeeming work of the Goēl, or Kinsman Redeemer (xix. 14, lxix. 18, lxxii. 14, lxxvii. 15, lxxviii. 35, ciii. 4, cvi. 10, cvii. 2, cxix. 154). In the forgiveness of sins through grace alone, which led Luther to call some of the Psalms "Pauline Psalms" because they teach Justification by Faith.

Several of the Psalms are "Penitential Psalms" (vi., xxxii., xxxviii., li., cii., cxxx., cxliii.), bringing out the exceeding sinfulness of sin, as shown in the depth of contrition of the Psalmists. May we not in some of these see Christ Jesus as our Sin-bearer? He who did no sin was made sin for us; and just as the righteous Ezra and Nehemiah and Daniel confessed the sins of their people as if they were their own, so in a much deeper and fuller sense we may see our Saviour's estimate of sin in these confessions on our behalf.

In the Book of Psalms we are given an insight into our Lord's inner feelings, and His sufferings for us, as nowhere else. He often quoted from the Book of Psalms, and in each case applied the quotation to Himself. He may have intended us to understand from this that all the Psalms are Messianic, though our eyes may not always be open to see Him in them. However this may be, it is doubtless the fact that they are so full of Christ which makes them so meet our need. The Jews are unanimous in applying a Messianic interpretation to those Psalms which are generally accepted as such by Christians. It is a remarkable fact that of all the citations in the New Testament from the Old which have a Messianic reference, nearly one-half are made from the Psalms.

THE KING. In several of the Psalms we see Christ in His

royal aspect as God's anointed King (Ps. ii., xx., xxi., xxiv., xlv. lxxii., cx.).

In Psalm ii. we have three of the special titles of our Lord. He is here called the Anointed, that is the Messiah (verse 2). He is the King of Zion (verse 6), and He is the Son of God (verses 6, 7).    He is then shown to be the possessor and Lord of all the earth (verses 8, 9), and loyal submission to Him is shown to be the only way of safety and reconciliation with God (verse 12).    Here, at the outset of the book, we see the Messiah, not in His suffering and humiliation, but in His ascended glory, and in His victory over all the earth.    Verses 1 and 2 had a first fulfilment at the time of our Lord's crucifixion, when "the heathen," "the kings of the earth," that is Pontius Pilate and Herod, on the one hand, and "the people," "the rulers," that is the Jews and the rulers of the Sanhedrin, on the other, banded themselves together against Christ.    But it waits a final fulfilment in the hostility of the last days, a hostility to be overthrown for ever, that the kingdoms of this world may become the kingdoms of the Lord and of His Christ.

Verse 6 : "But *I*," the King of heaven, "have set My own King, My Son, and My Viceregent, on the throne," "on My holy hill of Zion."    This was a kind of anticipative hint of the great truth taught in Psalm cx., that the anointed King should be the anointed Priest (Perowne).

Verse 7 : "Thou art My Son ; this day have I begotten Thee." Paul teaches us to see the fulfilment of these words in Christ's resurrection from the dead.    It was by *that* that with power He was declared—marked out as in a distinct and peculiar sense—to be the Son of God (Rom. i. 4 ; Acts xiii. 33).

Verse 8 : "Ask of Me, and I will give Thee the heathen for Thine inheritance, and the uttermost parts of the earth for Thy possession."    What a stimulus to all missionary effort to remember that the heathen are God's gift to the Son, as part of His inheritance.    Seeing the uttermost parts of the earth are His possession, with what alacrity should we fulfil His last command to carry the Gospel there.

Verse 12 : "Kiss the Son, lest He be angry."    Do homage to the Son, lest Jehovah be angry.    Christ said : "The Father hath committed all judgment unto the Son : that all men should honour the Son, even as they honour the Father.    He that honoureth not the Son, honoureth not the Father which hath sent Him" (John v. 22, 23).

Psalm xlv. tells of the marriage of the King.    It is the key to the Song of Songs, and a foreshadowing of the Marriage Supper of the Lamb. "Christ calls Himself the Bridegroom, and thus defends the joy of His disciples who did not fast. This word 'bridegroom' is an epitome of the whole Scripture."[1] This Psalm has a historical application, connected with the marriage probably of Solomon, but it is the sight of a greater King and a more glorious bride which makes the heart of the Psalmist to "bubble over" as he describes His eternal Kingdom. However little he understood the vision he seems to have seen that Face of glory, for he exclaims, "Thou art fairer than the children of men." He seems to have heard His voice, for he says, "Grace is poured into Thy lips."

The bride, "the king's daughter, is all glorious within; her clothing is of wrought gold. She shall be brought unto the King in raiment of needlework." "Let us be glad and rejoice, and give honour to Him: for the marriage of the Lamb is come, and His wife hath made herself ready. And to her was granted that she should be arrayed in fine linen, clean and white: for the fine linen is the righteousness of saints." The "King's palace" is to be her home for ever. "In My Father's house are many mansions."

Psalm lxxii. is one of the two Psalms ascribed to Solomon. It celebrates the coronation of the King. "The monarch grows fairer and larger than the Sons of Men; he is transfigured in the light of the promise made to David." "Like a man standing on high ground in a sunset, a glory not his own is on him. He casts a shadow much larger than himself!" In One, alone, is this glorious ideal realised. Christ stands out the true Prince of Peace, who is to reign from sea to sea, and whose dominion is to have no end; in whom all nations of the earth shall be blessed. "The handful of corn on the top of the mountains," that little group of unlearned and persecuted disciples sown in the unlikely soil of a corrupt Judaism, have already become like a forest of Lebanon, and the harvest shall one day fill the earth.

A double line of prophecy runs through the Psalms. One line speaks of the coming of the Messiah as an earthly King, the other of the coming of Jehovah, Israel's true King, her redemption and her glory. The earthly hope and the heavenly run on in parallel lines, but they never meet. In the light of the New Testament only do we see how David's Son is David's Lord (Perowne). Delitzsch, commenting on this fact, says: "In the night of the Old Testament there rise in two opposite

---

[1] *Christ and the Scriptures.* Adolph Saphir.

directions two Stars of Promise. The one describes its path from above downwards; it is the promise of Jehovah who is about to come. The other describes its path from below upwards; it is the hope which rests on the prophecy of the Son of David, which at first ran a course wholly human and only earthly. These two stars meet at last, they mingle so as to form but one; the Night vanishes, and it is Day. This one Star is Jesus Christ, Jehovah and David's Son in one person, the King of Israel, and at the same time the Redeemer of the world—in a word, the God-Man, blessed be He."

DAVID'S SON AND DAVID'S LORD. In Psalm cx. we see Christ in the united offices of King and Priest after the order of Melchizedek. The Jewish Rabbis all accepted this Psalm as Messianic, and this fact is recognised in the way it is quoted— with neither proof nor explanation—to the learned Jews to whom the Epistle to the Hebrews was written. Our Lord not only applies it to Himself, as the Messiah, as recorded in three of the Gospels, but gives it to us as an argument for His deity. And the logic of this argument rests absolutely on the fact of its authorship. "How say the scribes that Christ is the Son of David? For David himself said by the Holy Ghost, The Lord (Jehovah) said to my Lord (Adonai), Sit Thou on My right hand, till I make Thine enemies Thy footstool. David therefore himself calleth Him Lord; and whence is He then his Son?" (Mark xii. 35-37).

Our Lord puts this very solemnly, He says that *by the Holy Ghost* David called Him Lord. And yet some would have us believe that Christ was mistaken in this statement, and that the Psalm was not written by David but some hundreds of years later. About the time that Christ quoted Psalm cx., shortly before the last Passover, He said of His own words: "I have not spoken of Myself; but the Father which sent Me, He gave Me a commandment, what I should say, and what I should speak." The words of David and of David's Son were alike inspired words, the words of God. Mark adds as his comment on this incident: "The common people heard Him gladly." What a rebuke is this to those who tell us that ordinary folk cannot weigh the evidence for the truth of the Bible, but must surrender their judgment to experts! But Matthew throws further light upon the result of this conversation, and tells us that "no man was able to answer Him a word; neither durst any man, from that day forth, ask Him any more questions."

Immediately before this the most learned of the Jewish

Rabbis had been putting their heads together to know how they might entangle Him. Their enmity seems to have reached a climax. First came the Pharisees, with the Herodians, and when He answered them "they marvelled, and left Him and went their way." Then came the Sadducees, and were "put to silence" by His answer—an answer which hinged on a question of the tense of one word, "I am"—not "I was"—"the God of Abraham." When the Pharisees heard that He had put the Sadducees to silence they were stimulated to renew their attack. Having answered their question, our Lord propounded to them this problem about David's Son, "and no man was able to answer Him a word." If Christ had been mistaken about the authorship of this Psalm, how eagerly would He have been tripped up by these hostile scholars. And surely they in their turn were better able to pronounce judgment on a question of authorship than men of our day. They were astute scholars; their scholarship was directed to one study, the study of the Scriptures—the Law, the Prophets, and the Psalms; they were masters of the Hebrew language; they lived nearly two thousand years nearer the time when those books were written; they were in an incomparably better position to weigh the evidence than the most learned men of the Western world.

Christ's unanswerable argument convinced the doctors of the Law. It convinced the multitude also—"they were astonished at His doctrine." But there was this difference between the convinced people and the convinced scholars: "the common people heard Him gladly" (Mark xii. 37); "the chief priests and the scribes sought how they might take Him by craft, and put Him to death" (xiv. 1). God has condescended to make His revelation to man so simple that the wise and the mighty stumble at it, "but the wayfaring man, though a fool, shall not err therein."

Psalm cx. represents Messiah, by Jehovah's appointment, both as Zion's King and Zion's Priest. The kings of Judah were not priests. Uzziah was struck with leprosy for attempting so much as to burn incense. Of the tribe of Judah "Moses spake nothing concerning the priesthood" (Heb. vii. 14). The priests of Levi's line were not kings. But this is a royal Priest, after the order of Melchizedek, ruling in Zion, the seat of Melchizedek's kingdom and priesthood. Of this King-Priest it is declared in the second verse of this Psalm, "Jehovah will send Thy strong staff out of Zion." The word here used is not the sceptre, the usual mark of kingly power. It is the *matteh*, or ancestral staff. The mark of the hereditary and lineally descended ruler. It is borne by the head of each village, the sheik of each Bedaween tribe. And because in patriarchal times each head of a house appears in the character of a priest to his own family, the *matteh* marks the priest as well as the prince. It is here therefore most fitly said to be given to him who is described as bearing both offices, and as being the promised Prince of David's direct line. We read that this staff shall be "sent out of Zion." This mention of the sanctuary carries us back to Aaron and the way in which his authority as high priest was manifested. His staff, laid up "before Jehovah," was brought out from the Ark of the Tabernacle blossoming and bearing almonds, instinct with resurrection-life; indeed a strong staff of indisputable authority sent out of the sanctuary.

In like manner the Divine mission of our great High Priest was incontrovertibly established. He was with power declared to be the Son of God, according to the Spirit of holiness, *by the resurrection from the dead.* When the Jews demanded of our Lord a sign to prove His authority, He said unto them, "Destroy this temple, and in three days I will raise it up"; and He spake this of the temple of His body. Twice upon other occasions, when the Pharisees and Sadducees came and asked for a sign or miracle to establish His Messianic claims, He replied, "An evil and adulterous generation seeketh after a sign; and there shall no sign be given to it but the sign of the prophet Jonah," that is, as our Lord explains, His own resurrection from the dead on the third day. This is still the one sign, the one "token against the rebels," in Israel. The laying up of Aaron's rod in the Holy of Holies, which we are told is a type of heaven, prefigures Christ's ascension and His seat on the throne of God. The bringing out of the rod once more "from before Jehovah" to work further miracles, fitly foreshadows our Lord's second coming, amidst fresh miraculous signs, with power and great glory.[1] "We see not yet all things put under Him; but we see Jesus, crowned with glory and honour." "And the Father hath given Him authority to execute judgment also, because He is the Son of Man" (John v. 27).

ONE SACRIFICE. In Psalm xl. we again see Christ as Priest. "Lo, I come: in the volume of the book it is written of Me, to do Thy will, O God." These words are quoted in

---

[1] *Palestine Explored*, p. 171. Rev. James Neil.

the Epistle to the Hebrews in the argument against the perpetuity of the Jewish sacrifices.   These sacrifices were part of
a Law which was a shadow of good things to come; their
repetition proved their incompleteness.   The writer contrasts
Christ's sacrifice, the virtue of which lay in its being the
offering of an obedient will, and then he arrests the attention
of his readers by claiming these words of the Psalmist as
fulfilled by Christ.

PSALM XXIII.   We have already dwelt on the twenty-third
Psalm in connection with the life of David.   It is the first
Psalm we learned to love as children, the last to comfort us in
our passage through the dark valley.   It contains three secrets
—the secret of a happy life, a happy death, and a happy
eternity.   The setting of the twenty-third Psalm should not be
overlooked; it does not stand by itself, but in a group of
three.

| Psalm xxii. | Psalm xxiii. | Psalm xxiv. |
|---|---|---|
| The Good Shepherd in death, | The Great Shepherd in resurrection, | The Chief Shepherd in glory, |
| John x. 11. | Heb. xiii. 20. | 1 Peter v. 4. |
| My Saviour. | My Shepherd. | My King. |
| The Cross. | The Crook. | The Crown. |
| Past—Grace. | Present—Guidance. | Future—Glory. |

CALVARY.   Psalm xxii. brings us to "the place called
Calvary."   In its light we stand at the foot of the Cross.
Here and in Isaiah liii. the crucifixion is portrayed more clearly
than in any other part of the Old Testament.   Isaiah liii.
dwells mainly on the atoning aspect of Christ's death, Psalm
xxii. dwells more on His sufferings.   It begins with the cry
uttered by our Lord in the hour of darkness, "My God, My
God, why hast Thou forsaken Me?"   It closes with the words
"He hath done it," or "It is finished," as it stands in the
original Hebrew, identical with almost the last cry of our
Saviour.   It is a "Psalm of sobs."   The Hebrew shows not
one completed sentence in the opening verses, but a series of
brief ejaculations, like the gasps of a dying man whose breath
and strength are failing, and who can only utter a word or two
at a time.

Taken together with Psalm lxix., which also pictures the
crucifixion, we find the whole story of the Cross given here,
and the Evangelists have specially and repeatedly called our
attention to it.   "I am a worm, and no man; a reproach of

men, and despised of the people." Here is the offence of the
Cross. "All they that see Me laugh Me to scorn : they shoot
out the lip" (xxii. 6, 7). "The rulers derided Him." "The
soldiers also mocked Him" (Luke xxiii. 35, 36). "They
shake the head, saying, He trusted on the Lord that He would
deliver Him : let Him deliver Him, seeing He delighted in
Him" (verse 8). "They that passed by reviled Him, wagging
their heads. Likewise also the chief priests mocking Him, with
the scribes and elders, said. . . . He trusted in God ; let Him
deliver Him now, if He will have Him" (Matt. xxvii. 39, 41,
43). "Strong bulls of Bashan have beset Me round. They
gaped upon Me with their mouths" (verses 12, 13). "Sitting
down, they watched Him there. The thieves also, which were
crucified with Him, cast the same in His teeth" (Matt. xxvii. 36,
44). "They pierced My hands and My feet." "All My bones
are out of joint" (verses 16 and 14). The Roman method of
death by crucifixion—unknown to Jewish Law—is prophesied
here. The nailing to the Cross, the straining of bone and
sinew. The very action of the soldiers is given in the words,
"They part My garments among them, and cast lots upon My
vesture" (verse 18). "My tongue cleaveth to My jaws" (verse
15). "In My thirst they gave Me vinegar to drink" (Ps. lxix.
21). "Jesus . . . that the Scripture might be fulfilled, saith,
I thirst. And they filled a sponge with vinegar, and put it
upon hyssop, and put it to His mouth" (John xix. 28, 29).

A Broken Heart. "I am poured out like water : My heart
is like wax ; it is melted" (xxii. 14). "Reproach hath broken
My heart" (Ps. lxix. 20). Here we are told the immediate cause
of our Saviour's death. He died of a broken heart. Six times
over in Psalm lxix. the word "reproach" occurs. Reproach and
shame and dishonour borne for others. The bearing of our sins,
the hiding of His Father's face on account of it, was what broke
His heart. Oh, here we have the reproach of Christ, the offence of
the Cross in all its awful solemnity ! No wonder that to hold
this truth still brings reproach upon His followers.

"Jesus, when He had cried again with a loud voice, yielded
up the ghost. And, behold, the veil of the Temple was rent in
twain from the top to the bottom ; and the earth did quake,
and the rocks rent" (Matt. xxvii. 50, 51). When the soldiers
came to break the legs of those that hung upon the cross, they
found that Jesus was dead already, and brake not His legs.
"But one of the soldiers with a spear pierced His side, and
forthwith came there out blood and water. And he that saw

it bare record, and his record is true; and he knoweth that he saith true, that ye might believe." Death from a broken heart is very rare. It is caused by intense mental emotion. The loud cry, the fact of death occurring so soon, the effect of the spear-thrust, all point towards this being indeed the cause of our Lord's death. It tallies with His own words : "Therefore doth My Father love Me, because I lay down My life that I might take it again. No man taketh it from Me, but I lay it down of Myself." By wicked hands He was crucified and slain. By the determinate counsel and foreknowledge of God He was delivered to death. By His own will He laid down His life. These three statements are all true in the mystery of that great sacrifice for sin.

Surely we have in Psalm li. not merely the cry of the sinner, but a prophecy of this great sacrifice in the words : "The sacrifices of God are a broken spirit : a broken and a contrite heart, O God, Thou wilt not despise" (li. 17). This is "the plural of majesty." In Hebrew the plural is often put where the word *great* is to be understood. "The *great* sacrifice of God is a broken heart." This was the sacrifice that our Saviour offered for us. He clothed Himself in a human body that He might have it to offer (Heb. x. 5, 9, 10). He became possessed of a human heart that it might be broken. The way into the holiest is opened up for us through the broken heart of our Saviour.

This is the Gospel for us sinners. It is this that humbles us and brings us to know the power of the Cross of Christ to break the power of sin and set us free to serve Him. Psalm xxii. and Isaiah liii.—these two passages which unveil the power of the Cross, alike foreshadow also in their closing verses the resurrection triumph. The song of victory bursts upon our ear, victory through the blood of the Lamb. The Cross is the gateway to resurrection life for us now in this life. The crucified Lord must have crucified followers. Only as in our own lives we know the power of the Cross to separate us from the world, shall we know its power to move the hearts of others. "The Word of the Cross" is the power of God to-day, when proclaimed not in wisdom of words but in the demonstration of the Spirit.

### 3. PROVERBS

The Book of Esther closed the historical books of the Old Testament. Between these and the Prophets we have a series

of writings which have been said to deal with the exercises of
the hearts of God's people as to sanctification.  In *Job* we have
the death of the self-life.  In *Psalms* the resurrection-life and
the idea of worship.  In *Proverbs* "Laws from Heaven for life
on Earth" (Dr. Arnot).  In *Ecclesiastes* the powerlessness of the
world to satisfy the soul.  In the *Song of Songs* the satisfaction
of the soul in the Beloved.

SOLOMON'S WISDOM.  Apart from inspiration, Solomon was
peculiarly qualified to write this book.  God had given him
"wisdom and understanding exceeding much, and largeness of
heart, even as the sand that is on the sea-shore" (1 Kings iv.
29).  Solomon was a philosopher, an architect, and a man of
science, as well as a king.  Persons who have sought to catch
the "wise man" tripping in his science, have only displayed
their ignorance.  "The clouds drop down the dew" (ch. iii. 20)
our version says, and it has been rightly objected that dew only
falls on a cloudless night.  But the word in Hebrew means
"night-mist."  It is a copious mist, shedding small invisible
rain, that comes in rich abundance in Palestine, every night,
about midnight, in the hot weather when the west or north-
west winds blow, bringing the clouds from the sea.[1]

But beyond this wide knowledge of nature, Solomon
possessed keen intuition and discernment of character, and
insight into motives and springs of action.  This special power
was remarkably illustrated in the expedient he devised to discover the true mother of the living babe.  When all Israel
heard of this judgment at the beginning of his reign "they
feared the king : for they saw that the wisdom of God was in
him to do judgment" (1 Kings iii. 28).

LAWS FOR DAILY LIFE.  The object of the book is clearly
stated at the outset (i. 2-4).  "To receive the instruction of
wisdom, justice, and judgment, and equity ; to give subtilty
to the simple (literally the 'open,' the open-minded), to the
young man knowledge and discretion."  "It is the application of that wisdom which created the heavens and the earth
to the details of life in this world of confusion and evil."  It
is eminently practical in its teaching, and we should do well
to give it closer study for our guidance in daily life.

Coupled with "the fear of the Lord," filial piety finds a
prominent place in this book.  The duty of parents to chastise
their children is enforced, and is founded on God's chastening

[1] See *Palestine Explored*, chap. v.  Rev. J. Neil.

of His children (iii. 11, 12). The influence of a good mother is dwelt upon, and culminates in the description of the " virtuous woman " in the last chapter. This chapter forms a beautiful contrast to woman's influence for evil to which Solomon so grievously yielded in the latter part of his life, in spite of the solemn warnings he gives in this book.

The warnings against sin of various kinds in the Book of Proverbs come to us as God's message independently of the messenger. The writer urges his own experience of the wisdom of his father's instruction as a reason why his son should listen to his own advice, given with great tact and beauty of feeling. He warns the young especially against the influence of bad companions, against impurity and intemperance, against contentions, strifes, quarrels, anger ; against the liability to sin with the tongue through its too free use ; against lying, and deceitful dealings in trade, and against taking bribes. He earnestly denounces idleness and sloth, pride and an undue desire for riches, and he commends liberality to the poor.

THE FEAR OF THE LORD. Proverbs teaches " the fear of the Lord " as the beginning of knowledge. This is not the fear of fright, but the filial fear, the fear of grieving the Father's love.

WISDOM. But the beauty of the Book of Proverbs lies hidden in the meaning of the word *Wisdom.* Clearly this word, as used here, means more than an attribute. We cannot doubt that the Wisdom of Proverbs is identical with the Incarnate Word of the New Testament. Wisdom is represented as dwelling with God from all eternity, "from everlasting, from the beginning," as being " His Artificer " by which He founded the earth and established the heavens (iii. 19).

| WISDOM | THE WORD |
|---|---|
| Prov. viii. 23. I was set up from everlasting, from the beginning, or ever the earth was. | John i. 1. In the beginning was the Word. |
| Ver. 27. When He prepared the heavens, I was there. | And the Word was with God, and the Word was God. The same was in the beginning with God. |
| When He set a compass on the face of the deep. When He appointed the foundations of the earth. | Ver. 3. All things were made by Him ; and without Him was not anything made that was made. |
| Ver. 30. Then I was by Him, I was as His Artificer. | Heb. i. 2. His Son . . . by whom also He made the worlds. |

Ver. 22. The Lord possessed me in the beginning of the way, before His works of old.

Col. i. 17. He is before all things, and by Him all things consist.

Ver. 30. I was daily His delight,

rejoicing always before Him.

Luke iii. 22. Thou art My beloved Son, in whom I am well pleased.

John xvii. 24. Thou lovedst Me before the foundation of the world.

Ver. 14. Counsel is mine, and sound wisdom : I am understanding.

ii. 4. If thou searchest for her (Wisdom) as for hid treasure.

1 Cor. i. 30. Christ Jesus, who of God is made unto us Wisdom.

Col. ii. 3. In whom are hid all the treasures of wisdom and knowledge.

viii. 5. O ye simple, understand wisdom.

Luke x. 21. Hid from the wise and prudent . . . revealed unto babes.

i. 20, 23. Wisdom crieth . . . Turn ye at my reproof.

Matt. xviii. 3. Except ye be converted, etc.

i. 33. Whoso hearkeneth unto me shall be quiet from fear of evil.

Matt. xi. 28. Come unto Me, and I will give you rest.

viii. 1, 4. Doth not Wisdom cry ? Unto you, O men, I call.

John vii. 37. Jesus stood and cried, If any man thirst, let him come unto Me and drink.

ix. 5. Come, eat of my bread, and drink of the wine that I have mingled.

John vi. 35. I am the bread of life : he that cometh unto Me shall never hunger.

viii. 17. I love them that love me ;

Gal. ii. 20. The Son of God who loved me.

and those that seek me early shall find me.

Matt. vii. 7. Seek, and ye shall find.

Ver. 35. Whoso findeth me findeth life.

John vi. 47. He that believeth on Me hath everlasting life.

Ver. 32. Blessed are they that keep my ways.

John xv. 10. If ye keep My commandments ye shall abide in My love.

Ver. 6. Hear ; for I will speak excellent things.

Luke iv. 22. All wondered at the gracious words which proceeded out of His mouth.

Ver. 20. I lead in the way of righteousness.

Ps. xxiii. 3. He leadeth me in the paths of righteousness.

"WHAT IS HIS SON'S NAME ? " "Who hath ascended up into heaven, or descended ? who hath gathered the wind in His fists ? who hath bound the waters in a garment ? who hath established all the ends of the earth ? what is His Name, and what is His Son's Name, if thou canst tell ? " (xxx. 4). This is a most marvellous verse. If we ask a Jew the first question, "What is His Name ? " he would at once reply "Jehovah." But if we go further and say, "What is His Son's Name ? " the Jew is silent, or replies : "It is blasphemy to say God has a Son." But here is a verse which attributes ascension to heaven, and the creation and control of the world to God and to His Son. "And we know that the Son of God is come, and hath given us an understanding, that we may know Him that is true" (1 John v. 20).

## 4. ECCLESIASTES

This book is one long comment on the words of Christ, "Whoso drinketh of this water shall thirst again."

The expression "*under the sun*" occurs no less than twenty-eight times, and nowhere else in the Bible. It may be taken as the Key-note of the book. "Under the heaven" is thrice mentioned, and "upon the earth" seven times. The word "vanity" occurs thirty-seven times. Nearly forty times in this book does the Spirit of God name the earth and the things belonging to the earth. It is only in the last few verses that we get "above the sun."

If life be viewed apart from God it becomes an insoluble problem; all is vanity and vexation of spirit. Exclude God from the world, and scepticism and materialism must be the inevitable result. The chief design of the book is to test things in order to prove how inadequate they are to satisfy the deepest and truest longings of the human heart. Its problem is—Can the world, apart from God, meet man's need? The verdict is, "All is vanity."

WHAT SHALL IT PROFIT? Who is it that propounds this problem? It is one who was in the very best position to judge. One who possessed everything the world could give, not only of material things, but of intellectual gifts also. Solomon— "the peaceful one"—was intended to be the great ideal king. In the First Book of Kings we see the extent of his possessions. A large, well-defined, fertile territory, peace within and around his kingdom; an enormous revenue to spend, wealth practically limitless; all the interests of new commerce and exploration. Insight and penetration above all men, sympathy with all men and things, the interest of starting classifications of science, and of forming books of maxims and songs. The respect and admiration of all his contemporaries. The power of expressing his thoughts in words (1 Kings iv., viii., and x.; Eccles. ii. 1-11). Wealth, youth, and strength were all on his side at the commencement of his reign, and, unlike other Easterns, he was never idle. He spent a number of years in building the Temple, a worthy work for such a king. His actual possessions and his power of insight and penetration lift him into a position from which he can really view the whole of life, and the limit of what it can afford. Here is philosophical insight fully developed ; the great problem stated but not solved ; the diagnosis of the disease, but not the remedy. The book presents the world in its best aspect, yet says emphatically, "Satisfaction is not there."

"Only in the last two verses do we find the solution. Here Solomon gets above the sun, and things begin at once to disentangle and straighten. Love God, obey Him, trust Him, and all will be well with you ; for the judgment approaches in which all wrongs will be righted, and all mysteries cleared up, and you will be made glad with a joy unspeakable. This is the key to the book. Live under the sun, rise no higher, and doubt and unbelief will ensue. Live above the sun, spend the days with God, and light and peace you shall have." [1]

A NEW CENTRE. In chapter ii. we have a striking parallel to Romans vii. Both chapters are bristling with the personal pronoun "I," and the result in both is failure and disaster. In Ecclesiastes ii. Solomon says, "I said in mine heart, Go to now, I will prove thee with mirth. . . . I said, I sought, I made, I builded, I planted, I got, I gathered, *so* I was great. *Then I looked,* and behold all was vanity and vexation of spirit." The pronoun "*I*" occurs thirty-six times, and over thirty times in Romans vii. That New Testament chapter is the expression of what the Apostle's experience would be, any moment, apart from Christ. As he looks at himself all is failure, vanity, and vexation. But in Romans viii., as he looks at Christ, he loses sight of himself. The pronoun of the first person hardly occurs ; he is taken up with the contemplation of God, of Christ, of the Spirit. The Divine Name occurs abundantly all through the chapter, and the result is "No condemnation," "more than conquerors," "no separation."

When self is the centre of our life, and everything is looked at from that standpoint, all is failure. When we find in Christ a new centre and everything revolves round Him, then all falls into its right place, and we find rest and satisfaction to our souls. We begin then to ask about everything—not "How will this affect *me* ?" but "How will this affect my Lord and Master ?" Does it touch His honour ? Does it bring glory to Him ?

WHITE ROBES. There is a verse in Ecclesiastes which takes

[1] *Outline Studies in the Books of the Old Testament.* W. G. Moorehead, D.D.

us into the very atmosphere of John's first Epistle. "Let thy garments be always white ; and let thy head lack no ointment" (ix. 8). Obviously this does not allude to outward things. But how can we keep ourselves unspotted in such an evil world? and how can we be continually "unto God a sweet savour of Christ"? "The blood of Jesus Christ His Son cleanseth us from all sin." As we walk in the light as He is in the light, and abide under the power of His shed blood, we can be kept clean. "Ye have an unction from the Holy One . . . and the anointing which ye have received of Him abideth in you." As we abide under the anointing of the Holy Spirit, the Comforter, He will abide with us for ever.

THE LITTLE CITY. Again, this book contains a little parable. It is not a type, it is not a prophecy, but a simple little story with a beautiful truth hidden in it for those who believe that all parts of the Scriptures converge towards One Centre (Eccles. ix. 14, 15).

"*There was a little city, and few men in it*"—a picture of this earth which the Lord hath given to the children of men ; a speck in His great universe, yet He is mindful of man.

"*And there came a great king against it, and besieged it, and built great bulwarks against it.*" "The Prince of this world cometh," Christ said ; and he, the god of this world, has blinded the minds of men, lest the light of the glorious Gospel should shine unto them ; so successfully has he laid siege to the city of Mansoul.

"*Now there was found in it a poor wise man, and he by his wisdom delivered the city.*" We know the grace of our Lord Jesus Christ, who, though He was rich, for our sakes became poor, and was found in fashion as a man, and became obedient unto death, even the death of the Cross. The preaching of that Cross is unto them that perish foolishness, but unto us who are saved it is the power of God and the wisdom of God.

"*Yet no man remembered that same poor man.*" "My people have forgotten Me days without number," "forgotten that they were purged from their old sins." "Of the ten cleansed there were not found that returned to give glory to God save this stranger." Oh, redeemed children of men, "forget not all His benefits!"

"BOTH ALIKE GOOD." Chapter xi. contains words of encouragement to the worker for Christ. "Cast thy seed-corn on the waters : for thou shalt find it after many days." When the Nile overflows in Egypt, the rice grain is literally cast upon the fields while they are under water, to spring up in due season. In the parable of the sower, Christ tells us plainly that "the seed is the word." The ground, be it shallow, or trodden down, or preoccupied, or *good*—that is, soft and empty, and receptive—is the human heart. From this parable we see that the heart of man contains nothing of the good seed of the Kingdom to begin with—it has to be *sown*. The work of sowing the good seed of the Kingdom is always an act of faith. We cannot tell what sort of ground it will fall upon, but in this passage in Ecclesiastes God gives the faithful sower the benefit of the doubt as to its success. "Thou knowest not whether shall prosper, either this or that, or whether they *both shall be alike good*." Therefore, we are to be diligent in sowing, whether it be morning or evening, and whichever way the wind blows (xi. 6, 4). "Preach the word," Paul says to the youthful Timothy; "be instant in season, out of season; reprove, rebuke, exhort, with all long-suffering and doctrine."

"THOSE THAT SEEK ME EARLY SHALL FIND ME." The book closes with a call to the young: "Rejoice, O young man, in thy youth; and let thy heart cheer thee in the days of thy youth, and walk in the ways of thine heart, and in the sight of thine eyes: but know thou, that for all these things God will bring thee into judgment." The intention of the writer evidently is not to encourage the young to follow the dictates of their own heart without reference to God's will. He warns them of the result of such a course: "Therefore remove sorrow from thy heart, and put away evil from thy flesh: for childhood and youth are vanity. Remember *now* thy Creator in the days of thy youth, while the evil days come not, nor the years draw nigh, when thou shalt say, I have no pleasure in them."

This book is given as a danger-post, that we may be spared the bitterness of learning the vanity of the things of earth by finding their waters to fail; that we may choose the Lord's delightsome service of our own free will.

Those who have studied the subject have found that by far the largest proportion of men and women who are living to serve the Lord have chosen that service in childhood; that the proportion of those who are converted to God late in life is very small. How important then that the children should be won for Christ, that this most fertile soil should be claimed for Him, that the children should be led to accept His invitation: "Suffer the little children, and forbid them not, to come unto Me."

## 5. THE SONG OF SONGS

In all ages Christians have regarded this song as an allegory. It was in the Old Testament canon when the Septuagint version was made, 250 years before the advent of the Saviour; it has kept its place there ever since. Its mystic character has had the strongest hold upon some of the most spiritually-minded men the world has ever seen, such as Samuel Rutherford and Robert Murray M'Cheyne.

Adelaide Ann Newton has left us a little volume upon this Song which brings us into the very presence of the Lord of Glory. In her Preface she says: "The general character of this book in contrast to Ecclesiastes is very striking. Ecclesiastes from beginning to end tells of the vanity of the creature— Canticles of the sufficiency of the Beloved. . . . One verse in St. John's Gospel gives the contrast perfectly. Ecclesiastes is the first half of the verse 'Whosoever drinketh of this water *shall thirst again*'; Canticles is the latter half of the verse 'Whosoever drinketh of the water that I shall give him *shall never thirst.*' Thus the book is *full of Jesus*. But it is Jesus in a special character. He is not seen here as 'Saviour,' nor as 'King,' nor as 'High Priest,' nor as 'Prophet.' . . . No! it is a dearer and closer relation than any of these—it is Jesus as our 'Bridegroom'; Jesus in marriage union with His Bride, His Church.

"This is a great mystery, but it is one of most peculiar preciousness to 'all them that *love* our Lord Jesus Christ in sincerity.' It pervades every part of the Holy Scripture. It was first revealed in Adam and Eve in Eden. It was more fully brought out in the typical characters of the Old Testament; as, for example, in Boaz and Ruth; it was distinctly taught in the betrothment of the Jewish nation; and it is plainly declared in the spiritual language of the Epistles—'I have espoused you to one husband, that I may present you as a chaste virgin to Christ.'"[1]

THE NEED OF THE CHURCH TO-DAY. This characteristic makes the Song of Songs to contain a message which is peculiarly appropriate to the Church in our own day. In no age perhaps was Christ more the centre of interest both within and without the Church than He is to-day. His nature, His character, His work, His kingdom are freely discussed on all

---

[1] *The Song of Solomon compared with other Parts of Scripture.*

sides. But what a chill often creeps over our hearts as we listen, for we feel how little some of those who are thus discussing Him really *know* Him with that intimate personal knowledge which comes through communion with Him. When any one speaks who really knows and loves the Lord it awakens a response within us which no theoretical knowledge can do. The speaker may be an old country-woman in her cottage, or a policeman living amid the din of the London streets, but we feel at once "Here is one who has audience of the King."

Personal love to Christ is the greatest need of the Church to-day. A knowledge of sin forgiven and of our share in His redeeming work is the chief thing to draw out our love to Him. This is an age in which there is very little conviction for sin, so it is no wonder that love grows cold. For "to whom little is forgiven, the same loveth little." Simon the Pharisee asked our Lord to his house by way of patronising the Prophet, but he neglected to show Him any of the courtesies which civility demanded. The poor forgiven sinner drew near and lavished her love upon His feet. And the Master said: "Her sins, which are many, are forgiven; for she loved much."

REDEMPTION. In the Song of Songs the truth of Redemption is brought out in the beauty—not her own—with which the Bride is invested. She exclaims, "I am black, but comely, as the tents of Kedar, as the curtains of Solomon." Black as the goats' hair tents of the Bedaween; comely as the curtains of the Temple. "Perfect through My comeliness which I had put upon thee," as the Lord said to Israel. Our righteousness is as filthy rags, but He hath clothed us with the robe of His righteousness.

"O my dove, thou art in the clefts of the rock," the Beloved says to His Bride. Hidden in the cleft Rock of Ages, "crucified with Christ," and therefore dead to the world. "Thou art fair," is His reiterated assurance; "Thou art all fair, my love; there is no spot in thee." "For Christ also loved the Church, and gave Himself for it; that He might sanctify and cleanse it with the washing of water by the word; that He might present it to Himself a glorious Church, not having spot, or wrinkle, or any such thing; but that it should be holy, and without blemish" (Eph. v. 25, 27).

THE BELOVED. "As the apple tree among the trees of the wood, so is my Beloved among the sons. I sat down under

His shadow with great delight, and His fruit was sweet to my taste" (chap. ii. 3). There are four marks of the "apple" of our A.V.: (1) Pleasant and powerful perfume (chap. vii. 8); (2) Dense and delightful shade (chap. ii. 3); (3) Sweet and luscious fruit (chap. ii. 3); (4) Golden colour in the fruit, surrounded by a molten-silver setting of white flowers (Prov. xxv. 11). All these, in the highest degree, meet in the glorious evergreen orange and in it alone. It is doubtless the "apple" of Scripture.[1] Truly it is a very "tree of life," and, above all others, a fitting image of the Saviour.

"He is the Rose of Sharon and the Lily of the Valleys." The Rose of Sharon is a highly perfumed and very valuable white variety of the Damascene rose. The Lily of the Valleys is the wild crimson anemone. The one images our Lord's spotless, sinless character, the other His blood shed for us. The *Lamb slain* corresponding with chapter v. 10: "My Beloved is white and ruddy, the chiefest among ten thousand." The description of her Beloved in these words and the verses that follow is drawn from the Bride in response to the question of the daughters of Jerusalem, "What is thy Beloved more than another beloved?" "He is the chiefest among ten thousand. . . . Yea, He is altogether lovely. This is my Beloved, and this is my Friend."

We can trace through the Song how the Bride's love deepens through communion. Twice in the account that communion seems interrupted for a season, and this leads her to seek His presence more earnestly. These seasons when communion seems withheld may be the result of backsliding, or it may be that the Lord is leading her on into deeper fellowship with Himself. In either case that result seems clearly to be accomplished.

"*My Beloved is mine, and I am His*" (ii. 16). Here the chief thought is that of her possession in Christ. He is mine, for He has given Himself for me. The secondary thought is, "I am His"—bought with His own blood.

"*I am my Beloved's, and my Beloved is mine*" (vi. 3). Here the thought of His ownership of her holds the chief place.

"*I am my Beloved's, and His desire is toward me*" (vii. 10). Here His ownership swallows up every other thought.

In these three verses we have the double thought which is

---

[1] *Palestine Explored*, chapter vii., Rev. James Neil, who says also "Comfort me with apples" should be translated "straw me with orange," that is, with orange blossom. The strong perfume of the orange blossom, used to revive the Eastern brides, is the origin of our bridal wreath.

given us in the first chapter of the Epistle to the Ephesians. Christ the inheritance of the Church ; the Church the inheritance of Christ. "In whom also *we have obtained an inheritance*" (verse 11) ; "The riches of the glory of *His inheritance in the saints*" (verse 18).

RESULTS OF LOVE TO CHRIST. This leads us to the consideration of what should be the result in the Church to-day of a deepened personal love to Christ. We are not left in any doubt about it.

1. *Keeping His Commandments.* "If ye love Me, keep My commandments" (John xiv. 15). Where there is a real love to Christ there will be an intense sensitiveness not to grieve Him ; a great desire to become *in fact* what He sees us to be *potentially*— "undefiled," "all fair," "without spot."

2. *Feeding His Sheep.* Three times He said to Peter, "Lovest thou Me ? feed My sheep, feed My lambs." The longing to be of blessing to others comes out in various ways in this Song. In the Bride's care of the flock in chapter i. In her care of the garden in chapters iv. and vi. In her care of the vineyard in chapters vii. and viii.

3. *Fruit-bearing to His Praise.* "Herein is My Father glorified, that ye bear much fruit," our Lord said to His disciples. In this Song the thought of fruit-bearing is brought to perfection. "A garden enclosed is My sister, My spouse ; a well shut up, a fountain sealed" (iv. 12). In this fair picture of the garden the Lord has given us an idea of His inheritance in the saints. A quiet spot where He can delight to dwell, enclosed for His use, full of all manner of precious fruits and flowers. "Awake, O north wind ; and come, thou south ; blow upon my garden, that the spices thereof may flow out. Let my Beloved come into His garden, and eat His pleasant fruits" (iv. 16). His response is, "I am come into My garden ; I have gathered My myrrh with My spice ; I have eaten My honey-comb with My honey" (v. 1). But He will share it with others : "Eat, O friends ; drink, yea, drink abundantly, O beloved." His desire is that His fruitful Church shall be a blessing to others. The sealed fountain in the midst of the garden is first for the Master's use, for He says, "Give Me to drink" ; but it is also to flow out to others. "A fountain of gardens, a well of living waters, and streams from Lebanon" (iv. 15). How exactly this verse corresponds with the threefold description of the living water in John's Gospel. (1) "Whoso drinketh of the water that I shall give him shall never thirst"—the soul's thirst

quenched at the Fountain; (2) "The water that I shall give him shall be in him a well of water springing up unto everlasting life"—an unfailing supply in the soul of the believer; (3) "He that believeth on Me, out of him shall flow rivers of living water," "streams from Lebanon," flowing through the believer to a thirsty world.

SHINING AND VICTORIOUS. The Church which is really separated unto her Lord will be a power for Him in this dark world. "Who is she that looketh forth as the morning, fair as the moon, clear as the sun, and terrible as an army with banners?" (vi. 10). A glorious description of what the Church should be—shining with the reflected light of her absent Lord, a witness for Him in the night. "Terrible as an army with banners"—an all-conquering, victorious Church, pulling down the strongholds of Satan with the weapons of her warfare, which are not carnal, but mighty through God. Oh, how different is the Church of to-day! The blot of worldliness is lying like the shadow of the earth in an eclipse right across her fair face, preventing her being a light-bearer to the world. Instead of leading a victorious campaign against the enemy, she is suffering her walls to be broken down by his advance!

"Love is strong as death; jealousy is cruel as the grave: the coals thereof are coals of fire, which have a most vehement flame" (viii. 6). With a jealous love Christ yearns over His Church, that He may be able to present her to Himself a glorious Church.

LOOKING FOR HIS APPEARING. The Church that is really separated unto her Lord will be watching with intensity of desire for His appearing. With this thought the Song closes. "Make haste, my Beloved, and be Thou like to a roe or to a young hart upon the mountains of spices" (viii. 14). With the same thought the last book of the Bible closes: "The Spirit and the Bride say, Come. . . . And He which testifieth these things saith, Surely I come quickly: Amen. Even so, come, Lord Jesus."

# V. CHRIST IN THE PROPHETS

"The testimony of Jesus is the spirit of prophecy."—Rev. xix. 10.

## 1. GENERAL VIEW OF PROPHECY

BEFORE we consider the prophetical books one by one it may be well to take a general view of prophecy as a whole.

DEFINITION OF PROPHECY. The Bible itself furnishes us with an authoritative definition of the office and function of the prophet. "The Lord said unto Moses, See, I have made thee a god to Pharaoh ; and Aaron thy brother sh...ll be thy prophet." "And thou shalt put words in his mouth" (Exod. vii. 1, iv. 15). No statement could be clearer than this. By Divine appointment Moses was to be in the place of God to Pharaoh, and Aaron was to act as the prophet of Moses, receiving from him the message, and delivering it to the king (Moorehead).

IMPORTANCE OF PROPHECY. As Prophecy holds so important a place and occupies so large a part of God's revealed will, about a third of the whole Bible, how important it is that we should give it our earnest attention, and seek by the help of the Holy Spirit to understand its meaning. "Hebrew prophecy will be acknowledged by most to be a perfectly unique phenomenon in the history of religions" (Dr. Orr).

*Prophecy is God's revelation of His plans to His children.* It was given, not for a merely temporary use, but for all ages and for all people. Paul says concerning it, "Whatsoever things were written aforetime were written for our learning ; that we, through patience and comfort of the Scriptures, might have hope" (Romans xv. 4). Prophecy can only come from God, for He alone knows the end from the beginning. Christ said to His disciples, "I have called you friends ; for all things that I have heard of My Father I have made known unto you" (John xv. 15). Abraham was called the "friend of God" ; and when God was about to destroy Sodom, He said, "Shall I hide from

Abraham the thing that I do?" In studying the prophetical books we should realise that God is condescending to reveal to us His purposes. "Surely the Lord God will do nothing, but He revealeth His secret unto His servants the prophets" (Amos iii. 7).

There are three elements in the message of the prophets (Dr. Campbell Morgan).

1. *The Prophets bore a message to their own age.* Their standpoint was always the sovereignty of God. Whether they spoke with the voice of thunder or with the tenderness of love, they spoke in God's name and with His authority. Their protest against things that were contrary to His will was without compromise and absolutely fearless of consequences. Their one object was the glory of Jehovah; the failure of Israel to glorify God before the surrounding nations filled them with sorrow. And through everything their conviction is evident that in the end God will be victorious, and His purpose will be accomplished.

2. *The Prophets predicted future events.* A very large proportion of the message of the prophets was predictive. The main outline of prophecy is: the failure of God's chosen people, and God's judgment upon them; God's judgment on the surrounding nations; the coming of the Messiah and His rejection; His coming in glory, and the restoration of the chosen people; finally, the fact that Messiah's kingdom must ultimately be established over the whole earth.

"The element of prediction in Scripture has been lately undervalued, and under the specious plea that the moral and spiritual, the ethical element in the prophets, is the chief thing. This is a confusion of ideas. All prediction in Scripture is ethical, or rather spiritual, because it refers to the kingdom of God, and to its centre—Christ. But the spiritual element is intimately connected with the facts, the continued manifestations and gifts of God unto His people." [1]

3. *The prophetic books contain a living message to our own age.* The eternal principles of right and wrong are as applicable to our own times as to the times of the prophets. The rebuking of sin and the appeal to God's honour and glory are full of teaching for to-day. The prophets mainly denounced idolatry, the guilt and folly of worshipping stocks and stones, objects of men's own manufacture, and all the moral evils connected with it. Throughout the hundreds of millions of Christendom to-day idolatry, in the worship of images and pictures, still survives—to which is added the God-dishonouring worship of the wafer bread in the Mass as God Himself!

---

[1] *Christ and the Scriptures*, p. 49. Adolph Saphir, D.D.

PROPHECY HAD ITS ORIGIN IN MAN'S NEED. Man's fall called forth the first promise of the Great Deliverer in the person of the seed of the woman. Israel's bondage resulted in the call of Moses. Samuel was raised up at the time of Israel's rejection of God to be their glorious King. The idolatry of the kings of Israel called forth the prophecies of Elijah and Elisha. It was when Israel was apostatising from God by idolatry that the great galaxy of prophets appeared, uttered their solemn warnings, and made their passionate appeals. Peter speaks of the "more sure word of prophecy," and compares it to "a lamp shining in a dark place" (2 Peter i. 19); and often it shone the brightest when the darkness was most intense.[1]

PROPHECY DISTINCT FROM SOOTHSAYING. Prophecy is utterly distinct from divination and soothsaying. According to Scripture, it does not spring from any power of the human mind or spirit. Its origin is always traced to the supernatural working of the Spirit of God on the spirit of the prophet: "As He spake by the mouth of His holy prophets, which have been since the world began" (Luke i. 70). The prophets disclaim any part in the origination of their messages. Even the words in which the message is conveyed they ascribe to God. They invariably preface their message with some such words as these: "Thus saith the Lord," "The Word of the Lord came unto me," etc. The language of the Apostle Peter is final on the subject: "Knowing this first, that all written prophecy came not of [men's] own disclosure; for prophecy was not borne [in] in old time by the will of man, but holy men of God spake as they were borne [along] by the Holy Spirit" (2 Peter i. 21). God said to Jeremiah, "Behold, I have put My words in thy mouth" (i. 9); and to Ezekiel, "Thou shalt speak My word unto them" (ii. 7). The soothsayer and false prophet spoke out of their own hearts (Jer. xiv. 14, xxiii. 16).

Divination, moreover, professes to give prediction on all kinds of subjects and things without any reference to the Divine government or God's purposes of grace. It knows nothing of Christ, and cares nothing for Him. "It has no moral root and subserves no wider moral purpose, but is the result of a mere curious prying into the future" (Dr. Orr).

Prophecy, on the other hand, is never introduced as a mere wonder, or on its own account, but always in connection with,

[1] See *Outline Studies in the Books of the Old Testament*, p. 207. W. G. Moorehead, D.D.

and with a direct bearing upon, the kingdom of God. It announces nothing but what is in some way connected with His purpose of redemption. The object and centre of all prophecy is the Lord Jesus Christ and His salvation. " Of which salvation the prophets have inquired and searched diligently, who prophesied of the grace that should come unto you : searching what, or what manner of time the Spirit of Christ which was in them did signify, when it testified beforehand the sufferings of Christ, and the glory that should follow. Unto whom it was revealed, that not unto themselves, but unto us they did minister the things, which are now reported unto you by them that have preached the Gospel unto you with the Holy Ghost sent down from heaven ; which things the angels desire to look into " (1 Peter i. 10-13 ; Acts xxvi. 22, 23).

PERSPECTIVE OF PROPHECY. In foretelling future events the prophet resembles a traveller viewing a mountain range from afar. The perspective of the range is much foreshortened ; it appears as one ridge of hills. But as he gets nearer he sees range behind range. Peaks which appeared from afar to be at the same distance from him are perhaps miles behind each other. So it is with prophecy. The prophet sees the future in perspective. He cannot tell the immense distances of time which separate one event from another. Christ's first coming in humiliation and His second coming in glory are often seen as if they were one event. He does not realise the ages that should elapse before the kingdoms of this world become the kingdoms of our Lord and of His Christ. There is no such thing as *time* with Him who is the King of Eternity, and with whom one day is as a thousand years, and a thousand years as one day. In His presence it is but natural that the prophet should lose the sense of time and see things in the light of eternity.

THE INTERPRETER OF PROPHECY. It is evident that the prophets did not always understand the message themselves. We see this from the passage already quoted (1 Peter i. 10-13) ; also from various other passages (Dan. vii. 28, viii. 15-27, x. 7-15 ; Rev. i. 17, vii. 13, 14, xvii. 6). It follows from this that the very words must have been given them. Prophecy is an unimpeachable evidence of the inspiration of the Bible.

To understand prophecy we must follow the principle of interpretation always implied in the New Testament—that the Bible is an organic unity and Christ is its centre. We also need to depend continually on the Spirit of God who inspired prophecy, to be to us its Interpreter. It is a common saying that history is the expounder of prophecy, and that we must await its fulfilment to understand it. This view confounds the interpretation with the confirmation. If prophecy can only be understood after it is fulfilled, how can it be a lamp shining in a dark place for our guidance? Prophecy is intended for all God's people. But all cannot know the world's history; hence history is not its only interpreter.

Moreover our Saviour censured His disciples for not having understood from the prophets the things that were to happen to Him. "O fools, and slow of heart to believe all that the prophets have spoken : ought not Christ to have suffered these things, and to enter into His glory? And beginning at Moses and all the prophets, He expounded unto them in all the Scriptures the things concerning Himself" (Luke xxiv. 25-27). In like manner His second coming has been clearly foretold, and we shall be deserving of the same censure if we are not watching for it. "Therefore be ye also ready : for in such an hour as ye think not the Son of Man cometh" (Matt. xxiv. 42, 44).

Our Lord also shows that the Jewish nation ought to have recognised Him from the study of their own prophets. "Saying, If thou hadst known, even thou, at least in this thy day, the things that belong unto thy peace! but now they are hid from thine eyes. . . . They shall not leave in thee one stone upon another ; *because thou knewest not the time of thy visitation*" (Luke xix. 42, 44). As Stephen said : "Ye stiffnecked and uncircumcised in heart and ears, ye do always resist the Holy Ghost : as your fathers did, so do ye. Which of the prophets have not your fathers persecuted? and they have slain them which showed before of the coming of the Just One ; of whom ye have been now the betrayers and murderers" (Acts vii. 51, 52). Paul also said : "They that dwell at Jerusalem, and their rulers, because they knew Him not, nor yet the voices of the prophets which are read every Sabbath day, they have fulfilled them in condemning Him." "Beware therefore, lest that come upon you, which is spoken of in the prophets ; Behold, ye despisers, and wonder, and perish : for I work a work in your days, a work which ye shall in no wise believe, though a man declare it unto you" (Acts xiii. 27, 40, 41. See 2 Peter iii.).

COINCIDENCE AN IMPOSSIBLE EXPLANATION OF PROPHECY. Those who say that the correspondence of prophecy with its fulfilment is due to accidental coincidence have surely not studied the law of simple and compound probability. When a simple prediction is made, about which there is but one feature, it may or may not prove true ; there is therefore one chance in two of its being fulfilled. But if a second feature is introduced in the prediction, the region of compound probability is entered. Each prediction has a half chance of fulfilment, the two combined have only a quarter chance, *i.e.* there is one chance in four that both predictions will be verified. Every new feature added makes the fraction of probability smaller. The various events prophesied in the Scriptures, whether it be the destiny of the surrounding nations or of the Jewish people, are given with a precision and variety of detail which reduce the probability of their fulfilment to a minimum. The prophecies concerning Christ Himself, above all others, are so definite, and such a number of distinct features are given, that the probability of fulfilment apart from Divine foreknowledge, and as a matter of accidental coincidence, is reduced to a fraction too small for figures to represent.[1]

Fulfilled prophecy is one of the greatest miracles the world has seen. And these fulfilled prophecies are woven into the text of the Scriptures throughout.

INSTANCES OF FULFILLED PROPHECY. The whole work of Redemption was outlined in that first brief prediction which Adam heard from the voice of God Himself. "Noah sketched in three inspired sentences the great features of human history." The tenth chapter of Genesis contains a summary of the distribution of the race which is in perfect accord with the latest theories of ethnology.

"To Abraham was revealed the history of the descendants of his two sons Ishmael and Isaac ; the four hundred years' affliction of his posterity ; the blessing of all nations through his seed, etc. Abraham, Jacob, and Moses, all saw Christ's day and were glad ; Isaiah and Jeremiah revealed not only the proximate judgments and deliverances of Israel, but also incarnation and atonement. The visions of Daniel present not only a comprehensive, but an orderly and consecutive prophetic narrative of leading events from his own day to the end of all things : a miniature universal history. The fall of Belshazzar ; the rise of Cyrus, his conquests, the greatness of his empire ;

---

[1] See *Many Infallible Proofs*, p. 55, by A. T. Pierson, D.D., who shows that the twenty-five distinct predictions given by our Lord respecting the destruction of Jerusalem, by the law of compound probability reduce the chance of fulfilment to *one in nearly twenty millions!* Yet every one of these predictions was fulfilled in that event.

his successors, Cambyses, Smerdis, and Darius ; the character, power, and conduct of Xerxes ; the marvellous exploits of Alexander the Great, his sudden death, and the division of his empire ; the reigns of the Ptolemies and Seleucidæ ; the character and conquests of the Roman Empire ; the destruction of Jerusalem by Titus ; the decay and division of the Roman Empire ; the rise of the papacy and its career ; its cruel persecutions of God's saints ;—all this and much more is foretold by the man greatly beloved. The 'burdens' of the later prophets concern Syria, Egypt, Edom, Tyre, Sidon, Moab, Philistia, Kedar, Elam, Babylon, Gog and Magog, besides Judah and Ephraim." [1]

FULFILMENT OF PROPHECY IN THE JEWISH NATION. In an earlier chapter (p. 34) we touched upon the remarkable fulfilments of prophecy with regard to the Jewish nation. Let us now look a little more particularly into the prophecies regarding that nation which have already been fulfilled.

(1) *Their rejection of Christ foretold.* "He is despised and rejected of men . . . despised, and we esteemed Him not" (Isa. liii. 1-3) ; "The stone which the builders refused" (Ps. cxviii. 22). "One whom man despiseth—whom *the nation* abhorreth" (Isa. xlix. 7).

(2) *Their rejection of Christ to be long continued.* The prophet asks how long the doom of blindness is to rest upon Israel. "Till the land become utterly waste, and the Lord have removed men far away" (Isa. vi. 9-12). And Paul tells us that it is "until the fulness of the Gentiles be come in" (Rom. xi. 25). The Jew confirms by his very rejection the claims which he scorns.

(3) *The Romans to be used in the chastisement of Israel.* "The Lord shall bring a nation against thee from far, from the end of the earth, as the eagle flieth ; a nation whose tongue thou shalt not understand : a nation of fierce countenance" (Deut. xxviii. 49, 50. See also Jer. v. 15). How literally the Romans fulfilled the details of this prediction ! Instead of being one of the surrounding nations which had so often been used to chastise Israel, they came from far. Instead of the close similarity of the language of the surrounding nations with the Hebrew tongue, the language of the Romans was entirely foreign. The Roman eagle was their well-known ensign. They are "a nation of fierce countenance, which shall not regard the person of the old, nor show favour to the young." The merciless cruelty of the Romans at the time of the fall of Jerusalem is beyond words to describe.

[1] *The Approaching End of the Age,* p. 4. H. Grattan Guinness.

(4) *They were to be taken back to Egypt in ships.* "And the Lord shall bring thee into Egypt again with ships" (Deut. xxviii. 68). Of those saved at Jerusalem, all who were over seventeen years of age were sent to labour in the Egyptian mines, where prisoners were kept at work day and night without intermission, till they fell down and died.

(5) *The cities of Israel were to be besieged.* "He shall besiege thee in all thy gates, throughout all thy land, which the Lord thy God hath given thee" (Deut. xxviii. 52). The conquest of the land of Israel by the Romans, in contrast to previous wars, was almost entirely a war of sieges.

(6) *The method of attack.* "Until thy high and fenced walls come down, wherein thou trustedst." The strongest walls fell down before the terrors of the Roman battering-ram.

(7) *The extremities of famine.* "Thou shalt eat of the flesh of thy sons and thy daughters" (Deut. xxviii. 53; Jer. xix. 9). Literally fulfilled in the Siege of Jerusalem.

(8) *They should be left few in number.* "Ye shall be left few in number . . . and ye shall be plucked from off the land" (Deut. xxviii. 62, 63). "The whole land shall be desolate" (Jer. iv. 27). Many hundreds of thousands were slain during the war, besides those who perished by famine, disease, and fire, and besides multitudes carried away captive.

(9) *Their universal dispersion.* "And the Lord shall scatter thee among all peoples, from the one end of the earth even unto the other end of the earth" (Deut. xxviii. 64 and Hosea ix. 17). The Jew is found in every land to-day from North to South, from East to West.

(10) *They should be preserved as a nation.* "And yet for all that, when they be in the land of their enemies, I will not destroy them utterly" (Lev. xxvi. 44; Jer. xxx. 11, xlvi. 28). "Massacred by thousands, yet springing up again from their undying stock, the Jews appear at all times and in all regions. Their perpetuity, their national immortality, is at once the most curious problem to the political inquirer; to the religious man a subject of profound and awful admiration." [1]

(11) *Separateness.* "The people shall dwell alone, and shall not be reckoned among the nations" (Num. xxiii. 9). "That which cometh into your minds shall not be at all; in that ye say we will be as the nations, to serve wood and stone." Neither their own proclivities to idolatry, nor pressure and persecution from without have ever prevailed, since the Babylonian Captivity,

[1] *History of the Jews,* ii. 399. Milman.

to make them give up the faith of their fathers or become as the nations among whom they lived.

(12) *They should have no rest.* "And among these nations shalt thou find no ease, and there shall be no rest for the sole of thy foot. . . . Thy life shall hang in doubt before thee ; and thou shalt fear day and night, and shalt have none assurance of thy life" (Deut. xxviii. 65-67 ; Amos ix. 4). How literally these words have been fulfilled in the terrible massacres of the Jews down to our own day !

(13) *They should be deprived of central government and temple.* "For the Children of Israel shall abide many days without a king, and without a sacrifice" (Hos. iii. 4). These words have been fulfilled in spite of the strenuous efforts of the Jews to maintain among themselves some central authority.[1]

The following verse says : "Afterward shall the children of Israel return, and seek the Lord their God, and David their King ; and shall come with fear unto the Lord and to His goodness in the latter days" (Hos. iii. 5). How can we doubt that His word, which has been so literally fulfilled in the past in judgment, will be equally fulfilled in the future in mercy ? God expressly tells us that it shall be so. "Hear the word of the Lord, O ye nations. He that scattered Israel will gather him, and keep him, as a shepherd doth his flock" (Jer. xxxi. 10). "For thus saith the Lord God : Behold, I, even I, will both search My sheep, and seek them out. As a shepherd seeketh out his flock in the day that he is among his sheep that are scattered : so will I seek out My sheep, and will deliver them out of all places where they have been scattered in the cloudy and dark day. And I will bring them out from the people, and gather them from the countries, and will bring them to their own land, and feed them upon the mountains of Israel, by the rivers, and in all the inhabited places of the country. And I will set up One Shepherd over them, and He shall feed them, even My Servant David ; He shall feed them, and He shall be their Shepherd" (Ezek. xxxiv. 11-13, 23. See also Jer. xxx. 3).

FULFILMENT OF PROPHECY IN SURROUNDING NATIONS— TYRE (Ezek. xxvi. 7-11). After describing the vengeance which the king of Babylon should inflict upon Tyre, the prophet proceeds : "And *they* (*i.e.* 'many nations,' ver. 3) shall lay thy stones and thy timber and thy dust in the midst of

---

[1] *What are we to Believe ?* chap. x. Rev. J. Urquhart.

the waters, and thou shalt be built no more." Previous to the fall of their ancient city the Tyrians had removed the bulk of their treasures to an island in their possession half a mile from the shore. No attempt was made to rebuild the old city after the Babylonian army had retired, but the ruins still stood. Then Alexander came, and because the citizens would not hand over their city to him he resolved to build a solid causeway through the sea and take it. Every vestige of the ancient city was pulled down and laid in the midst of the sea, and so great was the demand for material that even the very dust seems to have been scraped from the ancient site. Though centuries had rolled away after the word was spoken, the word was literally fulfilled. The city has never been rebuilt; the site remains to-day without even a mound to mark it.

SIDON. Of the neighbouring city of Sidon a different fate is predicted (Ezek. xxviii. 20-23): "Behold, I am against thee, O Zidon; and I will be glorified in the midst of thee: and they shall know that I am the Lord, when I shall have executed judgments in her. For I will send into her pestilence, and blood in her streets; and the wounded shall fall in the midst of her, with the sword upon her on every side." No doom of extinction is pronounced against Sidon, but she is to suffer fearful slaughter. This has been abundantly fulfilled in every commotion which has troubled that unhappy land. Under the Persians 40,000 citizens set fire to their homes and perished rather than submit. Again and again blood has flowed in her streets, even as lately as 1840, when the place was captured by Admiral Napier. But Sidon still remains, possessing even now about 10,000 inhabitants.

If the prophecies concerning Tyre and Sidon had been reversed, how complete would have been the refutation of Ezekiel's claim to speak the word of the Lord![1]

FULFILMENT OF PROPHECY IN CHRIST. We have already, in a former section, "The Testimony of the Scripture to Christ," as well as in each succeeding section, traced many of the prophecies which have been so abundantly fulfilled in the life and death and resurrection and ascension of our Redeemer. "The Testimony of Jesus is the Spirit of Prophecy." "In the volume of the Book it is written of Me." There is only one Book, and only one Person to whom these words point. A perfect picture of the Messiah who was to come is traced for us in all its details in the prophecies of the Old Testament. A

[1] *What are we to Believe?* chap. viii. Rev. J. Urquhart.

perfect picture of His life is given in the historic records of the New. Place these two portraits one over the other and they correspond exactly. There can have been no collusion between the writers, for they are separated from each other by the silence of four hundred years. The Old Testament gives a portrait of the mysterious coming One, the New of One who had actually come. The hand that drew them both must have been Divine. This irresistible conclusion is a double one—it leads us to accept the prophetic Scriptures as inspired, and to accept the historic Christ, towards whom all these rays converge, as a Divine person (Dr. Pierson).

"When a lock and key are well-fitted, a fair presumption arises, even though they be of a simple character, that they were made for each other. If they are complex in their form, that presumption is considerably strengthened. But if the lock is composed of such strange and curious parts as to baffle the skill of the cleverest mechanic, if it is absolutely novel and peculiar, differing from everything which was before seen in the world—if no key in the universe will enter it except one, and by that one it is so easily and exactly fitted that a child may open it, then, indeed, are we absolutely certain that the lock and the key were made by the same master-hand, and they belong to each other. No less curiously diversified, no less hidden from the wisdom of man, no less novel and peculiar, are the prophecies contained in the Old Testament respecting Jesus Christ. No less easy, no less exact, is the manner in which they are fitted by the Gospel history. Who, then, can doubt that God was the author of these predictions, of the events by which they were fulfilled, and of the religion with which they are both inseparably connected?" (J. J. Gurney).

## 2. ISAIAH

There is something in the prophecy of Isaiah which makes it stand out from all the other books of the Old Testament. We are awe-stricken at the power and majesty of Jehovah, and yet our hearts sink into rest at the almightiness of a God who, in the same breath, says that He will gather the lambs with His arm, and carry them in His bosom, and yet hath measured the oceans in the hollow of His hand. Nowhere do the judgments of the Most High peal forth with a louder thunder. Nowhere do His consolations breathe more tenderly than when He bends down to say: "As one whom his mother comforteth, so will I comfort you." Nowhere is His glorious salvation more fully set forth than through him whom Jerome has well named the Evangelical Prophet.

THE VISION OF GLORY. The secret of this unique power in the book lies in Isaiah's vision in the Temple. "I saw the Lord," he says. It was this sight of the Lord that changed everything for the prophet. Henceforth he saw everything in the light of that glory. "Have not I seen the Lord?" Paul cried; and the sight of that Just One made him a minister and a witness, both to the Jews and Gentiles, of what he had seen and heard. From the Gospel of John it is manifest that it was the Eternal Son of God whom Isaiah saw, for he connects the hardness of heart of the Jews in not believing on Christ with the word of the Lord to Isaiah in the closing verses of this sixth chapter, and adds: "These things said Esaias, when he saw His glory, and spake of Him" (John xii. 37-41).

Isaiah saw the Lord as King of Glory, he heard the seraphim calling one to another, "Holy, Holy, Holy is the Lord of Hosts: the whole earth is full of His glory." We can trace the effect of what he then saw and heard throughout his entire prophecy :—

1. *An overwhelming sense of sin and God's judgment.*
2. *An all-pervading sense of God's power and holiness.*
3. *A clear vision of Christ and His salvation, and of His ultimate universal dominion.*

Let us briefly trace these three thoughts through the book :—

1. The sight of God's glory brought to Isaiah the *Conviction* of his own sinfulness and need, and made him cry : "Woe is me! for I am undone." It wrung from him the *Confession*, "I am a man of unclean lips." This brokenness of heart was very precious to the Lord, as Isaiah understood when he said that the High and Holy One would dwell with the humble and contrite heart (ch. lvii. 15). His Confession was immediately followed by *Cleansing*. The flying seraph caused a live coal to touch his lips, and his sin was purged. That live coal was taken from off the altar of burnt sacrifice. Cleansing can only rest upon the blood of atonement. To the question, "Whom shall I send, and who will go for us?" the cleansed soul was immediately ready to respond : "Here am I; send me." Here was *Consecration*. Then came the Lord's *Commission*, "Go." This should be the history of every messenger of the Lord A personal sight of the Saviour, a personal interview with the

Lord of Glory, contrition, brokenness of heart, cleansed lips, consecration, and a definite personal commission. The lips that are filled with the Lord's messages should be jealously guarded from evil speaking by the Lord's own garrison (Ps. cxli. 3). They should be *burnt* lips; not filled with excellency of speech in any thought of pleasing man with their eloquence, but declaring the testimony of God; determined not to know anything save Jesus Christ and Him crucified. The scorners of Isaiah's day complained of the simplicity of his reiterated message, precept upon precept, line upon line, as if they were little children, and the Lord's message came to them as through stammering lips.

SIN AND JUDGMENT. The date of Isaiah's vision was "the year that King Uzziah died." Uzziah had been one of the best kings Jerusalem had ever seen. For fifty years he had reigned with justice and judgment. But his heart seems to have been lifted up with pride, and, for daring to usurp the priestly office, he was smitten with leprosy, and dwelt an outcast in a separate house. The sense of this sin and of the defilement of leprosy seems to have been weighing heavily on Isaiah's heart, from the way he connects his vision with the year of Uzziah's death. "I dwell in the midst of a people of unclean lips." It is not only his own sin, of which he gets a sight as he sees the Lord's glory, but the sin of his king, of his people, of his nation.

Possibly this vision was the commencement of Isaiah's work as a prophet, and it may be that in this sixth chapter he goes back in thought to his first call. Henceforth he denounces sin with unflinching boldness. It is a message of judgment to his own people that the Lord entrusts to him in his first commission. "The vision of Isaiah, the son of Amos, which he saw concerning Judah and Jerusalem." Thus commences the first chapter, and he proceeds to lay bare the natural corruption and depravity of the human heart in its rebellion and revolt against God. "The whole head is sick," the centre of all power of thought; "the whole heart is faint," the centre of all the power of will and affection; "no soundness from sole of foot to crown of head," corruption showing in the outward life. He dwells on the sin of hypocrisy—on drawing near to God with the lips while the heart is far from Him—and the life full of cruelty to others, and then he makes his earnest appeal for repentance: "Wash you, make you clean; put away the evil of your doings from before Mine eyes; cease to do evil; learn to do well; seek judgment;

relieve the oppressed ; judge the fatherless ; plead for the widow "
(i. 16, 17).

He who learned in the presence of God to cry " Woe is me "
is now sent to proclaim *Woe* to others.  " Woe to their soul :
for they have rewarded evil unto themselves"; "Woe to the
wicked" (iii. 9, 11) ; "Woe to the covetous" (v. 8); "Woe to
the drunkards" (v. 11, 22, xxviii. 1); "Woe to the self-
righteous " (v. 20, 21); " Woe to those that oppress the poor "
(x. 1, 2); "Woe to Jerusalem" (xxix. 1); "Woe to the
rebellious children " (xxx. 1); " Woe to him that striveth with
his Maker " (xlv. 9).  Isaiah shows God's people how their sins
have hidden His face from them, and how they have rebelled
and vexed His Holy Spirit (lix. 2-15, lxiii. 10).  He tells them
that their very righteousnesses are as filthy rags (lxiv. 6, 7).  He
proclaims the plumb-line of God's righteousness, and that His
hail shall sweep away the refuge of lies (xxviii. 17).  With
scathing words he rebukes the vain and careless women for
their haughtiness of mien and the excesses of their attire
(iii. 16, xxxii. 9).  He speaks in clear terms about the sin of
spiritualism (viii. 19, 20), and the blessing on those who keep
the Sabbath from polluting it ; not doing their own way, nor
finding their own pleasure, nor speaking their own words on the
Lord's holy day (lvi. 2, lviii. 13, 14).  In how many of these
things God's warning is just as applicable to this twentieth
century as it was when Isaiah first uttered it.

IDOLATRY.  The crowning sin against which Isaiah denounces
God's judgment is the sin of Idolatry.  The book is full of this
subject from beginning to end.  In the second chapter the land
is pictured as full of idols, rich and poor uniting together in
their worship (ii. 18-20).  But God's promise follows that He
will utterly abolish the idols, and that men shall cast them to
the moles and to the bats.  This promise is repeated in other
words again and again (see x. 11, xvii. 7, 8, xxvii. 9, xxxi. 7).
Chapters xl., xli., xliv., and xlvi. contain the most vivid descriptions of the making of idols.  The rich man is described as
lavishing gold out of the bag and weighing silver in the balance,
and hiring a goldsmith to make him a god.  The goldsmith is
pictured at work : melting the gold in the fire, holding it with
his tongs, fashioning it with his hammer on the anvil, smoothing
it, graving it with a tool, casting silver chains for it, fixing it in
its place so that it cannot be moved.

Then the poor man's action is described.  He cannot afford
to pay a goldsmith to make him an idol of gold, so he chooses

a good sound tree—anything from the stately cedar to the common ash—and sets a carpenter to work to carve him an image of wood. The carpenter takes his rule, he marks out the form with red ochre, and works it with a sharp tool, and carves it according to the beauty of the human form, and then it is set up in the home to be worshipped. The chips that are left over are gathered together to make a fire to cook food by, or for warmth—so commonplace is the origin of this god !

The sin of idolatry is charged home to God's own people. "A people that provoketh Me to anger continually to My face ; that sacrificeth in gardens . . . which have burned incense upon the mountains, and blasphemed Me upon the hills" (lxv. 3-7). "Enflaming yourselves with idols under every green tree, slaying the children in the valleys under the clifts of the rocks. Among the smooth stones of the stream is thy portion" (lvii. 5, 6). Idolatry was Israel's besetting sin before the Captivity—a sin from which they have been completely delivered, as a nation, ever since that time.

In denouncing the whole system of idolatry, Jehovah draws the contrast with Himself, and this brings us to the second part of the effect of the vision upon Isaiah. It produced in him

2. *An all-pervading sense of God's power and holiness.* Nowhere does this come out more forcibly than in the contrast God puts in his mouth between Himself and the idols. With the opening promise that the idols shall be utterly abolished is the corresponding promise that the Lord alone shall be exalted in that day. Again comes the contrast that, instead of a man looking to the images which his fingers have made, he shall look to the One who made him. The account of the making of the idols in the fortieth chapter is set off against the glorious description of God as the Creator of all things. The Creator of the ends of the earth, of the mountains and the seas ; the Creator and sustainer of the heavenly host, before whom the inhabitants of the earth are as grasshoppers, and all flesh as grass. The description of the Lord's power in creation in these chapters is not surpassed in any other part of the Bible.

The scientific accuracy of chapter xl. is marvellous. Verse 12 : "Who hath measured the waters in the hollow of His hand ?" The figure is that God held the water in the hollow of His hand, and saw to it that the exact quantity was there, and then placed it in its earthy bed. Science tells us the same thing. We have the exact quantity we require to produce the right amount of rain to make the earth fruitful. "And meted out heaven with the span?" The extent of the atmosphere was fixed by the Creator, and is exactly proportioned for us to breathe without difficulty. "And comprehended the dust of the earth in a measure?" The soil on the earth's surface has been measured and spread out to prepare the world for the abode of man. "And weighed the mountains in scales, and the hills in a balance?" The height of the mountains on every coast is in direct proportion to the depth of the sea which beats upon the shore. "It is He who sitteth upon the circle of the earth." That word *khug*, translated "circle," does not mean a circle drawn upon a plane surface. It means an arch or sphere. It occurs in two other places, where it refers to the vault of heaven, and here it teaches us the true form of the earth. "That stretcheth out the heavens as a curtain." The word *dōk*, here translated "curtain," does not mean curtain at all; it means "thinness"; and no better word could be used to describe the ether which modern science assures us is the element in which all the heavenly bodies move. It is matter in its most attenuated form, it has never been seen or weighed, yet scientists are assured of its existence. "God stretched out the heaven as thinness." [1]

The forty-first chapter contains a solemn challenge from God to the false gods to declare future events as a proof of their right to be worshipped. This Divine challenge is renewed again and again (see xlii. 9, xliv. 7, 8, xliii. 9, 10, xlviii. 3-5).

The forty-sixth chapter contains the striking contrast between the idols of Babylon that have to be borne upon men's shoulders, and the Almighty God carrying His children, not only as lambs, but to their old age and hoar hairs, in His fatherly arms.

THE HOLY ONE OF ISRAEL. The Divine title, "The Holy One of Israel," is almost peculiar to Isaiah, being used elsewhere only in three Psalms (lxxi., lxxviii., lxxix.), twice in Jeremiah (l., li.), and in 2 Kings xix. 22, where Isaiah is the speaker. Twenty-three times he uses it in this book as if it were the reflection on his inmost soul of the vision he saw when he heard the seraphim crying one to another, "Holy, Holy, Holy is the Lord of Hosts"; the name is stamped upon the book throughout, from the first chapter to the sixtieth, as if it were Isaiah's peculiar prophetic signature.

There is an intimation of the revelation of the Trinity in the question, "Whom shall I send, and who will go for Us?"

[1] Abridged from *Roger's Reasons*, by Rev. John Urquhart.

The personality of God the Holy Spirit is clearly brought out in the Book of Isaiah (see xi. 2, xlii. 1, xliv. 3, xlviii. 16, lix. 21, lxi. 1, lxiii. 10, 11, 14). As we have already seen, John identifies the Jehovah, God of Hosts, of this vision with Christ Jesus the Lord. The Divinity of the Messiah is elsewhere manifest in the book. This brings us to the third effect of the vision upon Isaiah, and at the same time to the great central theme of the whole book.

3. *A clear vision of Christ and His salvation and of His ultimate universal dominion.* The Key-note of the book is *Salvation.* Isaiah's own name means "Salvation is of Jehovah"; and it forms the subject of the book from the blessed invitation in chapter i. : "Come now, and let us reason together, saith the Lord : Though your sins be as scarlet, they shall be as white as snow," to the similar promise in xliii. 25 and xliv. 22 : "I have blotted out, as a thick cloud, thy transgressions, and, as a cloud, thy sins ; return unto Me ; for I have redeemed thee."

*Peace,* the effect of righteousness, the result of salvation, in like manner runs as a silver thread throughout the chapters from the Prince of Peace in ix. 6, 7, to the proclamation of peace in lvii. 19, and peace as a river in xlviii. 18 and lxvi. 12.

The universal spread of Messiah's Kingdom was foreshadowed in the vision in the words of the seraphim, "The whole earth is full of His glory." The truth finds expression throughout the book. In ii. 2 all nations shall flow to the mountain of the house of the Lord, which is to be established in the top of the mountains ; in xi. 9, "The earth shall be full of the knowledge of the Lord, as the waters cover the sea"; and in the last chapter we have the declaring of His glory among the Gentiles.

THE MESSIAH. The glorious salvation of this book centres round a Person, the Coming One, the promised Messiah. There is something very remarkable in the way in which He fills the vision of the prophet ; a certain abruptness with which the prophecies about Him are introduced, as if to arrest attention. It is so in the sign which God promised to give in the birth of a Divine Person from a human virgin. The promise in chapter vii. is blended with the promise in chapter ix., and in the two prophecies we get a picture of the Child which was to be. He is identified with our race, for He is "a child born, a son given." He is to be of the family of David. But He is much more : His birth is to be supernatural. He is to be

Divine, "God with us" — *Immanuel*; "Wonderful," the name by which God revealed Himself to Manoah and his wife; "Counsellor," corresponding with the Wisdom of Proverbs, He who of God is "made unto us Wisdom"; "The Mighty God,"—the word for God, *El*, links this verse to the name Immanu*el*; "The Everlasting Father" or "Father of Eternity," which is equivalent to "the author of everlasting salvation" of Heb. v. 7; "The Prince of Peace," the name foreshadowed in the priestly King of Salem, and in Solomon, the Peaceful One.

All these predictions have met and been fulfilled only in one event, the birth of the Lord Jesus Christ, our Saviour, of whom the angel said to Mary, "That holy thing which shall be born of thee shall be called the Son of God." "Unto us a child is born" were the words of Isaiah. "To you is born this day, in the city of David, a Saviour," was the word of the angel to the shepherds. "His name shall be called the Mighty God, the Prince of Peace," prophesied Isaiah. And the multitude of the heavenly host took up the refrain, "Glory to God in the highest, and on earth peace, good will toward men." "The people that walked in darkness have seen a great light: they that dwelt in the land of the shadow of death, upon them hath the light shined," ran the prophecy. "Mine eyes have seen Thy salvation," said the aged Simeon; "a light to lighten the Gentiles, and the glory of Thy people Israel."

Once more abruptly comes the prophecy: "There shall come forth a rod out of the stem of Jesse, and a Branch shall grow out of his roots" (xi. 1). "The Spirit of the Lord shall rest upon Him, the spirit of wisdom and understanding, the spirit of counsel and might, the spirit of knowledge and of the fear of the Lord." This description of the Messiah in the eleventh chapter corresponds perfectly with the description in the sixty-first, which our Lord applied to Himself in His first sermon in the synagogue of Nazareth. "The Spirit of the Lord God is upon Me." In both descriptions the result of that anointing is the same, making Him the Friend of the poor and the meek and the oppressed. Our Lord stopped in His reading at the proclamation of mercy and applied it to Himself. He did not go on to read of judgment; for at His first coming He came not to condemn the world, but to save it (John iii. 17). Both these passages in Isaiah speak as certainly of judgment as of blessing; for Christ is coming again to judge the world, as He said, His Father "hath given Him authority to execute judgment also, because He is the Son of Man." "Marvel not at this: for the hour is coming, in the which all that are in the graves shall hear His voice, and shall come forth; they that have done good, unto the resurrection of life; and they that have done evil, unto the resurrection of damnation" (v. 27-29).

Chapter xxviii. gives us the precious Corner-Stone. Chapter xxxii. tells of a King reigning in righteousness; of a Man being as a hiding-place, as the shadow of a great Rock in a weary land—the Rock of Ages of chapter xxvi. 4 (margin).

THE SERVANT OF JEHOVAH.   From chapter xlii. to lii. the Messiah is set before us as the Servant of Jehovah: "Behold My Servant."   Some of these verses have a preliminary reference to Cyrus, whom the Lord revealed to Isaiah as the future deliverer of His people.   But many of the expressions look forward to a greater Deliverer who was to come, and to a greater deliverance than from Babylon.   The words used to describe the glorious gathering to Jerusalem would be altogether out of place as a description of the return of the remnant under the decree of Cyrus.   Many of the words used of the Servant of the Lord in whom He could delight can only describe the one great Deliverer.   The blessings which are to extend to all nations through God's chosen people Israel, point forward to "the time of their receiving again," as Paul shows us in Romans xi., where he quotes from this book (Isa. lxvi. 22).

In chapter xlix. we begin to see the suffering Messiah.   The One whom man despiseth, whom the nation abhorreth, yet who shall be worshipped of kings, and given for a covenant to the people.   The sufferings deepen in the next chapter.   He who is given "the tongue of him that is taught" is not rebellious. He gives His back to the smiters, He hides not His face from shame and from spitting.   In chapter lii. we see again the Servant of the Lord, His visage marred more than any man, and His form more than the sons of men.   We see Him sprinkling many nations.

This brings us to the fifty-third chapter, the most perfect picture of our suffering Saviour in all the Old Testament Scriptures.   Seven times we are told He has borne our sins: (1) Wounded for our transgressions; (2) Bruised for our iniquities; (3) The Lord hath laid on Him the iniquity of us all; (4) For the transgression of My people was the stroke upon Him; (5) Thou shalt make His soul an offering for sin;

(6) He shall bear their iniquities; (7) He bare the sin of many.

How marvellously this prophecy has been fulfilled in all its details will be seen by a study of the corresponding verses from the New Testament.

### ISAIAH LIII. AS FULFILLED BY CHRIST

Reference.

Ver. 1. Who hath believed our report ?
John xii. 37. Yet they believed not on Him.

To whom is the arm of the Lord revealed ?
Luke x. 21. Thou hast revealed them unto babes.

Ver. 2. He shall grow up before Him as a tender plant.
John xv. 1. I am the true Vine.

And as a root out of a dry ground.
Isa. xi. 1. A rod out of the stem of Jesse, a Branch shall grow out of his roots.

He hath no form nor comeliness.
Isa. lii. 14. His visage was so marred more than any man.

And when we shall see Him, there is no beauty that we should desire Him.
1 Cor. ii. 14. The natural man receiveth not the things of the Spirit of God.

Ver. 3. He is despised.
Matt. xxvii. 29. They mocked Him.

And rejected of men.
John xviii. 40. Not this Man, but Barabbas.

A Man of Sorrows.
Mark xiv. 32. My soul is exceeding sorrowful unto death.

And acquainted with grief.
John xi. 35. Jesus wept.

And we hid as it were our faces from Him.
John v. 40. Ye will not come to Me that ye might have life.

He was despised, and we esteemed Him not.
1 Cor. i. 23. Unto the Jews a stumbling-block, and unto the Greeks foolishness.

Ver. 4. Surely He hath borne our griefs.
Heb. iv. 15. Touched with the feeling of our infirmities.

And carried our sorrows.
John xi. 38. Jesus again groaning in Himself, cometh to the grave.

Yet we did esteem Him stricken, smitten of God and afflicted.
Luke xxiii. 35. Let Him save Himself, if He be the Christ, the Chosen of God.

Ver. 5. He was wounded for our transgressions.
1 Pet. iii. 18. Christ also hath once suffered for sins, the Just for the unjust.

He was bruised for our iniquities.
John xix. 1. Pilate took Jesus and scourged Him.

The chastisement of our peace was upon Him.
Col. i. 20. Having made peace through the blood of His Cross.

And with His stripes we are healed.
Heb. x. 10. Sanctified through the offering of the body of Jesus Christ once for all.

**Ver. 6.** All we, like sheep, have gone astray.

We have turned every one to his own way.

And the Lord hath laid on Him the iniquity of us all.

**Ver. 7.** He was oppressed.

And He was afflicted.

Yet He opened not His mouth.

He is brought as a lamb to the slaughter.

And as a sheep before her shearers is dumb, so He opened not His mouth.

**Ver. 8.** He was taken from prison and from judgment.

And His manner of life who shall declare.[1]

For He was cut off out of the land of the living.

For the transgression of My people was He smitten.

**Ver. 9.** His grave was appointed with the wicked, but it was [viz. His grave was] with the rich in His death.[2]

Because He had done no violence.

Neither was any deceit in His mouth.

**Ver. 10.** Yet it pleased the Lord to bruise Him, He hath put Him to grief.

When Thou shalt make His soul an offering for sin.

Rom. iii. 23. All have sinned, and come short of the glory of God.

Phil. ii. 21. All seek their own, not the things which are Jesus Christ's.

2 Cor. v. 21. He hath made Him to be sin for us.

Luke xxii. 44. Being in an agony He prayed more earnestly.

John xix. 5. Wearing the crown of thorns.

1 Peter ii. 23. When He suffered He threatened not.

Matt. xxvii. 31. And led Him away to crucify Him.

Matt. xxvii. 14. He answered him to never a word.

John xviii. 24. Now Annas had sent Him bound unto Caiaphas.

John xviii. 20, 21. I spake openly to the world . . . ask them that heard Me . . . behold they know what I said.

Acts ii. 23. By wicked hands crucified and slain.

John xi. 51, 52. That Jesus should die for that nation.

Matt. xxvii. 57-60. A rich man named Joseph . . . begged the body of Jesus, and laid it in his own new tomb.

1 Peter ii. 22. Who did no sin.

1 Peter ii. 22. Neither was guile found in His mouth.

Rom. viii. 32. He that spared not His own Son, but delivered Him up for us all.

John iii. 16. God so loved the world that He gave His only begotten Son.

---

[1] It was a custom before the death of a condemned person for a proclamation to be made that others might bear witness to his innocency. That no such proclamation was made for our Lord was part of the injustice of His trial. See *Lowth on Isaiah*, p. 363.

[2] The intention was to give Him the burial of a criminal along with the two thieves. But Joseph of Arimathea, hitherto a secret disciple, came to Pilate and craved the body of Jesus, and with reverent hands it was laid by the rich man in his own new tomb. That is the Gospel record. It was written seven hundred years before on the prophetic page.

He shall see His seed.

He shall prolong His days.
The pleasure of the Lord shall prosper in His hand.

John iii. 16. That whosoever believeth in Him should not perish.
John iii. 16. But have everlasting life.
John xvii. 4. I have glorified Thee on the earth: I have finished the work which Thou gavest Me to do.

Ver. 11. He shall see of the travail of His soul, and shall be satisfied.
By His knowledge shall My righteous Servant justify many.

For He shall bear their iniquities.

Heb. xii. 2. Who for the joy that was set before Him endured the Cross.
John xvii. 3. This is life eternal, that they might know Thee the only true God, and Jesus Christ.
1 Pet. ii. 24. His own self bare our sins in His own body on the tree.

Ver. 12. Therefore will I divide Him a portion with the great.
And He shall divide the spoil with the strong.

Phil. ii. 9. Wherefore God also hath highly exalted Him.
Col. ii. 15. Having spoiled principalities and powers.
Heb. iii. 2. Appointed heir of all things.

Because He hath poured out His soul unto death.
And He was numbered with the transgressors.
And He bare the sin of many.

And made intercession for the transgressors.

John x. 15. I lay down My life for the sheep.
Mark xv. 27. And with Him they crucify two thieves.
Heb. ix. 28. Christ was once offered to bear the sins of many.
Luke xxiii. 34. Father, forgive them.
Heb. vii. 25. Ever liveth to make intercession for us.

ATONEMENT. "In His death" in the Hebrew is in the plural, "in His deaths," possibly "the plural of majesty," signifying "His *great* death," that great atoning death which was a sacrifice for sin. Or it may shadow forth the truth that "if one died for all, then all died." His death represented the great multitudes for whom He died. From that moment in the prophetic record the song of triumph begins, as we traced it in the twenty-second Psalm, as we may trace it in Phil. ii., which descends step by step in humiliation till "death, even the death of the Cross," is reached, and then bursts forth in an ever-ascending scale of triumph, till it reaches "the glory of God the Father." Thus it is in this chapter. The future triumph is revealed; the satisfaction of the soul of the Redeemer in the spoil that He has won; the great multitude who have been redeemed to everlasting life through His death.

The next chapter breaks forth afresh into a description of the glorious future. Then follows the Gospel invitation in chapter lv.—"Ho, every one that thirsteth, come ye to the waters—in which we can see our Saviour standing on the last great day of the feast, and saying, "If any man thirst, let him come unto Me and drink."

CHRIST'S REIGN.  The closing chapters are full of the note of victory, but full also of the time of judgment by which Christ's glorious millennial reign is to be ushered in.  Israel having been gathered to their own land in unbelief, must undergo a time of awful tribulation; but when they see Him whom they have pierced (Zech. xii. 10), returning in power and great glory, accompanied by His Church, to execute judgment upon the earth (Jude 14, 15), the veil of unbelief shall be taken away (2 Cor. iii. 15, 16), and they shall receive Him as their Messiah, and He shall reign over them on the throne of His father David (Isa. ix. 7, xvi. 5), and Jerusalem shall become a praise in the midst of the earth (lxii. 7).  During this reign Satan shall be bound (Isa. xxiv. 21, 22; Rev. xx. 1-3); universal peace shall be established among the nations (Isa. ii. 4); the very fierceness of the animal creation shall be completely subdued (Isa. lxv. 25, xi. 6-9).  Human life shall be prolonged, as in the days before the flood (lxv. 20-22); water shall once more be plentiful in the land of Palestine (xxx. 23, 25, xli. 18), and its deserts shall become fruitful as the garden of the Lord (li. 3, xliii. 19, 20, xli. 18, 19, xxxv. 1, 2, 7).  All Israel shall be saved with an everlasting salvation (xlv. 17), and God's purpose of blessing to the whole world through His own chosen people shall be fulfilled (Gen. xii. 2, 3; Rom. xi. 15; Isa. ii. 2, 3, lxvi. 12, 19, lx., lxi., and lxii.).

FULFILMENT OF PROPHECY IN THE HISTORY OF BABYLON. The predictions of the prophet Isaiah with regard to Babylon have been most remarkably fulfilled, both in its fall and subsequent desolation.  The army which is to accomplish its fall is summoned from the mountains, from a distant land : Persia, no doubt, is meant (xiii. 4).  But Persia is not to act alone; Media is to join the mustering squadrons (xiii. 17).  The Lord of Hosts calls them to execute His judgments upon the guilty city (xiii. 2, 3, 11, 19), and the earth trembles beneath the tread of marching men in response.  In chapter xxi. 2 we are told that it is the Medo-Persian army that is to capture the

Chaldean capital. The steady advance of the hostile army, with its battalions of horses and asses and camels, is seen by the watchman (xxi. 7). Herodotus tells us the Persian army had just such adjuncts as are here mentioned.

The fall of the city is to take place at the time of a feast (xxi. 5; Dan. v.). It is declared that fear shall take possession of the doomed city; panic-stricken it shall make no defence (xiii. 8). How exactly this was fulfilled, Daniel assures us. The consternation which seized the king on the night of Babylon's assault is read in the graphic language of Dan. v. 6: "His knees smote one against another." "On that night was Belshazzar, the king of the Chaldeans, slain." The gates of Babylon were to be open for Cyrus's entrance (xlv. 1). History relates that on the night of the capture this actually occurred. Marching into the heart of the city by the river channel, which he had drained, Cyrus found the gate within the city, leading from the streets to the river, providentially left open in the general disorder occasioned by the great feast. Otherwise the army would have been shut up in the bed of the river, as in a trap, and destroyed. Finally, there is the sudden cry of the capture and overthrow: "Babylon is fallen, is fallen!" and her chief gods, Bel, Nebo, and Merodach, are for ever discredited (xxi. 9, xlvi. 1, 2). The absolute accuracy of the prediction is fully attested by the history of Babylon's fall. It came about as here foretold.

The future condition of Babylon was also foretold. "It shall never be inhabited, neither shall it be dwelt in from generation to generation: neither shall the Arabian pitch tent there; neither shall the shepherds make their flocks to lie down there. But wild beasts of the desert shall lie there; and their houses shall be full of doleful creatures; and ostriches shall dwell there, and satyrs shall dance there. And the wolves shall cry in their castles, and jackals in the pleasant palaces" (xiii. 19-22). This exactly describes the unutterable desolation of Babylon. Not one human dwelling rests on the site of the ancient city. The Bedaween, though he pastures his flocks in the immediate neighbourhood, regards the ruins themselves with superstitious awe. The tents of the Arabs are freely pitched on the Chaldean plains, but not one of them is pitched amid the ruins of Babylon. Other ancient cities seldom become complete solitudes; their sites are marked by some village or group of huts or fold for flocks, but Babylon has ever been an exception.

Maundeville in the fourteenth century wrote: "It is alle

deserte, and full of dragons and grete serpentes." It remains
the same to-day. Owls start from the scanty thickets, lions
make their dens in the buried dwelling-places, and the foul
jackal skulks through the furrows. The surface is covered
with shapeless heaps, and the foot sinks in loose dust and
rubbish, exactly fulfilling the prediction: "Babylon shall
become heaps" (Jer. li. 37). "Come and sit in the dust, O
virgin daughter of Babylon" (Isa. xlvii. 1). The riches of the
city seemed to bid defiance to the constant ravages of man, in
fulfilment of the words, "All that spoil her shall be satisfied"
(Jer. l. 10). "Her cities are a desolation, a dry land, and a
wilderness, a land wherein no man dwelleth, neither doth any
son of man pass thereby" (Jer. li. 43). In the time of its
glory the country round the great city had been drained and
irrigated at enormous cost, till it was unsurpassed for fertility.
Now through centuries of neglect it has sunk back to its
original state, "a stinking morass and a barren steppe"; a vast
waste wilderness, with nothing but an occasional black Bedaween
tent or a wandering camel here and there to mark the existence
of man.

## ANALYSIS

The Book of Isaiah may be divided into three parts. The
first part and the third are composed of most magnificent
poetry. The beauty of the style is well reproduced in Bishop
Lowth's translation, which is worth careful study.

These two parts are, as it were, clasped together by the
second portion, which is history, and mainly written in prose.
Two chapters are connected with the first part of the book,
and relate the story of the Assyrian invasion and its results;
and two chapters are connected with the third part of the
book, and tell of Hezekiah's sickness and recovery, and the
incident of the Babylonian ambassadors.

## PART I. CHAPS. I.–XXXV.

(1) Chaps. i.-xii. Reproofs mainly addressed to Judah and
    Jerusalem. Coming glory, chaps. xi. and xii.
(2) Chaps. xiii.-xxiii. Judgments on nations hostile to Judah,
    *e.g.* Babylon, Syria, Egypt, Tyre.
(3) Chaps. xxiv.-xxxv. Judgment on the world, on Samaria
    and Judah. Sins provoking judgment. Assyrian
    invasion and destruction of Jerusalem. Coming glory,
    chap. xxxv.

### Part II. Chaps. XXXVI.–XXXIX.

(1) Chaps. xxxvi., xxxvii.   Assyrian invasion and results.
      (Closely connected with Part I.)
(2) Chaps. xxxviii., xxxix.   Hezekiah's sickness and recovery.
      Babylonian ambassadors.   Babylonian Captivity foretold.
      (Closely connected with Part III.)

### Part III. Chaps. XL.–LXVI.

(1) Chaps. xl.-xlviii.   *Comfort.*   Antithesis of Jehovah and
      idols, Israel and the nations.   Section ends with knell
      of judgment: "There is no peace, saith the Lord, to
      the wicked."
(2) Chaps. xlix.-lvii.   *The Servant of Jehovah.*   Antithesis between
      sufferings of the Servant and the glory that should
      follow.   Section ends with knell of judgment : "There
      is no peace, saith my God, to the wicked."
(3) Chaps. lviii.-lxvi.   *Promised glory.*   Antithesis between the
      hypocrites and the faithful; between present sin and
      sorrow, and future holiness and blessedness.   Section
      ends with still heavier note of judgment (lxvi. 24).

THE CROSS THE CENTRE.   The twenty-seven chapters of
Part III. constitute one grand Messianic poem, subdivided into
three books.   Each book consists of three sections of three
chapters each, nearly corresponding with the divisions of our
English Bible.   Chap. liii. (with the last three verses of lii.) is the
middle chapter of the middle book of this great prophetic poem,
the heart of the prophetic writings of the Old Testament.   And
the central verse of this central chapter enshrines *the central
truth of the Gospel* :—

> He was wounded for our transgressions,
> He was bruised for our iniquities :
> The chastisement of our peace was upon Him ;
> And with His stripes we are healed.

> (Dr. Pierson.)

### THE UNITY OF ISAIAH

A summary of the Book of Isaiah would hardly be complete
without allusion to the question that has been raised of late
years as to the duality or plurality of authorship.   It is asked,
"What difference does it make whether the prophecy is the
work of one man or of two or of twenty?"   On the surface

it makes no difference—provided its inspiration is established. If we are sure the Spirit of God is speaking, the human channel matters little.

But it is just because we see that this question of inspiration is doubly involved that we feel it does matter.

(1) *In the first place, the denial of the unity of Isaiah has its root in an unwillingness to admit the supernatural power of prediction in prophecy.*

(2) *In the second place, to maintain the denial of its unity sets aside the authority of the New Testament.*

In considering this question we will lay aside for the time the foregoing division of the book into three parts, and speak of Isaiah 1 (chaps. i.-xxxix.) and Isaiah 2 (chaps. xl.-lxvi.); the former written by Isaiah, the son of Amos, the latter supposed to have been written by some great Unknown Prophet during the time of the Babylonian Captivity.

LANGUAGE. At first the supposed difference in language was assigned as the reason for doubting the unity of the book. But on the authority of great Hebrew scholars, with scarcely an exception, it is proved that there is no linguistic necessity for the theory of a dual or plural authorship. Indeed, the resemblance in style between Isaiah 1 and 2, we are told, is closer than that between either of them, and any other book of the Old Testament. The similarity between the two parts of the book is so striking that some who hold to the theory of two authors have come to the conclusion that the second Isaiah has imitated the style of the first!

When we consider the long period during which Isaiah himself tells us he used the prophetic gift—from the days of Uzziah to Hezekiah, probably sixty years—and the very varied matter of which he wrote, there is more than sufficient reason to account for any difference of style. "The second Isaiah employs words only known otherwise to the first Isaiah, of which the meaning was lost by Jeremiah's time. The second Isaiah shows himself otherwise possessed of a scientific and technical vocabulary, which the first Isaiah only shares with him." [1]

Professor Birks, in studying the words used in 1 and 2 Isaiah, and nowhere in the later prophets, finds the instances so numerous that he limits his examples to those beginning with the first letter of the Hebrew alphabet—the letter *aleph*— of which he cites forty.

[1] *Lines of Defence of the Biblical Revelation*, p. 139.   Prof. Margoliouth.

PREDICTION. The reason for the denial of the unity of the authorship of Isaiah lies deeper than a question of language—it originated in the denial of the supernatural in prophecy. "Remove the great stumbling-block, the fact of prediction, and everything is in favour of its authenticity" (Dr. Payne Smith).

That the prophet should predict the fall of Babylon when it had not yet risen to its supremacy as a great world-power, and when *Assyria* was still the dreaded foe of the Jewish nation; that he should predict the deliverance from captivity before the people were carried captive; that he should foretell that deliverance should come from Medo-Persia when these two nations were still separate and insignificant; that he should call the deliverer by name [1]—Cyrus—more than a hundred years before his birth,—these matters are stumbling-blocks to those who see in prophecy only the human intuition of a good man who has understanding of the times. But to the devout believer it is a confirmation of his faith in an almighty God who claims to inspire His prophets with the Holy Spirit.

In Isaiah 2 God Himself, through His prophet, appeals to the fulfilment of the earlier predictions as the ground for believing that the later predictions will be fulfilled (Isa. xlviii. 3-5). This appeal would have no meaning if there were no earlier predictions to refer to. Among the predictions of Isaiah 1 were the invasion and destruction of Samaria by Sennacherib, his threatened invasion and the final deliverance of Jerusalem, and the prolongation of Hezekiah's life.

And now God appeals to His people Israel to be His witnesses to the fulfilment of His predictions in chapters xl.-lxvi. (see xliii. 9, 10). He challenges the idols, the gods of the nations, to prove their right to be worshipped by foretelling future events (xli. 23, xlii. 7-9).

The mention of Cyrus by name is expressly declared to be a miracle, wrought in order that the whole world, from east to west, might know that Jehovah is the only God (xlv. 4-6).

This is exactly the effect it had both upon the great world-conqueror himself and upon the people of Israel.

Josephus tells us that it was the reading of the prophecy of Isaiah concerning himself that led Cyrus to issue the decree: "Thus saith Cyrus king of Persia, All the kingdoms of the earth hath the Lord God of heaven given me; and He hath charged me to build Him a house in Jerusalem, which is in Judah" (2 Chron. xxxvi. 23). If the prophecy had only been

---

[1] See *The Unity of Isaiah*, p. 71.  John Kennedy, D.D.

written a few years before in Babylon, when his name was well known, and by a contemporary, is it credible that it would have so impressed the great conqueror as to lead him to take this step?

We have already touched upon the effect of Isaiah's prophecy upon the Jews. They went down to Babylon with what seemed to be an ineradicable tendency to idolatry. They returned from it what they have remained to the present day, the most monotheistic of nations. No nation can pass through such a change as that except under some overpowering conviction. Such a conviction would be produced as they gradually watched the prophecies of Isaiah fulfilled to the letter, and realised that God had foreseen these events and had "declared this from ancient time" (xlv. 21), and the heart of the nation would be turned for ever from idols unto the Holy One of Israel.

HISTORY. History, again, uniformly attributes the second part of the book to Isaiah. It is not known historically to have ever existed in a separate form. The conjunction of the two parts was certainly established as early as the days of Ezra. If the second part was written by a contemporary, or by a prophet of the immediately preceding age, Ezra must have known this. To ascribe either carelessness or deceit to Ezra would be contrary to all that is known of his character. The Septuagint translation, made 280 B.C., contains the whole book as the Book of Isaiah. The apocryphal Book of Ecclesiasticus, 200 B.C., says: "He (Esaias) saw by an excellent spirit what should come to pass at the last, and he comforted them that mourn in Zion; he showed what should come to pass for ever, and secret things or ever they came."

In the face of the universal testimony of history, the burden of proof rests with those who deny the Isaianic origin of the second part. "The rules of ordinary criticism require us to accept Isaiah as the author until it is shown that he cannot have been so" (Sir Edward Strachey).

THE NEW TESTAMENT. The witness of the New Testament is explicit and abundant. Isaiah is mentioned by name as the writer of this prophecy no less than twenty-one times. Of these, *ten* are in connection with passages contained in the first part of the prophecy, and *eleven* with passages from the second part. According to Westcott and Hort, the whole Book of Isaiah is quoted or referred to more than 210 times; chapters xl.-lxvi. more than 100 times.

With the New Testament writers the book is "the words of the prophet Isaiah, who spake by the Holy Spirit." Matthew declares that the writer of chapter xlii. was Isaiah (Matt. xii. 17, 18). Luke testifies that chapter liii. was written by Isaiah (Acts viii. 28-35), that chapter lxvi. was written by Isaiah (Luke iv. 17). John in the same breath ascribes chapter liii. and chapter vi. to Isaiah by name (John.xii. 38-41). Paul ascribes chapter liii. and lxv. to the same prophet (Rom. x. 16, 20). In every possible way the New Testament writers attribute the entire book to Isaiah, distinguishing between the "Book of Isaiah" and the "prophet Isaiah" who wrote the book (see Luke iv. 17 and iii. 4, etc.).

UNITY OF PURPOSE. The unity of thought and purpose throughout the book is a final testimony to the unity of authorship.

Professor Margoliouth, quoting Aristotle, tells us that a work of art should be so constructed that the removal of any part should cause the whole to fall to pieces, and says that if this rule be applied to Isaiah, we shall be disposed to find the unity of the works ascribed to that prophet brilliantly vindicated. It has been found impossible by those who would divide Isaiah to keep consistently to an early date for the whole of Isaiah 1 and to a late, or Babylonian, date for the whole of Isaiah 2. The fall of Babylon is predicted in Isaiah xiii. and xiv., to these and other portions of Isaiah 1 a late date has therefore been assigned.

The form of idolatry of which the Jewish nation is accused in chapter lvii., as also that described in the earlier part of the book, is peculiar to Israel in her own land before the Captivity. The surroundings of that chapter are likewise the surroundings of Palestine ; the high mountains, the rocky torrent-beds, and the smooth stones of the stream are foreign to the great alluvial plain of Babylon, and an earlier date is therefore assigned to this and other passages in Isaiah 2. This reduces both parts of this magnificent prophecy to a mere literary patchwork.

It is held by some that the Book of Isaiah is a collection of various writers put together for the sake of convenience. But in the parallel case of the Minor Prophets the name is carefully prefixed to each, even to those who only wrote one short chapter. The unity of thought and style is a strong argument against such a plurality of authorship, and the brilliance and power of the prophet make it most unlikely that he should be unknown, even by name. It was the custom of the Hebrew prophets to give their name at the commencement of their writings, and Isaiah is no exception to this (see i. 1). That this verse is not the preface to the first chapter only, or to any small portion of the book, is evident from the enumeration of the four kings during whose reigns he prophesied. It is evidently intended as a seal to the whole volume.

In the lines of thought which we have traced in studying Isaiah it will have been noticed that those lines were unbroken and that *the references have been taken from each part of the book*. Isaiah's vision in the Temple when he received his call to the prophetic office formed a fit introduction to the whole prophecy. We have seen how the influence of that vision may be traced throughout in the impression he received of the holiness and majesty of God, imprinting the name of the Holy One of Israel on all his prophecies, as if to anticipate the difficulty now before us. The influence of the vision may be traced again in the catholicity of the Divine purpose toward the whole world.

Most of all the unity of the book may be seen in the central figure of the person of the Messiah, in His glorious work of redemption, and in His universal reign of righteousness. Salvation and Judgment, Peace the effect of Righteousness, the power and majesty of God in creation as contrasted with idols, the work of men's hands,—these form the great themes of the prophet Isaiah, and are to be found flowing in unbroken connection throughout the entire volume of his writings.

### 3. JEREMIAH

God chooses unlikely instruments to do His work. He chose the sensitive, shrinking Jeremiah for what seemed a hopeless mission, with the words : " Say not, I am a child : for on whatsoever errand I shall send thee thou shalt go, and whatsoever I shall command thee thou shalt speak. Be not afraid. I am with thee to deliver thee " (Jer. i. 7-9, R.V.). And Jeremiah proved worthy of the trust. Though his heart was wrung with the severe denunciations he had to give, and with the stubborn rejection of them by his people, though he often poured out his complaints to God, and even went so far as to say that he would not speak any more in His Name, yet we never once find him turning back from the path of duty. Imprisoned again and again, put in the stocks (xx. 2), lowered by ropes into a miry dungeon (xxxviii. 6)—probably an empty cistern—mocked, derided (xx. 7), a man of strife and contention to the whole world (xv. 10), accused of treachery to his country (xxxviii. 4), opposed by false prophets (xxiii., xxviii.), confronted by an angry people who clamoured for his life (xxvi.), carried, against his will, by his countrymen into Egypt (xliii. 1-7),—under all these circumstances Jeremiah went steadily on delivering his message with unswerving fidelity for over forty years.

Jeremiah prophesied for eighteen years during the reign of Josiah, then during the reigns of the four kings of Judah till after the capture of Jerusalem and the end of the kingdom. He was thus about a hundred years later than the prophet Isaiah. His home was in the village of Anathoth, a few miles north of Jerusalem, and he was by birth a priest. It is possible, though not certain, that his father, Hilkiah, was the High Priest who discovered the book of the Law in the Temple during the reign of Josiah (see the *Cambridge Bible for Schools*). In any case the discovery had as marked an effect upon the ministry of the young prophet as upon the conduct of the young king. Jeremiah, no doubt, strengthened Josiah's hands in his work of reform and against forming an alliance with Egypt. Though Jeremiah had many enemies, God gave him some true friends, from Josiah the king down to Ebedmelech the Ethiopian who rescued him from the dungeon.

COURAGE. Jeremiah's fearlessness in the face of danger is shown most conspicuously in chapter xxvi., where the Lord sends him to give His message in the Temple court and admonishes him not to diminish a word. So incensed were the priests and the people, that they took him, saying: "Thou shalt surely die." "As for me," replied the prophet, "behold, I am in your hand; do with me as seemeth good and meet unto you: but know ye for certain, that, if ye put me to death, ye shall surely bring innocent blood upon yourselves: for of a truth the Lord hath sent me unto you, to speak all these words in your ears."

THREE GREAT EVENTS. There were three great events in the life of the prophet: (1) The battle of Megiddo, between Judah and Pharaoh Necho, where the good king Josiah was slain, and was deeply mourned by his people, Jeremiah writing a lament concerning him. (2) The battle of Carchemish, near the same spot, four years later, in the reign of Jehoiakim, who had become the vassal of Egypt. In this battle the Egyptians were wholly defeated by the Babylonian forces under Nebuchadnezzar, and it was followed by the first deportation of Jews to Babylon. (3) The third great event was the capture of Jerusalem by Nebuchadnezzar, the destruction of the city and the Temple, and the exile of the greater part of the remainder of the people to Babylon.

In such troublous times as these Jeremiah lived. The life of the nation from the time of Manasseh, the grandfather of Josiah, was corrupt in the extreme. The reforms of Josiah seemed only to touch it on the surface, and temporarily ; after his death the nation sank back into the worst forms of idolatry and into every kind of iniquity. Jeremiah's mission was to endeavour to turn his people back to their God. During the reign of Josiah he began to prophesy the dreadful calamity threatening them from the North, unless they would repent. Judah's salvation was still possible, but each year her guilt became heavier and her doom more certain.

The Lord raised up Nebuchadnezzar to execute His judgment upon Judah. He gave him universal dominion, and even called him " My servant." It was because God revealed this to Jeremiah that we find him advocating submission to Nebuchadnezzar, and it was for this that his people accused him of treachery. After the destruction of Jerusalem, Jeremiah was given his choice whether he would go to Babylon or remain with the remnant that were left in the land. He chose the latter. Days of darkness followed. Jeremiah exhorted his people to obey the voice of the Lord and remain in the land, and not flee into Egypt. But they refused to obey, and they carried Jeremiah with them into Egypt, where, tradition says, he was stoned to death.

BRICKWORK IN EGYPT. When Johanan and the chief of the captains refused to obey the voice of the Lord by Jeremiah, and persisted in going down into Egypt with all the remnant of Judah—men, women, and children, including the King's daughters—they came and dwelt at Tahpanhes. At the commandment of the Lord, Jeremiah took great stones and hid them under the large platform, or pavement of brickwork, at the entry of Pharaoh's house in Tahpanhes, and prophesied that over these stones Nebuchadnezzar should one day set his throne and spread his royal pavilion. Dr. Flinders Petrie has discovered " the palace of the Jew's daughter " at Tahpanhes. Tahpanhes seems to have been an old fort on the Syrian frontier, guarding the road to Egypt, and evidently a constant refuge for the Jews. In front of the fort is a large platform, or pavement of brickwork, suitable for outdoor business, such as loading goods, pitching tents, etc.—just what is now called a *mastaba*. Dr. Petrie says: "Now Jeremiah writes of the pavement (or brickwork) which is at the entry of Pharaoh's house in Tahpanhes; this passage, which has been an unexplained stumbling-block to translators hitherto, is the exact description of the *mastaba* which I found, and this would be the most likely place for Nebuchadnezzar to pitch his royal tent as stated by Jeremiah." [1]

THE HEART. "Jeremiah was, of all the prophets of the Old Testament, the supreme prophet of God to the human heart. In season and out of season, for a long lifetime, he laid siege to the hearts of his hearers. The cure of all your famines, he cried, and all your plagues and all your defeats and all your captivities—the cause and the cure of them all is in your own heart: in the heart of each inhabitant of Jerusalem and each captive in Babylon." [2]

"His ministry was one of admonition and antagonism. Against the whole land, against the kings of Judah, against the princes, against the priests, against the prophets was he to stand. He was to gird up his loins and arise, and speak all that God commanded him. He was to be the solitary fortress, the column of iron, the wall of brass, fearless, undismayed in any presence; the one grand, immoveable figure who pursued the apostatising people and rulers, delivering his message in the Temple court or the royal chamber or the street, whether they would hear or whether they would forbear. In consequence he was the prophet of unwelcome truths, hated of all, but feared as well by all. It was a mission requiring courage, faith, strength, will; a mission no weakling could fill, no coward would undertake. Jeremiah is one of the very great men of the world." [3]

To Jeremiah was committed the hopeless task of trying to bring back his people at the eleventh hour. He prophesied the seventy years' servitude of the Jews to Babylon, urging them to settle down to the life of that city and to seek its peace. He prophesied as certainly the restoration of his people and the unalterable love of God to them. At the very time of

[1] *Ten Years' Digging in Egypt*, pp. 50-54.
[2] *Bible Characters*, p. 153. Dr. Alexander Whyte.
[3] *Outline Studies*. Moorehead.

the siege of Jerusalem, and from his prison cell, Jeremiah, at the bidding of the Lord, purchased a field from his cousin Hanameel as a proof that Israel should be restored to their land.

PREDICTION. Chapters l. and li. give us a picture of the whole of Babylon's future. Those who deny the miracle of prophetic prediction for the same reason deny that these chapters were written by Jeremiah. They suppose them to have been written by a follower of the prophet, accustomed to use similar phraseology, and that he wrote them not long before the fall of Babylon. Against this theory we have the following facts:—(1) Even those who deny that Jeremiah was the author admit that the style of those two chapters presents all the characteristics of the special style of that prophet. (2) Those two chapters in particular are more carefully authenticated as being by Jeremiah than any other portion of the book: chapter l. beginning with the words, "The word that the Lord spake against Babylon by Jeremiah the prophet," and chapter li. closing with, "Thus far are the words of Jeremiah." To impugn their authorship is to impugn their honesty. (3) To place the prophecy at the time when Babylon was about to be taken by Cyrus does not do away with the miracle of prediction, for many of the details of the prophecy were not fulfilled for more than five centuries later. At the time of the conquest the walls were not thrown down; neither sower nor reaper was cut off from Babylon; she was not deserted of her population; and the utter desolation described in these two chapters did not take place at that time, but was fulfilled to the letter long years after.

SACRIFICE. In Jeremiah vii. 22, 23 we read, "I spake not unto your fathers, nor commanded them in the day that I brought them out of the land of Egypt, concerning burnt offerings or sacrifices: but this one thing I commanded them, Obey My Voice." These words are not opposed to the history as contained in the Pentateuch, nor a proof, as some allege, that "the Levitical Code" was not in existence in Jeremiah's day. This sentence is a figure of grammar, of frequent occurrence in both Old and New Testaments, as scholars have pointed out over and over again. The figure is this: That a negative followed, generally though not always, by an adversative particle (generally the conjunction "but") is frequently not a negative at all, but a·form of comparison. For instance, "For I desired mercy, and not sacrifice; and the knowledge of God *more than* burnt offerings" (Hos. vi. 6); "You sent me not hither, but God" (Gen. xlv. 8). These words of Joseph in no way deny the historical fact that it *was* his brethren who sent him. "Your murmurings are not against us, but against Jehovah" (Exod. xvi. 8). This only means more against Jehovah than against Moses and Aaron. So also, "They have not rejected thee, but have rejected Me" (1 Sam. viii. 7), only means, it was *more* against Jehovah than against Samuel. "Receive my instruction, and not silver; and knowledge *rather than* choice gold" (Prov. viii. 10). "Rend your heart and not your garments."

In the New Testament this figure of grammar occurs over and over again. "Labour not for the meat which perisheth, but for that meat which endureth unto everlasting life" (John vi. 27). "In this rejoice not, that the spirits are subject unto you; but rather rejoice, because your names are written in heaven" (Luke x. 20). "The word which ye hear is not Mine, but the Father's which sent Me" (John xiv. 24). See also Matt. vi. 19, 20; John vii. 16; Col. iii. 2, 22, 23, etc. etc. In all these places the negative is not a literal negative at all, but is a strong and striking form of the comparative. In this form, or figure, the negative does not exclude the thing denied, but only implies the prior claim of the thing set in opposition to it (Rev. James Neil).

The essence of the covenant He made with them at Sinai was obedience: "If ye will obey My voice, and keep My covenant, then ye shall be Mine own possession." The appointment of the Levitical Law was a *part* of the obedience which formed the essence of the covenant.

A TYPE OF CHRIST. Jeremiah was a true foreshadowing of Christ. It is hardly to be wondered at that some mistook the Man of Sorrows for the prophet of the broken heart (Matt. xvi. 14). He wept over his people as Jesus wept over them (ix. 1). His fearless rebuking of sin brought him reproach and rejection and suffering as it brought our Lord. He compares himself to a lamb or an ox brought to the slaughter (xi. 19).

THE MESSIAH. Jeremiah does not unfold to us as much of the coming Messiah as Isaiah does, but we have glimpses of Christ as the Fountain of Living Waters (ii. 13), as the Great Physician (viii. 22), as the Good Shepherd (xxxi. 10, xxiii. 4), as the Righteous Branch (xxiii. 5), as David the King (xxx. 9), as the Redeemer (l. 34), as the Lord our Righteousness (xxiii. 6). At the very time that David's throne was imperilled, and justice and equity almost unknown, the prophet announced the coming of a King of the House of David, a righteous Branch, who should reign and prosper, and execute judgment and justice in the earth. "In His days Judah shall be saved, and Israel shall dwell safely; and this is His name whereby He shall be called, THE LORD OUR RIGHTEOUSNESS"— *Jehovah Tsidkenu.* In this majestic name the Godhead of our Saviour is predicted, and, as a descendant of David, His humanity.

THE NEW COVENANT. God says by His servant that He will make a New Covenant with the House of Israel and with the House of Judah (xxxi. 31-37). In the New Testament this is distinctly applied to the Jews of the future (Rom. xi. 26, 27; Heb. viii. 8, 13). Christ is the Mediator of this better Covenant (Heb. xii. 24). The prophecy points forward to His day, and includes, not the Jews only, but all who know Him as their Saviour and Mediator. It shows the spiritual nature of His kingdom, in which His Laws will be written on our minds to make us *know* them, and on our hearts to make us *love* them, and he will give us His Spirit to enable us to *do* them.

BACKSLIDING. The grievous famine of chapter xiv. 1-9 may be applied spiritually, as a picture of the heart that has known the Saviour and has backslidden from Him. It is a parched land. No water, no rain, no grass, no herbage (R.V.). The Lord as a stranger in the land, "as a mighty man that cannot save." How graphically this describes many a heart whose own sin and unbelief are "limiting the Holy One of Israel." Jeremiah is the book for backsliders. It reveals the tenderness of the Lord's love, and contains His gracious invitation to them, and their resolve with regard to Him: "Return, ye backsliding children, and I will heal your backslidings. Behold, we come unto Thee; for Thou art the Lord our God" (iii. 22).

QUESTIONS.—The book contains various questions, the answer to which can only be found in the Gospel of our Lord Jesus Christ.

"How shall I pardon thee?" (Jer. v. 7; Eph. i. 7).

"How shall I put thee among the children?" (iii. 19; John i. 12).

"Is there no balm in Gilead? is there no Physician there?" (viii. 22; Matt. ix. 12).

"Can the Ethiopian change his skin, or the leopard his spots?" (xiii. 23; Acts viii. 37; 2 Peter iii. 14).

"How wilt thou do in the swelling of Jordan?" (xii. 5; 1 Cor. xv. 55-57).

"Where is the flock that was given thee, thy beautiful flock ?" (xiii. 20 ; Col. i. 28 ; Heb. xiii. 17).

GOSPEL TEXTS.—It contains likewise various texts which would supply subjects for Gospel sermons.

"What wilt thou say when He shall punish thee ?" (xiii. 21).

"The heart is deceitful above all things, and desperately wicked" (xvii. 9).

"Flee, save your lives, and be like the heath (juniper) in the wilderness" (xlviii. 6).

"My word is like a fire, and like a hammer that breaketh the rock in pieces" (xxiii. 29).

"Break up your fallow ground" (iv. 3).

"Her sun is gone down while it is yet day" (xv. 9).

"I know the thoughts that I think toward you, saith the Lord, thoughts of peace and not of evil" (xxix. 11).

"I have loved thee with an everlasting love ; therefore with loving-kindness have I drawn thee" (xxxi. 3).

"Ye shall seek Me, and find Me, when ye shall search for Me with all your heart" (xxix. 13).

"Ask for the old paths . . . and ye shall find rest for your souls" (vi. 16).

"They shall ask the way to Zion, with their faces thitherward" (l. 5).

"My people have been lost sheep . . . they have forgotten their resting-place" (l. 6).

"The time of their visitation" (viii. 7, 12).

"The harvest is past, the summer is ended and we are not saved" (viii. 20).

"There is nothing too hard for Thee" (xxxii. 17).

THE PENKNIFE. The Book of Jeremiah throws much light on the subject of inspiration. It is a helpful study to take one's Bible, and beginning with the first verse to mark all the expressions which assert or imply that God spake by Jeremiah, such as, "Thus saith the Lord," "The Lord said unto me," "The word of the Lord came," etc. Such expressions occur sometimes a dozen times in one chapter, and in them Jeremiah unhesitatingly claims inspiration.

As we read on a scene rises before us. We see Jeremiah in prison. The rulers have bound him that they may be no longer troubled by the word of the Lord. God tells him to take a roll and write in it all the words that He had spoken unto him from the days of Josiah unto that day. We can picture the prophet in the dimly lighted dungeon, with his faithful friend Baruch at his side, busily writing down the words on the roll as the prophet spoke them. "And Baruch wrote from the mouth of Jeremiah all the words of the Lord, which He had spoken unto him, upon a roll of a book. And Jeremiah commanded Baruch, saying, I am shut up; I cannot go into the house of the Lord; therefore go thou, and read in the roll, which thou

hast written from my mouth, *the words of the Lord*, in the ears of
the people, in the Lord's House upon the fasting-day." What
Baruch holds in his hand, and what he reads in the ears of the
princes, priests, and people, are "the words of the Lord." The
roll is long. It contains every prophecy which Jeremiah has
uttered up to that time. But none of the words, many as they
are, are given as *his* words. They are all of them *God's* words.

But this is not all. After Baruch had read the roll to the
people, he was sent for by the Royal Council and commanded to
read it to them. The great officials of Jerusalem said to Baruch,
"Tell us now, How didst thou write all these words at his mouth?
Then Baruch answered them, He pronounced all these words
with his mouth, and I wrote them with ink in the book." They
afterwards brought the roll to the King. Here another scene
rises before us. We are no longer in the dark dungeon, but in
the winter palace of Jehoiakim, surrounded by all the magnificent
luxury of an Eastern Court. When the monarch had heard three
or four leaves of the roll he had heard enough. He asked for
the roll, cut it in pieces with a penknife, and cast it into the fire
that was upon the hearth. "It was his last chance, his last offer
of mercy : as he threw the torn fragments of the roll on the fire
he threw there, in symbol, his royal house, his doomed city, the
Temple, and all the people of the land " (*Speaker's Commentary*).

Jeremiah and Baruch were ordered to be taken, and would,
no doubt, have been treated with like ferocity, "but the Lord
hid them." And now in their seclusion another task was set them.
The Lord commanded Jeremiah to take another roll, and to write
in it "all the words of the book which Jehoiakim king of Judah
had burned in the fire ; and there were added besides unto them,
many like words." Other words were added, but the body of
the sacred book was word by word the same as the first.[1]

Man may cut God's Word to pieces with the penknife of his
intellect. Like Jehoiakim he may cast his hope of salvation in
the fire. But "the word of the Lord endureth for ever" and
by that word shall he be judged in the last day (1 Pet. i. 25 ;
John xii. 48).

"MY WORD—FIRE." The stern messages Jeremiah had to
give were so foreign to his sensitive nature that it could only
have been the deep conviction that they were the words of the
Lord that enabled him to give utterance to them. Like Job he
deplores the day of his birth ; he sits alone because of the Lord's

[1] *The Inspiration and Accuracy of the Holy Scriptures*, pp. 44-47
Urquhart.

hand ; he complains that he is in derision daily ; the word of the Lord was made a reproach unto him, for His sake he has suffered rebuke ; cursed by every one, mocked, defamed, watched by all his familiars for his halting,—is it likely that Jeremiah would have gone on if he had not been certain that the Lord had commissioned him ?  As we have already seen, he contemplates speaking no more in the name of the Lord, " But," he says, " His word was in my heart as a burning fire shut up in my bones, and I was weary with forbearing, and I could not stay."  With such a fire burning in his heart is it any wonder that the Lord's promise was fulfilled, " Behold, I will make My words in thy mouth fire " ?  The Lord also promised him, " If thou take forth the precious from the vile, *thou shalt be as My mouth.*"  " Thy words were found," he says to the Lord, " and I did eat them ; and Thy word was unto me the joy and rejoicing of mine heart."  In his prayers to God, Jeremiah reveals the secret workings of his heart.  He was emphatically a man of prayer, a man who understood the meaning of communion with his God.

## 4. LAMENTATIONS

" THE CITY OF THE GREAT KING."   " ' How doth the city sit solitary, that was full of people !  how is she a widow that was great among the nations !  and princess among the provinces, how is it she became tributary ! '  So bursts forth the elaborate dirge of which the oldest Jewish tradition tells us that 'after the captivity of Israel and the desolation of Jerusalem, Jeremiah sat down and wept, and lamented his lamentation over Jerusalem.'  In the face of a rocky hill, on the western side of the city, the local belief has placed ' the grotto of Jeremiah.'  There in that fixed attitude of grief, which Michael Angelo has immortalised, the prophet may well be supposed to have mourned the fall of his country." [1]

The desolation of the city by the Chaldean army is described by Jeremiah in his Book of Lamentations with all the vividness of an eye-witness.

Six hundred years have passed, and now from the opposite or eastern side of the city a procession of rejoicing children with a lowly King winds up the slopes of the Mount of Olives.  A sudden bend in the road brings the city of Jerusalem full upon the view.  The sight of that proud city in the morning sunlight, with the marble pinnacles and gilded roofs of the Temple, brought such a mighty rush of compassion to the soul of our

[1] Stanley's *Jewish Church.*

Saviour that He wept aloud.   "If thou hadst known, even thou, at least in this thy day, the things that belong unto thy peace!" —and there sorrow interrupted the sentence, and, when He found voice to continue, He could only add, "but now they are hid from thine eyes.   For the days shall come upon thee, that thine enemies shall cast a trench about thee . . . and they shall not leave one stone upon another; because thou knewest not the time of thy visitation."[1]

The weeping prophet was a type of the weeping Saviour. The one had foretold the destruction of the city by the Chaldeans, the other by the Romans.

JUDGMENT FOR SIN.   Throughout the Book of Lamentations, Jeremiah points out plainly that the judgment that has come upon the city is on account of her sin.   The Key-note of the book is *Destruction*.   It contains five Laments corresponding with the five chapters.   Each Lament is arranged in acrostic form, every verse beginning with one of the twenty-two letters of the Hebrew alphabet, except that in the fifth Lament, though it contains the right number of stanzas, the acrostic form disappears.   Moreover, in the third or middle Lament—the climax of the poem—each initial letter is repeated three times.

*Lament I.*   In the first part of this Lament the prophet speaks, and describes the city as a woman bereft of her husband and children.   In the second Zion speaks, and bewails her misery.   She acknowledges that her punishment is from the Lord, and confesses "The Lord is righteous; I have rebelled."

*Lament II.* is spoken by the prophet.   A remarkable description of the ruin of Jerusalem.

*Lament III.*   The prophet speaks, but makes the miseries of the people his own.   Out of the midst of the misery he stays himself upon the Lord's faithfulness and His unfailing compassion, and asserts unhesitatingly that "He doth not afflict willingly, nor grieve the children of men" (iii. 33).

*Lament IV.*   The prophet again describes the fearful judgments which have befallen Jerusalem.

*Lament V.*   The Jewish people speak and make confession, and appeal to God for forgiveness and deliverance.

"NO REST."   In chapter i. we have the description of desolation.   No rest; no pasture; no Comforter (ver. 3, 6, 9). Such is the desolation of every soul that is without Christ.

[1] See Farrar's *Life of Christ*, vol. ii. p. 199.

| Without Christ. | | With Christ. | |
| --- | --- | --- | --- |
| Chap. i. 3. | No Rest. | Matt. xi. 28. | I will give you rest. |
| Chap. i. 6. | No Pasture. | Ps. xxiii. 2. | Green pastures. |
| Chap. i. 9. | No Comforter. | John xiv. 16. | Another Comforter. |

CALVARY. Jeremiah weeping over the city reminds us of our Lord. There are several verses, moreover, which seem to be a foreshadowing of Calvary: "Is it nothing to you, all ye that pass by? behold, and see if there be any sorrow like unto My sorrow" (i. 12). Again: "All that pass by clap their hands at thee; they hiss and wag their head" (ii. 15, 16; Matt. xxvii. 39); "All thine enemies have opened their mouth against thee" (ii. 16; Ps. xxii. 13); "He shutteth out my prayer" (iii. 8; Matt. xxvii. 46); "I was a derision to all my people, and their song every day" (iii. 14; Ps. lxix. 12); "The wormwood and the gall" (iii. 19; Ps. lxix. 21); "He giveth his cheek to him that smiteth him: he is filled with reproach" (iii. 30; Isa. l. 6; Ps. lxix. 20).

In the verse "For the sins of her prophets, and the iniquities of her priests, that have *shed the blood of the just* in the midst of her," we are reminded, first, of our Lord's own words: "O Jerusalem, Jerusalem, thou that killest the prophets, and stonest them which are sent unto thee"; and, secondly, of Peter's words of accusation to the people of Jerusalem: "Ye denied *the Holy One and the Just*, and killed the Prince of Life."

## 5. EZEKIEL

The Lord set Jeremiah to be an iron pillar in the land of Judah. In the same way He set Ezekiel for a pillar among his own captive people by the river Chebar, in the land of the Chaldeans, and told him that as an adamant, harder than flint, had He made his forehead (iii. 9). Strength characterised the ministry of the prophet whose name means "*God will strengthen.*" For a time Jeremiah and Ezekiel were contemporary; for the latter began his prophecy in the fifth year of Jehoiakim's captivity and prosecuted it for twenty-two years at least (i. 2, xxix. 17). He took up the theme of Jeremiah concerning the future of his people and developed it.

"A SANCTUARY." Like Jeremiah, Ezekiel was a priest as well as a prophet, and in all probability the "thirtieth year" of which he speaks in the first verse was the thirtieth year of his own age—the age when the priests entered upon their sacred duties. God withdrew His presence from His sanctuary at

Jerusalem, and His chosen people were henceforth represented by the captives in Babylon. To these He promised to be "as a little sanctuary" in the land of their captivity, indicating that He would not confine His glory to any particular spot. Ezekiel was called to be a sort of ministering priest to his people in this spiritual sanctuary.

This book may be divided into three parts :—

Part I., chaps. i.-xxiv. Testimonies from God against Israel in general and against Jerusalem in particular.

Part II., chaps. xxv.-xxxii. Judgments denounced against surrounding nations.

Part III., chaps. xxxiii.-xlviii. The subject of Israel is resumed, and their restoration and blessing foretold.

Ezekiel himself divides his prophecies into fourteen parts, which may be traced by his prefixing the date to each. The main object of his message seems to be to comfort the exiles in their desolation, to fortify them against the idolatry by which they were surrounded, and to inspire them with the glorious prospect the future held in store for them if, with true hearts, they would turn to their God. His wealth of imagery imparts a singular beauty to his prophecies. They glow with life and action and brilliant colouring, and for this very reason are more difficult to understand. But with the assurance that "whatsoever things were written aforetime were written for our learning," we may count on the Holy Spirit to unfold their teaching to our understanding.

VISION OF THE CHERUBIM. Ezekiel stands out as a man entirely abandoned to God's use. To prepare him for service the Lord granted him a double vision. In the vision of the cherubim Ezekiel saw four living creatures which were absolutely at God's disposal. "They went every one straight forward : whither the Spirit was to go, they went; and they turned not when they went" (i. 12). Such unswerving following the Lord expected from His prophet, and such He expects from us. The lion, the strongest animal; the ox, the most enduring; the eagle, the highest soaring; man made in the image of God,—these four bring before us the highest forms of natural life. These four living ones, with their wings and their wheels full of eyes, moving with the symmetry of one organism, and the rapidity of lightning in the midst of "the enfolding fire," give us a picture of God's will perfectly executed, as His redeemed saints will be enabled to fulfil it when they see Him as He is, and as they should aim at fulfilling it here below.

VISION OF THE LORD. We have not far to seek to find "Christ in Ezekiel." The prophet beholds Him in vision in the very first chapter. For surely the "Man" upon the throne can be none other than the only-begotten Son, the representative of the invisible God. We recognise in this vision the prophetic announcement of the Holy Incarnation. The details of the vision seen by the captive on the banks of the Chebar correspond minutely with the details of the vision of the captive in the isle called Patmos. Over eighty points of contact may be found between the two books. As there is no doubt who is designated by John, we cannot but recognise in the vision of Ezekiel the Glory of God in the person of our Lord Jesus Christ. Ezekiel saw "a throne as an appearance of a sapphire stone, and the likeness as the appearance of a Man above upon it." John saw "a throne set in heaven, and One sat on the throne." They both saw the rainbow, the token of the covenant; they both saw "the terrible crystal" of the purity of God's presence, which nothing can evade. To Ezekiel it appeared as a firmament; to John as a sea of glass. They both had a vision of burning lamps of the fire of God's Spirit, and of the four living creatures, whose sound was as the sound of many waters (i. 24; Rev. xix. 4-6). To both was given by the One encircled by the rainbow the roll of a book, which he was commanded to eat, and then go and prophesy (Ezek. i. 28, ii. 1, 8-10, iii. 1-4; Rev. x. 1, 2, 8-11).

"This," said Ezekiel, "was the appearance of the likeness of the glory of the Lord" (i. 28). When we read of the "glory of the Lord" in this book, we see in it the manifested presence of God as revealed in the Eternal Son, who, in the fulness of time, "became flesh, and dwelt amongst us, and we beheld His glory, the glory as of the only-begotten of the Father."

The sight of Christ upon the Cross—bearing our sin—brings us salvation. The sight of Christ upon the throne—baptizing with the Holy Ghost—sets us free for service. Ezekiel says that the Spirit entered into him, and that then he heard Him that spake unto him. The personality of the Holy Spirit finds frequent expression in this book.

A MAN AT GOD'S DISPOSAL. *The Lord sent Ezekiel to be a prophet.* Whether they accepted or rejected him, they could not but "know that there had been a prophet among them."

Often we read "the hand of the Lord was upon me," and often such words as "the Spirit took me up." Do we, as workers, know what it is to have the Lord's hand so strong upon us that His Spirit can take us up and wield us as He wills? Ezekiel was a faithful and obedient prophet; he spoke when the Lord opened his mouth, and was willing to be dumb when the Lord closed it, and therefore "they knew that it was the Word of the Lord."

*Ezekiel was sent to his own people.* It may be easier to some to go as a missionary to India or China than to speak the Lord's message to their own relations, or the members of their own church; but perhaps He is saying to them as He said to Ezekiel: "Thou art *not* sent to many people of a hard language, whose words thou canst not understand . . . go, get thee unto the children of thy people, and speak to them" (iii. 5, 11). Ezekiel had to give the Lord's message to very difficult people: to the prophets, the elders, the shepherds, the princes; to Jerusalem and the land of Israel; to the leading heathen nations; to inanimate objects—dry bones, wind, fowls, beasts, forests.

A WATCHMAN. *The Lord sent Ezekiel to be a watchman.* He told him not to be afraid of the people, but to give them warning, and that if he did not do so He would require their blood at his hands (chaps. iii. and xxxiii.). These chapters set before us very plainly our personal responsibility in giving the Lord's message and warning men of sin. Paul was so faithful in doing this that he was able to say, "I am pure from the blood of all men" (Acts xx. 26).

A SIGN. *The Lord sent Ezekiel to be a sign.* "Ezekiel is unto you a sign" (xxiv. 24, iv. 3, xii. 11). The portrayal of the imaginary siege of Jerusalem was no doubt exactly calculated to make the men of those times *think*; for God fits His signs to the times. In the British Museum part of a similar tile of the same date may be seen, with a plan of Babylon drawn upon it. To be God's sign to the people, Ezekiel willingly sacrificed all his private interests. He was willing to lie in any position God told him; to smite with his hand or strike with his foot; to go forth into the plain, or shut himself up within his house; to sacrifice his personal appearance (v. 1); to eat his food by weight, or move house at a day's notice. The severest test of all was when God took away the desire of his eyes and commanded him not to weep. He who wept by the grave of Lazarus understands the sorrow of our human hearts, and does not rebuke us for it. But He needed Ezekiel as a sign, and so He commanded him not to weep for his own private grief, but to weep bitterly for the sins of his people (xxiv. 15, 16, xxi. 6, 7).

The Lord will not ask the same extraordinary things of us that He asked of Ezekiel, but the line of following Him who was despised and rejected of men is certain to lie across the will of nature, right athwart the course of this world. Does the Lord find in us those who are absolutely pliant in His hands, as Ezekiel was? He is seeking such. "I sought for a man to stand in the gap before Me for the land, that I should not destroy it ; but I found none" (chaps. xxii. 30, xiii. 5).

THE GLORY OF THE LORD. The Key-note of the book of Ezekiel is *The Glory of the Lord*, that is, His manifested presence. It occurs twelve times in the first eleven chapters. Then there is a great gap, and we do not meet with it again till the forty-third chapter. The glory of the Lord was grieved away from the Temple at Jerusalem by the idolatry of the people, and not till the city had been overturned to the uttermost could the glory come back and take up its abode in the new Temple. The message was, "Ye have defiled My sanctuary"; therefore "I will make thee waste." Through several chapters the prophet is commanded to declare the judgments that were coming on the land on account of the "detestable things" and "the abominations" which the people had introduced into the sanctuary. In the eighth chapter Ezekiel is spiritually transported from the land of the Chaldeans to Jerusalem, and in a vision sees the four kinds of grievous idolatries which were practised in the courts of the Lord's house, even to the worshipping of the sun with their faces to the east and their backs to the sanctuary.

We see the glory of the Lord gradually removing. Grieved away from the inner sanctuary by the sin of idolatry, the brightness fills the court. Then it departed from the threshold and rested over the cherubim, those beings who perfectly fulfilled God's will and responded to His power. As the cherubim mounted from the earth, the glory of the Lord abode above their free pinions and mounted with them, forsaking the city and removing to the mountains. In the same way it is possible for a Christian so to provoke, resist, grieve, straiten, limit, vex, quench the Holy Spirit, that the heart may become like a ruined temple bereft of the glory.

There is many a blighted life from which the early glow has

departed through simple disobedience—refusing to give the Lord's message, it may be. "God can do so much with a spark, and it is dreadful when He cannot get a conductor for it" (Bramwell Booth). We *grieve* the Holy Spirit when we do not allow ourselves time for communion with God; we *limit* Him by doubting His power to cleanse and keep and fill. We *provoke* and *resist* Him by the idols in our hearts. We *vex* the Holy Spirit by our rebellion, by not really saying in very truth "Thy will be done." And if rebellion is persisted in, the Holy Spirit may be *quenched*.

The spirit of worldliness is one of the chief idols that is grieving the Holy Spirit away from His temple. It is sapping the very life of the Church to-day. How much of the worldly spirit of utter selfishness there is in the business life, in the undue estimation of wealth and position, in love of display, and in friendships made with the people of the world, forgetting that "whosoever will be a friend of the world is the enemy of God." Christians conform to the world's ways, and read the world's books, and dress in the world's fashions, instead of being a people separated unto the Lord. The real cure for this worldliness is such a vision of Christ Jesus as shall make the earthly lights pale before the splendour of it. If our hearts are satisfied with Him, the world will have no hold upon us. He said: " The Prince of this world cometh and hath nothing in Me." Are we able to say: "The world knoweth us not, because it knew Him not"?

SHEPHERDS. Chapter xxxiv. contains a warning to the false shepherds who feed themselves and feed not the flock. It closes with a most beautiful prophecy of Christ as the Good Shepherd, which our Lord evidently applies to Himself in the tenth chapter of John. His promise of searching out His sheep, and bringing them back to their own land, is primarily for the Jews; but Jesus Himself spoke of His " other sheep," which are not of the Jewish fold, which should also hear His voice, and that all should ultimately be gathered in one fold with one Shepherd.

A CLEAN HEART. Chapter xxxvi. is also first for Israel, and points forward to the time of the restoration of God's chosen people, when they shall be gathered out of all the countries and brought into their own land, and there cleansed from all their iniquities, and become God's witnesses among the nations.

But it contains also a glorious picture of the Gospel and of Christ's power to cleanse and save to the uttermost. Verses 16-28 show the deep and universal defilement of sin and God's judgment of it. They show that there is nothing in us as sinners to commend us to God; that the salvation which is in Christ Jesus is all of His free grace and for the honour of His Holy Name, which we have profaned by our iniquities. The cleansing from all sin is promised, and with it the corresponding promise of the new heart; that He will take away our stony heart, and give us a heart of flesh, and put His Spirit within us to enable us to walk so as to please Him.

DRY BONES. Chapter xxxvii. again refers primarily to the Jews. "Son of man, these bones are the whole house of Israel." It is again a promise of salvation and restoration to God's chosen people. But it contains a beautiful Gospel picture of God's power to raise those who are dead in trespasses and sins. It corresponds with His words to Nicodemus about the necessity of the new birth, and the mighty action of the Holy Spirit, coming unseen as the wind, to quicken the dead. The chapter closes with the renewed promise of the future David to be the Shepherd-King of God's people.

JUDGMENT. Chapters xxxviii. and xxxix. contain an account of the judgment that the Lord will bring upon His people through the instrumentality of Gog and his northern army. This is thought to be the final terrible trial of the chosen people, known as the time of Jacob's trouble. In chapter xxi. the Lord says He will send a sword against Jerusalem, and "I will overturn, overturn, overturn it: and it shall be no more, until He come whose right it is; and I will give it Him." In chapter xxii., after speaking of Israel's dispersion, He says He will gather them together into the midst of Jerusalem as they gather metal into the midst of a furnace to melt it, so will He gather His people and melt them in the fire of His wrath. These terrible final judgments will be blessed to the conversion of the Jewish people and their restoration to the Divine favour.

THE TEMPLE. The last nine chapters contain Ezekiel's vision of the New Temple. This vision has never yet been fulfilled. The Temple built by Zerubbabel, and that by Herod, fell far short of the size of the New Temple of which Ezekiel was given the plan by the angel. "Just what the meaning of this vision is, it is by no means easy to determine. . . . The new distribution of the land according to the twelve tribes and the prince and his portion, and the suburbs ; the new city and the immense Temple area,—all combine to point to a future re-establishment of Israel and to the millennial glory. It has never yet had its appropriate fulfilment. To spiritualise it, as some do, exhausting all its splendours and hopes in the Christian dispensation, is to mistake its meaning and dwarf its magnificent proportions. For unmistakably the vision has to do with Israel in the last and glorious days when all God hath promised for that people shall have its accomplishment." [1]

When the Temple was complete, Ezekiel saw the glory of the Lord returning by the way of the east gate—the direction in which it had left the city—and filling the house of the Lord. If we have grieved the Spirit of the Lord away from our hearts, we must expect His return by the way that He went. That is to say, we must come back to the very point where we failed, and confess that particular sin to the Lord, and obey Him on that point, before we can expect Him to return. "The Holy Ghost, whom God hath given to them that *obey* Him." In this chapter we read of the glory definitely coming back, and taking up its abode in the Temple, and *continuing* to fill it. This is what God expects shall be the normal condition of every Christian. "Be filled with the Spirit" (Eph. v. 18).

THE RIVER. If we are filled with the Spirit there must be an overflow to others ; and this brings us to the vision of the river (chap. xlvii.). Whatever is the future application of this chapter to Israel, its spiritual application to us to-day is clear. The Lord wants to make His rivers of blessing flow out through every saved soul (John vii. 37-39). Are we, as workers for Christ, "ministering the Spirit" to others ?

The rivers issued out from the sanctuary. It is only from the presence of the Lord that we can go forth to bless others. It was from the south side of the altar—pointing again to the place of sacrifice as the source of blessing. "A pure river of water of life, clear as crystal, proceeding out of the throne of God and of the Lamb" ; "A Lamb as it had been slain." The river rose to the ankles, to the knees, to the loins, for the Lord means His power in us to increase till it becomes "waters to swim in, a river that *I* could not pass over"—self lost in the fulness of the Spirit. Wherever the river came the fish *lived*, the banks grew green, clothed with trees, bearing fruit

---

[1] *Outline Studies in the Books of the Old Testament*, p. 274.   Moorehead.

for meat and leaves for medicine. God wants to use us wherever we go to bring life to dead souls, and blessing and healing to all around us. The only places that were not healed were the *marshes*. They were given up to salt. A marsh is something that is always taking in and never giving out. Unless we are giving out, in some way, to others, we shall become stagnant and useless.

"Rivers of living water." This is God's purpose for us. Do not let us reason from our old past experience of failure, nor from the parched condition of the Church around us. God says He will do a *new thing*: "Behold, I will do a *new thing*: now it shall spring forth; shall ye not know it? I will even make a way in the wilderness, and rivers in the desert—viz. in the most unlikely places—to give drink to My people, My chosen."

LIFE. Throughout the Book of Ezekiel we see Christ as the Giver of Life. The cherubim, in the vision of the first chapter, were illustrations of the abundant *life* of His redeemed. The Man clothed in linen, who is thought by many to be the Angel of the Covenant, our Great High Priest, set the mark of *life* upon God's faithful ones, that their *lives* should be spared in the destruction of the city (chap. ix. 2). His first word to the out-cast babe—which represented Israel, and became "perfect through His comeliness," which He had put upon it —was *Live* (chap. xvi. 6). His word through the watchman was: "I have no pleasure in the death of the wicked . . . turn ye, turn ye, why will ye die, O house of Israel?" (xxxiii. 11). His care as a Shepherd is over the *life* of His sheep (xxxiv.). He answered His own question, "Can these dry bones *live*?" with the words, "Behold, I will cause breath to enter into you, and ye shall *live*" (xxxvii. 3, 5). Finally, as we have seen, His promise was, "Everything shall *live* whither the river cometh."

"SON OF MAN." Throughout the book God addresses Ezekiel as the "Son of man." It is part of His wondrous grace that He has chosen man to be His messenger to his fellow-men, instead of choosing angels. The greatest exhibition of this grace is the fact that the Son of God became the Son of Man to fit Him to be God's messenger to us. "For verily He took not on Him the nature of angels; but He took on Him the seed of Abraham"; in all things made like unto His brethren, that He might be able to succour and to save us.

The book closes with the promise of God's continual presence. "The name of the city from that day shall be *Jehovah-shammah*, The Lord is there."

## 6. DANIEL

The omnipotence of God is exhibited as much in His power to keep Daniel pure and true and faithful to Himself amidst all the corruptions of a heathen Court, as it is in the outward deliverances which He wrought for His servant as recorded in this book. Carried captive as a youth, Daniel found himself in this position of extreme difficulty through no choice of his own, and we may learn from this history that there is no position, however full of temptation, in which the Lord is not able to keep us from falling, if we have not placed ourselves there wilfully.

Daniel's character is beautiful in its simplicity. It shows the same consistency throughout, attributing every power, every success, every deliverance to God. A chief statesman in the first empire of the world, a chief adviser of a great monarch, a great protector, doubtless, of his own people, he never introduces himself or his own actions, except as illustrations of God's power. From the first picture we have of him, as a youth of royal descent, refusing to defile himself with the heathen king's meat (no doubt as being connected with idol sacrifices), and carrying his companions with him by the power of his influence, to the aged statesman in the last days of the Captivity, we see the same undeviating faithfulness. Even his enemies confessed that they could find no fault in him, and no occasion to accuse him except they found it against him concerning the law of his God.

A MAN GREATLY BELOVED. Daniel was a man greatly beloved. We read that God had brought him into favour and tender love with the Court official Ashpenaz. The proud and despotic Nebuchadnezzar seems to have had a real affection for the man whom he honoured throughout his long reign. The regard Darius felt for him is undisguised. When he found what a trap he had fallen into, he "was sore displeased with himself, and set his heart on Daniel to deliver him." We can well imagine that Daniel's great age added poignancy to the king's remorse at having to pass such a sentence upon him. Cyrus, no doubt, was greatly influenced by his aged statesman, who in all probability showed him the prophecy of Isaiah which led to his issuing the decree for the building of the Temple at Jerusalem.

But, best of all, Daniel was greatly beloved by his God. We are thrice told this. He was a man of prayer, as we see on various occasions. The interpretation of Nebuchadnezzar's dream was given him in answer to the united prayer of himself and his companions, and he did not fail to acknowledge publicly that it was so. Later on, in spite of the decree of Darius, he quietly pursued his usual custom, and prayed to God with his windows open towards Jerusalem "as he did aforetime." Again, believing Jeremiah's prophecy as to the restoration of his people, he set himself to seek the Lord by prayer and fasting, and, in the memorable prayer of chapter x., made a full confession of sin on behalf of his people. Again, in the third year of Cyrus, after three weeks of fasting and prayer (x. 1, 2), another vision of the future is granted to him. In this account we are allowed a glimpse into one of the mysteries of delayed answers to prayer. How little we realise the unseen forces of darkness which are arrayed against us! The thought of this should lead us to pray more earnestly. We cannot understand the mystery of prayer; but we have God's promise, and we know by experience that He does hear and answer prayer, and this is enough for us.

A CONTRAST OF POWER. The great object of the Book of Daniel is to bring out the power of God as contrasted with the great world-power. This thought is brought out in the two sections into which the Book of Daniel is divided. The first six chapters are mainly *Narration*, the last six mainly *Revelation*.

*Chapter I.* God's power is shown, as we have already seen, in the character of Daniel and his three companions, and in the wisdom and understanding which God gave them above all the wise men of Babylon. All of them had before borne names commemorative of the true God. The change of names, though in two cases at least they were named after idols, did not change their hearts. They were trained in all the learning of Chaldea, as Moses had been trained in the learning of the greatest country of his time.

*Chapter II.* God's power is shown in His revelation to Daniel of Nebuchadnezzar's dream and the interpretation thereof, which the wise men of Babylon were unable to give.

*Chapter III.* It is shown again in His deliverance of the three companions of Daniel from the fiery furnace when they had refused to worship the golden image. It was no uncommon thing for sovereigns of vast empires to claim Divine honours; and it may have been with some idea of this kind that Nebuchadnezzar set up this huge golden image, probably representing himself, and sent for all the officials of his kingdom to come and worship it. History has no finer picture than that of these three young men standing alone against a nation with the calm faith that God would deliver them, yet adding, "*but if not*—be it known to thee, O King, that we will not worship the golden image." According to His promise (Isa. xliii. 2), the Lord was with them in the fire, "and the form of the fourth was like the Son of God." Here is our first sight of Christ in this book; and He is still with His own when they pass through the fire, and many a saint has proved since then, as they did, that the only effect of the fire is to burn the bonds. "Lo, I see four men *loose*, walking in the midst of the fire, and they have no hurt."

*Chapter IV.* Again we see God's power in His dealings with Nebuchadnezzar. First He warned him in a dream of his coming madness, and revealed to Daniel the interpretation of it. Daniel's respectful regard for his monarch comes out in his reluctance to tell him the interpretation: "He sat astonied for one hour, and his thoughts troubled him." The king had to encourage him to speak, and then with what mingled tenderness and boldness he exhorted him to repentance. At the end of twelve months, as the proud monarch was boasting of his power on the roof of his magnificent palace, the stroke of God fell, and he was driven far from among men, and had his dwelling among the beasts of the field. There he repented, and God restored him according to His promise. This whole chapter is of special interest as being, not a record by Daniel, but a State Paper sent out by Nebuchadnezzar to his people.

*Chapter V.* God's power is shown again in the awful handwriting on the wall, when Belshazzar's sacrilege received God's retribution. The prophet who had pleaded so deferentially with Nebuchadnezzar had only words of fearless condemnation for the foolish and sensual young king his grandson. A bad reign came to a sudden termination. "In that night was Belshazzar king of the Chaldeans slain"—we are not told how; "and Darius the Mede received the kingdom." The Medo-Persian army took the city in all likelihood without fighting. Darius probably received the kingdom from Cyrus as his vicegerent over some portion of it. His identity is still to some extent a puzzle to historians, but so was Belshazzar's until recently. "For history testifies that the last king of Babylon was Nabonidus; that he was absent from the capital when Cyrus entered it, and that he lived many years after the Persian conquest. The contradiction between history and Scripture was complete. But the since-deciphered inscriptions have disclosed that Belshazzar was eldest son and heir to Nabonidus, that he was regent in Babylon during his father's absence, and that he was killed the night the Persian army entered the inner city" (Sir R. Anderson).

*Chapter VI.* Once more God's power was shown in the deliverance of Daniel from the lion's den, when the incorruptibility of his conduct had made enemies for the aged statesman, and they had successfully intrigued against him.

MANIFESTATION OF POWER. The time of the captivity in Babylon was a special occasion for God to manifest His power. When His chosen people were captives in Egypt He wrought wonders for them by the hand of Moses, and showed, both to them and to the great Egyptian nation, that He was Lord over all. So now once more when His people were in captivity He made bare His arm, and showed forth His mighty power, so that even these great world emperors were brought to confess that He is the Living God, the Most High, the King of Heaven, whose dominion is an everlasting dominion. In this very centre of Pagan world-power Jehovah visits His exiles by miracle and prophecy, to show His power and comfort them by glimpses of the future. "Fulfilled prophecy is miracle in the highest sphere, that of mind. It is the ever-growing proof of Divine prescience in the authors of sacred Scripture" (H. Grattan Guinness).

This revelation of the future became an added confirmation to God's people as they saw it gradually fulfilled before their eyes. But how far more is it a confirmation to our faith, to us who can look back on the wide sweep of revelation already fulfilled in the world's history. God makes a special appeal to fulfilled prophecy as the seal of the truth of His word (Jer. xxviii. 9 ; 2 Peter i. 19-21).

UNIVERSAL DOMINION. The first revelation in this book occurs in the historic portion of it, in Nebuchadnezzar's dream of the great image with its head of gold, its breast and arms of silver, its belly and thighs of brass, and its legs of iron, its feet and toes of iron and clay, brought to nothing by a stone cut out without hands which smote the image, and broke it to pieces ; and the stone became a great mountain and filled the whole earth.

No human ingenuity could have hit upon the interpretation. The image symbolises the world-kingdoms in their historic succession. God makes known to Nebuchadnezzar "what shall come to pass hereafter," in the glorious future Kingdom of Christ. He reveals first the Gentile dominion. Four great empires, and only four, were to succeed each other in the government of the world from the Chaldean to the end. The first was the Babylonian with Nebuchadnezzar at its head: "Thou art this head of gold." The grant of Empire was made to him by God Himself (ver. 37, 38 ; Jer. xxvii. 5-7).

The breast and the arms of silver denote the Medo-Persian Empire which overthrew the Chaldean, and became its successor in the government of the world. The brass, or rather copper, is the Grecian, which overturned the Persian ; and the iron is the Roman, which succeeded the Greek. From the Book of Daniel itself we learn which are the world-kingdoms symbolised. Chapter ii. 38 shows us that the head of gold is Babylon. In viii. 20 we see that the Medo-Persian empire was to succeed the Chaldean ; and viii. 21 declares that Grecia follows Persia, while ix. 26 plainly indicates that Rome is the fourth. After that the power is divided.

In the stone cut out without hands we see the Kingdom of Christ, whose kingdom shall never be destroyed ; it shall break in pieces and destroy all these kingdoms and it shall stand for ever.

THE FOUR BEASTS. *Chapter VII.* In Daniel's vision of the four beasts we have these four kingdoms under another symbol. In the great image of Nebuchadnezzar's dream we have the magnificence of these kingdoms in man's view. In Daniel's vision we have the same in God's view. He sees them as a set of devouring wild beasts. The first, or Babylonian, was like a lion with eagle's wings. Jeremiah had likened Nebuchadnezzar both to the lion and eagle (xlix. 19, 22). Persia was the cruel bear, the animal who delights to kill for the sake of killing, and to tear for the sake of tearing—a heavy beast, well portraying the ponderous Persian armies. The third is the leopard or panther, an animal insatiable above every other beast of prey, gifted with a swiftness which scarce any prey can escape, represented yet further with four wings. Here we see the rapid marches of Alexander's army and his insatiable love of conquest. In thirteen brief years he had subdued the world.

The fourth beast was "dreadful and terrible, and strong

exceedingly, and had great iron teeth." This is the Roman Empire.

THE SON OF GOD. With the close of the vision of the four beasts we have a further revelation of Christ in Daniel. We see the throne of God, and the Ancient of Days sitting there in judgment, and the books opened. And there, on the right hand of God the Father, Daniel sees God the Son. "One like the Son of Man coming in the clouds of heaven," and everlasting dominion and glory given to Him. We see in act what was said in words in David's Psalm, which Jesus quoted as written of Himself, "The Lord said unto my Lord, Sit Thou on My right hand until I make Thine enemies Thy footstool." When the High Priest said to our Lord, "I adjure Thee by the living God, that Thou tell me whether Thou be the Christ, the Son of God," Jesus saith unto him, "Thou hast said : nevertheless, I say unto thee, Hereafter shall ye see the Son of Man sitting on the right hand of power, and coming in the clouds of heaven." Then the High Priest rent his clothes, saying, "He hath spoken blasphemy." Our Lord applied these words of Daniel to Himself, and the High Priest immediately recognised in them His claim to deity.

*Chapter VIII.* Next we have a vision of the ram and the he-goat, the kingdom of Medo-Persia overthrown by the kingdom of Grecia. It contains the prophecy of the division of the latter kingdom, on the death of Alexander, between his four generals. Daniel had this vision at Shushan, the capital of Persia, where, seventy years later, the events recorded in the Book of Esther took place.

SEVENTY WEEKS. *Chapter IX.* This chapter contains, as we have already seen, Daniel's discovery from the prophecy of Jeremiah that the Captivity was nearing its close. This shows the great importance of the study of the Holy Scriptures ; and the eleventh verse of this chapter contains a testimony both to the antiquity and to the Mosaic authorship of the Pentateuch. Daniel's prayer was followed by the vision of the seventy weeks. The angel Gabriel tells Daniel that seventy weeks are determined or measured off, upon his people and the holy city ; within which period of time God will perform His whole work, promised and predicted throughout all Scripture.

Seventy weeks. The word "week" is retained, because there is no English word which exactly expresses the idea of the original. It is seventy times seven years that is meant, 490 years in all. It was a form of reckoning familiar to the Jews from earliest times.

The seventy weeks are divided into three groups, viz. seven weeks, sixty-two weeks, one week. The seventy weeks began with the edict of Artaxerxes to rebuild the walls of Jerusalem, in the Jewish month Nisan of the year 445 B.C. "The language of the prophecy is clear : 'From the going forth of the commandment to restore and to build Jerusalem unto *Messiah the Prince*, shall be seven weeks and threescore and two weeks.'" Sir Robert Anderson, with the assistance of astronomical calculations supplied by the Astronomer-Royal, Sir G. B. Airy, has calculated that this interval (173,880 days, or seventy times sixty-nine prophetic years of 360 days) brings us to the very day of Christ's triumphal entry into Jerusalem, the climax of His ministry, when the prophecy of Zechariah was fulfilled, "Behold thy King cometh unto thee," and the day of Zion's irrevocable choice. The correct translation of our Lord's words is : "If thou hadst known, *even on this day*, the things that belong unto thy peace, but now they are hid from thine eyes." The prophecy continues : "And *after* threescore and two weeks shall Messiah be cut off, but not for Himself."

Then follows the prophecy of the destruction of Jerusalem. In A.D. 70 the Roman eagles swooped down on the devoted city and destroyed both city and temple. But the prophecy points onward to a time yet to come. The last week is rent off from the other sixty-nine and stands by itself. There is a mighty break between the sixty-ninth and the seventieth in the series. The death of Christ broke the chain for the weeks ; for that event sundered the relation then existing between God and the chosen people.

Verses 24-27 refer plainly to the manifestation of Jesus Christ to fulfil all righteousness and to make full atonement for the sins of His people (compare 1 John iii. 8 and 2 Cor. v. 19).

"THE TIME OF THE END." The last three chapters of Daniel contain one vision. Chapter x. reveals the influence of supernatural beings in the affairs of earth. Chapters xi. and xii. point on to the "Time of the end," and the appearance of anti-Christ. Daniel, Paul, John (2 Thess. ii. ; Rev. xix.), prophesy of the mighty scenes and events of this time, the Day of the Lord. They severally declare that the great adversary will

be destroyed by the coming of Jesus Christ Himself. Our
Lord's own testimony is identical with theirs (Matt. xxiv.
and xxv ; Mark xiii. and Luke xxi.). Our Lord quotes the
words of Daniel about the daily sacrifice being taken away, and
the abomination that maketh desolate being set up.

RESURRECTION. Chapter xii. 1, 2 predicts a time of unparalleled trouble. Our Lord speaks of the same (Matt. xxiv.
21). It is the great tribulation. Here the resurrection of the
dead is more plainly foretold than anywhere else in the Old
Testament : "Many of them that sleep in the dust of the earth
shall awake, some to everlasting life, and some to shame and
everlasting contempt." The future joy of those that turn
many to righteousness is revealed.

The vision closes with a word of personal comfort to the
faithful prophet : "Go thy way till the end be : for thou shalt
rest, and stand in thy lot at the end of the days."

AUTHENTICITY. A book which contains such exact predictions is one which is likely to be assailed. "The Book of
Daniel is especially fitted to be a battle-field between faith and
unbelief. It admits of no half measures. It is either Divine
or an imposture." With these words Dr. Pusey begins his
most valuable volume on Daniel. He shows that to write any
book under the name of another, and to give it out as his, is
in any case a forgery. But in this case, if the writer were not
Daniel, the book would be one continued lie in the name of
God ; for, as we have seen, the book ascribes everything to
God.

The proofs of the authenticity of the book can barely be
touched upon here.[1]

(1) WITNESS OF DANIEL. The book claims Daniel for its
author (viii. 1, 2, etc. etc.)

(2) WITNESS OF EZEKIEL. Ezekiel testified both to the
existence and character of Daniel (xiv. 14, 20, xxviii. 3).

(3) WITNESS OF THE MONUMENTS. The records of the
monuments testify with ever-increasing clearness, as more of

[1] For convincing proofs see *Lectures on Daniel the Prophet*, Dr. Pusey ; *The
Coming Prince* and *Daniel in the Critics' Den*, Sir R. Anderson ; *The Biblical
Guide*, and *The Inspiration and Accuracy of the Holy Scriptures*, Rev. J.
Urquhart.

them are deciphered, to the absolute accuracy of the details of Daniel's description. The local colouring is true to life, such as could not have been invented by a forger in Palestine of later date

The inscriptions show that there was a school in connection with the palace of Babylon, where youths, including captive princes, were trained in the learning of Chaldea, which embraced a wide circle of subjects.

The monuments vouch, either directly or indirectly, for each one of the classes into which Daniel divides the wise men of Babylon; also for the articles of dress worn by his companions: they are such as would have been worn by nobles on a great festive occasion.

Casting into a fiery furnace and into a den of lions were punishments well known in Babylon.

On the plains of Dura there stands to-day a rectilinear mound, about twenty feet high, an exact square of about forty-six feet at the base, resembling the pedestal of a colossal statue. Everything leads to the belief that Nebuchadnezzar's golden image was set up in this place.

Nebuchadnezzar's proud and imperious personality has been stamped upon our imaginations from childhood. The monuments bear abundant testimony to the same. "*To astonish mankind*, I reconstructed and renewed the wonder of Borsippa, the temple of the seven spheres of the world." The Arabs still use the ruins of Babylon as a large quarry, and carry off its bricks. Nine out of every ten of these bricks is stamped with the name of Nebuchadnezzar, a silent answer to the truth of his question, "Is not this great Babylon which I have built?"

(4) WITNESS OF LANGUAGE. Another proof of the date of this book is the languages in which it is written. From chapter ii. 4 to the end of chapter vii. it is in Aramaic or Syriac, the common language of the Gentile nations, the language of commerce and diplomacy over the then known world. The rest is in Hebrew. The part written in Aramaic relates to the Gentile supremacy over Israel. The use of this language signifies that God had for a time set aside the Jew. During the Captivity, just at the time that Daniel wrote, both languages, the Aramaic and the Hebrew, were understood by the Jewish people, and they would be able to follow the whole book. The Jews did not understand Aramaic in the reign of Hezekiah (2 Kings xviii. 26), and they had ceased, as a nation, to understand Hebrew by the time of Ezra, for when he read to them

the Law, he had to give the sense or translate as he went. If the book had been written, as is alleged, during the time of Antiochus Epiphanes, or immediately before it, in order to console the Jews under their persecutions, is it likely that the writer would have wrapped up his words of comfort in a language they could not understand ?

The presence of certain Greek words in the Book of Daniel is supposed to point to the book having been written after the conquests of Alexander. Most of these supposed Greek words have been found to be really Aramaic, their actual number has been reduced to two, and these are the names of two musical instruments. Modern discovery has revealed the widespread interchange of thought and commerce between the most ancient nations of the earth. A busy commercial intercourse existed between Greece and Babylonia, about a century before the time of Daniel. The harp with seven strings was invented by Terpander, a Greek poet and musician in the year 650 B.C. This seven-stringed harp was introduced into Babylon within twenty-five years of that date, for we find it sculptured then on the monuments. This *kitharis* is one of the two remaining Greek words in Daniel !

WITNESS OF CHRIST. There remains yet one more proof which can hardly be put alongside the foregoing, as it transcends them all. It is the testimony of our Lord Himself. He quoted from this book as recorded in Matthew xxiv. 14, 15, 30 ; Luke xxi. 24 ; and again in Matthew xxvi. 63, 64, when, as we have seen, He applied the prophecy of Daniel about the Son of Man coming in the clouds of heaven as a proof of His Messiahship and His deity. He speaks expressly of the "Prophet Daniel" by name, with the words added, "whoso readeth, let him understand." It is a remarkable fact that our Lord thus commends to our study this Book of Daniel, and also the Book of Revelation, both full of unfulfilled prophecy, both difficult to understand ; and the Book of Revelation, which is the most difficult of all, opens with a blessing on him that readeth, and those that hear and keep this word of the testimony of Jesus Christ, and it closes with a solemn warning to those who shall either add or take away from the words of the prophecy of this book (Rev. i. 1-3, xxii. 16, 18, 19).

## 7. THE MINOR PROPHETS

These twelve were classed by the Jews as one book. The period which they cover, within which the major prophets also fall, extends from about 870-440 B.C. For the sake of better understanding their teaching, they may be grouped round the four greater prophets.

(1) Isaiah is illustrated by Hosea, Amos, and Micah.
(2) Jeremiah is illustrated by Obadiah, Habakkuk, and Zephaniah.
(3) Ezekiel is illustrated by Joel, Jonah, Nahum.
(4) Daniel is illustrated by Haggai, Zechariah, Malachi.

The connection of *time* with the first group is obvious. Obadiah is connected with Jeremiah by his prophecies against Edom. Habakkuk and Zephaniah are closely connected with the same prophet. The last three of the twelve, with Daniel, lived to see the return after the Captivity. Joel, Jonah, and Nahum contain prophecies concerning the Gentiles which may be taken as linking them with Ezekiel, who prophesied in a Gentile land during the Captivity.[1]

"The prophecies contained in these twelve books present one complete view. The kingdom of David is seen as rent asunder, and its riven portions end in apparent ruin. But a believing remnant always survives the wreck, and a restoration will come when David's Son will rebuild the ruined nation and re-establish the throne. There is a constant look forward, past Macedonian conquests and Maccabean successes, the apostasy of the Jews and the destruction of Jerusalem, beyond even the dispersion of the elect nation, to the *final conversion* and *ultimate restoration* of *God's chosen people*. The Old Testament outline of Messiah and His Kingdom, which at earlier periods of prophecy was like a 'drawing without colour,' now reaches completeness, and every prophetic book adds at least another touch or tint to the grand picture. . . . Once let the reader of prophecy get clear conceptions of this fact, that *Christ is its personal centre* and *Israel its national centre*, and that round about these centres all else clusters, and that in them all else converges, and, 'whether he walks or runs, he will see all things clearly,' for the vision is written in large letters as upon tablets by the wayside."[2]

[1] *Hosea*, by Chas. H. Waller, D.D.
[2] *The Keywords of the Bible*. A. T. Pierson, D.D.

## 8. Hosea

The prophet Hosea was a contemporary of Isaiah and continued to prophesy for sixty-five or seventy years. He was God's messenger to the northern kingdom of Israel and only mentions Judah incidentally. He addresses Israel sometimes as Samaria and Jacob and *Ephraim*—the last because that tribe was the largest of the ten and the leader in rebellion. The book abounds in expressive metaphors. Ephraim is "a cake not turned," "a silly dove without a heart"; her king is "cut off as foam upon the water." Hosea began to prophesy during the reign of Jeroboam II. king of Israel, one of the most powerful of her kings, and during the reign of his successors, whom the prophet does not even name because they were not of the Lord's choosing (viii. 4). There was not one of them found who would risk his throne for God. This was a striking illustration of the Law in Deuteronomy xvii. 15, "Thou shalt in any wise set him king over thee, whom the Lord thy God shall choose." That Israel possessed the written Law in the days of Hosea is shown from various passages, notably viii. 12.

WICKEDNESS OF THE LAND. The moral state of Israel was as bad as it could possibly be. The idolatry inaugurated by Jeroboam I., the son of Nebat, had continued for upwards of two hundred years, and had diffused every form of vice among the people. "The Lord hath a controversy with the land," said Hosea, "because there is no truth, nor mercy, nor knowledge of God in the land. By swearing, and lying, and killing, and stealing, and committing adultery, they break out" (iv. 1, 2). Drunkenness and shameful idol festivals were spread over the land. The idolatrous priests even waylaid and murdered the wayfarers.

JUDGMENT AND MERCY. Hosea was sent both to denounce the sins of the people and to proclaim to them the compassionate love of God, and His willingness to have mercy upon them if they would but return to Him. He himself was made a sign to the people. His longsuffering love for a wife who proved faithless to him, and whom he bought back from a life of shame, was a picture of God's love to His rebellious people, who had broken their covenant with Him and had given themselves up to the worship of idols.

God first pronounces His judgment upon His people. He

will be to them as a moth and rottenness, as a young lion, as a leopard, as a bear robbed of her whelps. He says He has hewed them by the prophets and slain them by the words of His mouth. He foretells the awful destruction of Samaria, the sword that shall slay them, and the fire that shall destroy them. But along with judgment He makes known His mercy, His earnest desire for their repentance. "I will go and return to My place, till they acknowledge their offence, and seek My face : in their affliction they will seek Me early" (Hosea, v. 15). Nothing can exceed the earnestness and love with which the Lord entreats Ephraim to return to Him. "How shall I give thee up Ephraim?" Four times over this "How" is repeated. "O Israel, thou hast destroyed thyself; but in Me is thy help." "O Israel, return unto the Lord thy God; for thou hast fallen by thine iniquity. Take with you words, and return to the Lord: say unto Him, Take away all iniquity, and receive us graciously. . . . I will heal their backsliding, I will love them freely." And then follows His gracious promise of restoration, that He will be as the "summer night-mist" to Israel, and it shall grow with the beauty of the lily, with the strength of the cedars of Lebanon, with the fragrance of the undergrowth of those mountains, and with the fruitfulness of the olive, and the corn, and the vine, and the perennial greenness of the fir-tree.

THE MESSIAH. Messianic allusions in this book are clear and beautiful. Both Peter and Paul show us that the prophecy of i. 10 has been fulfilled in Christ (1 Pet. ii. 10; Rom. xi. 25, 26).

In iii. 4 the present state of Israel is described. "Without a king, without a prince, without a sacrifice, without an ephod"—the sign of the priest—because they have rejected their King, their true Priest after the order of Melchizedek, and are still rejecting the sacrifice He offered. And, on the other hand, they are "without an image, and without teraphim," for they are free from idolatry. The next verse describes their glorious future, when they shall return and seek the Lord their God, and David their King—the Lord Jesus Christ.

RESURRECTION OF CHRIST. Chapter vi. 2: "After two days He will revive us : in the third day He will raise us up, and we shall live in His sight." The resurrection of Christ, and our resurrection in Him, could not be more plainly fore-told. The prophet expressly mentions *two days*, after which life should be given, and *a third day*, on which the resurrection should take place. Verse 3 : " His going forth is prepared as the morning ; and He shall come unto us as the rain, as the latter and former rain unto the earth." He who should so go forth is the same as He who was to revive them and raise them up—even Christ, who as " the Day-spring from on high hath visited us," coming forth from the grave on the resurrection morning, and of whom it was foretold that He should " come down like showers upon the mown grass."

" OUT OF EGYPT." xi. 1. " I called My Son out of Egypt." This had a primary fulfilment in Israel as a type of Christ. Its real fulfilment, as we are told by Matthew (ii. 15), was in Christ, the Only-begotten Son of God.

ONE SAVIOUR. xi. 4. " I drew them with cords of a Man, with bands of love." Christ drew us with cords of a man when for us He became man and died for us. " I, if I be lifted up, will draw all men unto Me."

xiii. 4. " There is no Saviour beside Me." " Thou shalt call His name Jesus (Saviour) ; for He shall save His people from their sins." " Neither is there salvation in any other : for there is none other name under heaven given among men whereby we must be saved."

xiii. 14. " I will ransom them from the power of the grave ; I will redeem them from death." " The word rendered *ransom*, signifies rescued them by the payment of a price ; the word rendered *redeem*, relates to one who, as the nearest of kin, had the right to acquire anything as his own, by paying the price. Both words in their most exact sense describe what Jesus did for us " (Dr. Pusey).

" O death, I will be thy plagues ; O grave, I will be thy destruction," is a burst of triumph at the promised redemption, when Christ being risen from the dead became the first-fruits of them that slept.

## 9. JOEL

Joel was the first to prophesy the outpouring of the Spirit upon all flesh. His prophecy seems to have been delivered all at one time—not like that of Hosea, spread over a period of many years—and its scope extends from his own day to the end of time.

He was probably the earliest of the prophetic writers, but

he tells us nothing about himself beyond the few words necessary to authenticate his book and give it its Divine authority. "The word of the Lord that came to Joel the son of Pethuel" (i. 1).

Locusts. He was prophet to Judah, and, using God's present judgment of a plague of locusts, with urgency he calls his people to repentance in order to avert the still severer judgment upon their sins by means of hostile armies, of which the army of locusts was a type.

In graphic language he describes the plague, calling first on the old men to confirm its unparalleled severity. The drunkards feel the effects of it, for the vines have perished. The priests have no meat offering of corn, nor drink offering of wine to offer. The husbandmen and vine-dressers are ashamed. The cry of the cattle and sheep goes up to God. Joel urges the people to call a fast, and then, in the beginning of the second chapter, he continues his description of the plague.

Before the army of locusts the land is as the Garden of Eden—behind them it is a desolate wilderness (ii. 3). An army of locusts is incredible to those who have not watched it. They fill the air, and darken the sun like an eclipse (ii. 2), and spread for miles over the land. The advance columns will attack all that is green and succulent; in half an hour every leaf and blade is destroyed (i. 11, 12). Others coming on in succession will strip the bark from the trees (i. 6, 7). A land so devastated takes years to recover (i. 17-20). The noise of their wings can be heard for miles, and the noise of their browsing is like a fire (ii. 5), and the land over which they have passed has the appearance of being fire-swept (ii. 3). Having stripped the country, they scale the walls of the cities, in serried ranks like mailed horsemen and chariots, and marching into the houses consume everything which can be consumed in their resistless onslaught (ii. 4, 7-9).

"The Day of the Lord." "Blow the trumpet in Zion . . . for the day of the Lord cometh, for it is nigh at hand. Sanctify a fast, call a solemn assembly; gather the people" (ii. 1, 15-17). Joel urges all classes of the people to repent, from the priests—the ministers of the Lord—and the elders, to the bride and bridegroom, and the children, even the little ones. "*The day of the Lord*" always signifies judgment; the expression occurs five times in this short book, and is its Keynote. It refers, doubtless, to a series of judgments—the

present locusts, the coming armies of invasion which were
about to come as a scourge of God upon the land, and the final
Day of the Lord described in the third chapter.

Joel calls on the Lord to spare His people, and, like Moses,
urges the plea that the heathen would question "Where is
their God?" (ii. 17). His call to repentance is enforced by
promises. The pity of the Lord, His readiness to bless if the
conditions are fulfilled, the removal of the scourge, the plentiful rain and abundant crops, and the outpouring of the Spirit.

PROMISE OF THE SPIRIT. This brings us to the great central
promise of the book. Other prophets have foretold details of
our Lord's life on earth and of His future reign; to Joel was
committed the privilege of telling that He would pour out His
Spirit upon all flesh, alike on Jew and Gentile, bond and free,
male and female; for all should be one in Christ Jesus. He
tells us that the blessing shall flow forth from Jerusalem (ii. 32,
iii. 18). This prophecy, we are distinctly told, was fulfilled on
the day of Pentecost; for Peter said, "This is that which was
spoken by the prophet Joel." And again: "This Jesus hath
God raised up, and having received of the Father the promise
of the Holy Ghost, He hath shed forth this, which ye now see
and hear" (Acts ii. 16, 32, 33). It no doubt has a further
fulfilment yet to come after the great Day of the Lord, which
is described in the third chapter, when unquestionably the
prophet looks forward to a final day when the Lord shall come
in judgment. Christ speaks of this day in the same figure of a
great harvest (iii. 13; Matt. xiii. 36-43), and we find the figure
of the wine-press again in the Book of Revelation (iii. 13; Rev.
xiv. 18-20).

A LESSON FOR TO-DAY. The whole book contains a beautiful
spiritual lesson for to-day. First, the desolated condition of
the Church of Christ. It is laid waste by many spiritual foes,
well described in chapter i. 4. There is famine and drought on
all sides. The call goes forth afresh to-day to the Church of
God to come down into the very dust before the Lord in true
repentance of heart. This repentance should begin with the
leaders, the ministers, the elders, the vine-dressers. But it may
be the work will begin with the little ones, as it has been so
often in times of revival. If only there is this turning of heart
to the Lord we may count on the fulfilment of His promise of
the abundant outpouring of His Spirit, and that He will restore
the years that the canker-worm hath eaten.

Although the third chapter is one of judgment we may take it also in a spiritual sense, and see the Church, prepared by the fulness of the Spirit, ready to fight the battle of the Lord against the hosts of darkness, ready for a great ingathering of souls, and multitudes, multitudes shall be brought into the valley of decision.

## 10. Amos

The "man of God from Judah" was sent to Bethel in the northern kingdom to rebuke Jeroboam I. as he was sacrificing to the golden calves. Another man of God from Judah was sent to prophesy at Bethel, during the reign of Jeroboam II., in the person of the herdman, or shepherd, Amos. Amos is one of the many instances in the Bible of the Lord calling a man to some special service while occupied with his ordinary daily work.

On the wild uplands of Judah beyond Tekoa, which is twelve miles south of Jerusalem, Amos, inured to hardship and danger, received his training as a prophet straight from the hand of the Lord. His beautiful style abounds in illustrations drawn from his mountain home. He had learnt the power of the Creator in the mountains and the wind, in the dawn and in the darkness. Like David he had gazed upon the stars and looked beyond them to their Maker. Like him also, as he had "followed the flock" (vii. 15), he had known what it was to defend them from the wild beasts, both the lion and the bear, and is probably describing his own experience when he speaks of a shepherd taking out of the mouth of the lion "two legs or a piece of an ear." [1] The snare of the fowler and the snake concealed in the rough stone wall were alike familiar to him. He was also a "gatherer," or "dresser," of sycamore fruit. This fruit, which is a very inferior sort of fig, only eaten by the very poor, has to be scarified at one stage of its growth with a special instrument for the purpose, in order to enable it to swell and ripen properly. Many of the figures which Amos uses are taken from the milder lowlands; these also may have been familiar to him in his earlier life, or, as a keen observer of nature, may have struck him as he prophesied in the plains of Samaria. He speaks of the oaks and the cedars, the vines and fig-trees and

[1] "The common Syrian goat, *Capra mambrica*, may be at once recognised by its enormous pendent ears a foot long, often reaching lower than its nose, and its stout recurved horns" (*The Natural History of the Bible*, p. 93, by Canon Tristram).

olive-trees, the gardens, the ploughmen, the sower, the reaper, and the cart pressed down with its weight of sheaves.

THE EARTHQUAKE. Amos opens his prophecy by quoting the words of Joel, "The Lord will roar from Zion, and utter His voice from Jerusalem." He tells us in the verse before, that his prophecy was uttered "two years before the earthquake." Joel also says, "The heavens and the earth shall shake." They no doubt refer to the same earthquake, and it must have been one of exceptional severity ; for Zechariah speaks of it nearly three hundred years later, as an event well remembered, though the whole captivity in Babylon had intervened (Zech. xiv. 5). The Hebrew word *Ra'ash* suggests the English word *Crash*, "two years before the crash." Dr. Waller, in his little book on Amos, shows how perfectly the prophet's description of the coming catastrophe fitted the event, though probably at the time he prophesied he did not realise that it was an earthquake he was describing. Twice over (viii. 8, ix. 5, R. V.) we read that "The land is to rise up wholly like a flood, and sink again as the flood of Egypt." This is a most terrible form of earthquake. "If the widespread effect of the earthquake in Amos is indicated literally by the clause seven times repeated in chapters one and two, 'I will send fire which shall devour the palaces,' then the shock must have extended from Tyrus to Gaza on the coast of the Mediterranean and from Damascus to Rabbah of the children of Ammon on the east of Jordan. The whole of the bed of the Jordan is said to be volcanic—which means that the underground forces are there, and available if the Lord of creation should choose to set them at work." [1] Fires almost invariably follow severe earthquakes.

Reading Amos in the light of the earthquake we can account for various things he foretells. The fires throughout the book. "The waters of the sea poured upon the face of the earth" (v. 8). "If there remain ten men in one house they shall die" (vi. 9). "He will smite the great house with breaches, and the little house with clefts" (vi. 11). "Shall not the land tremble ?" (viii. 8). "Smite the lintel of the door, that the posts may shake" (ix. 1). "He toucheth the land and it shall melt " (ix. 5).

But behind the primary fulfilment of his words in the earthquake there was the terrible invasion of the Assyrians, and the people carried into captivity (v. 27, vi. 14). And behind all this "the day of the Lord." "Prepare to meet thy God, O Israel" (iv. 12).

[1] *Amos*, by Chas. H. Waller, D.D.

JUDGMENT ON THE NATIONS. Amos opens the way for his message to Israel by proclaiming the Lord's judgment upon six surrounding nations—Damascus (Syria), Gaza (Philistia), Tyrus (Phœnicia), Edom, Ammon, Moab. Then he comes nearer home and pronounces judgment against Judah (ii. 4), and against Israel itself (ii. 6), and finally against the whole nation (iii. 1, 2).

It would seem that the people questioned his authority, for he proceeds by a series of seven questions to show that the Lord has revealed His secret to him, and that therefore he can do no other than prophesy (iii. 3-8).

He denounces the sins of Israel in more graphic detail than Hosea, dwelling especially on the careless ease and luxury, the oppression of the poor, the extortion and lying and cheating which prevailed, and the utter hypocrisy in worship. The Lord grieves over the people for not attending to His judgments, with the refrain, " Yet have ye not returned unto Me, saith the Lord," and the renewed invitation, " Seek ye Me and live."

FIVE VISIONS. The last three chapters contain a fivefold vision of judgment which the Lord showed Amos. First the locusts, and second the fire, which judgments are removed in answer to his intercession. Third the plumb-line. There was no hope of deliverance from this last. The Lord said, " I will not again pass by them any more." This unqualified pronouncement of judgment stirred up the smouldering animosity of Amaziah, the priest of Bethel, to a flame, and he denounced the prophet to the king, saying, " The land is not able to bear his words," so mightily had they shaken the nation. At the same time he urged Amos to flee away back to the land of Judah and prophesy there—but not here at the Court of the king. Amos fearlessly told of the Lord's call, " I was no prophet, neither was I a prophet's son ; but the Lord took me as I followed the flock, and said, Go, prophesy unto My people Israel." He then pronounced the Lord's judgment upon Amaziah, and proceeded with the account of the remaining visions regardless of the interruption. The fourth vision was of the basket of summer fruit, the last basket. "The end has come upon My people." The prophet saw the guilty nation ripe for judgment. The fifth vision is of the Lord Himself, standing upon the altar, and closes with the glorious promise of restoration for the fallen Tabernacle of the House of David, the promise of the Messiah who was to come at the moment of its greatest humiliation. This passage is quoted in Acts (xv. 15-17) by James, and applied to the ingathering of the Gentile believers, and God's favour at the same time to the House of David, when His purpose for Jew and Gentile alike will be accomplished.

## 11. OBADIAH

Between the Gulf of Akaba and the Dead Sea lies a range of precipitous red sandstone heights, known as Mount Seir.

Here Esau settled after he had despised his birthright, and his descendants, having driven out the Horites (Gen. xiv. 6), occupied the whole of the mountain (Deut. ii. 12). The capital city Selah, or Petra, "Rock," was a city unique of its kind amid the works of man. Perched like an eagle's nest (ver. 4) amid inaccessible mountain fastnesses, the dwellings were mostly caves, hewn out of the soft rock (ver. 3, 6), and placed where you could scarce imagine a human foot could climb.

JUDGMENT OF EDOM. Against this people the prophecy of the unknown prophet Obadiah, "a worshipper of Jehovah," was directed.

To Israel God had commanded (Deut. xxiii. 7), "Thou shalt not abhor an Edomite; for he is thy brother." But Edom had shown an implacable hatred to Israel from the time that he refused him a passage through his country on the way from Egypt to Canaan (Num. xx. 14-21) to the day of the destruction of Jerusalem by the Chaldeans, when Edom malignantly cried "Rase it, rase it" (Ps. cxxxvii. 7).

For his pride and cruel hatred the total destruction of Edom was decreed (ver. 3, 4, 10). The people were driven from their rocky home five years after the destruction of Jerusalem, when Nebuchadnezzar, passing down the valley of Arabah, which formed the military road to Egypt, crushed the Edomites. They lost their existence as a nation about a century and a half B.C., and their name perished at the capture of Jerusalem by the Romans. "As thou hast done, it shall be done unto thee."

DELIVERANCE FOR ISRAEL. The book closes with the promise of deliverance for Zion: "And the House of Jacob shall possess their possessions." "The first step in the future successes of the Jews is the recovery of what was previously their own" (*Speaker's Commentary*).

Obadiah predicts the coming of the Day of the Lord and the establishment of Messiah's kingdom.

### 12. Jonah

Carved in rude outline on the walls of the catacombs of Rome, there is no more favourite representation than that of Jonah as a type of the resurrection.

"On the horizon of the Old Testament there has always blazed this sign of the death and resurrection of the Lord Jesus—the sign of the prophet Jonah." Our Lord declared that no sign should be given to the men of His generation, save the sign of the prophet Jonas (Matt. xii. 39). And since then "age after age the Jew has been confronted with that sign. He killed the Messiah, and out of the grave of the Crucified has arisen a power which has changed the lives of myriads all down the ages. Our Lord gave a promise, the rising from the dead, and He has kept it. He has proved His claim to be the Son of God and the world's Saviour." [1]  "Declared to be the Son of God with power, by the resurrection from the dead" (Rom. i. 4).

The Prophet.     Jonah was the son of Amittai, the prophet, a native of Gath-hepher, a Galilean village, a little to the north of Nazareth, the home of his great Anti-type. Jewish tradition says that he was the son of the widow of Zarephath, whom Elijah restored to life. But though we have no sufficient ground for this tradition, Jonah was the successor of Elijah and Elisha, and was probably acquainted with them both, and was the link between them and Hosea, Amos, and Isaiah. It is likely that he was trained in the schools of the prophets, and that he exercised his ministry during the reign of Jeroboam II., and perhaps before it.

His name signifies "the dove," and his first prophetic utterance was one in keeping with his name. It was a message of comfort to Israel, that the Lord had seen the affliction of His people, and that He would save them by the hand of Jeroboam, the son of Joash, and restore to them the border lands which they had lost through the invasion of the Syrians. We are told this in 2 Kings xiv. 25-27, a record which was probably written long after Jonah wrote his book; and it would seem that the writer took special care to do honour to God's prophet who has been so unsparing of his own character in his faithful record.

The fact that Jonah was a historic character tells against

---

[1] *The Biblical Guide*, Rev. J. Urquhart, vol. viii. p. 146.

the idea that the book is a mere parable. The writer of a parable would not have been likely to invent an imaginary story about a real man. Jonah's candid record of his own faults is another evidence of the truth of the account, as also the fact that the Jews admitted the book to the Canon of Scripture, though it militated against their national prejudices in exhibiting God's mercy to another nation.

WHY DID JONAH DISOBEY? "The word of the Lord came to Jonah, Arise, go to Nineveh, that great city, and cry against it; for their wickedness is come up before Me. But Jonah rose up to flee unto Tarshish from the presence of the Lord" (Jonah i. 1, 2).

What was the reason of the prophet's deliberate disobedience? It was not cowardice, as we see from his attitude in the storm; nor was it the length of the journey, for a voyage to Tarshish on the coast of Spain was a far more hazardous undertaking than even the long overland journey to Nineveh; for the caravans of camels bearing merchandise plied regularly in those days to the great Assyrian capital. His reluctance was, no doubt, partly to be found in the prevalent idea of his country, that all other nations were outside the pale of God's mercy. But beyond this, Assyria was the dreaded foe of Israel, the scourge with which Jonah perhaps knew that God was going to punish his country (see Hosea ix. 3). For generations Assyria had been making fierce raids on the lands bordering on the Mediterranean, and the punishments which she inflicted upon her captives were cruel beyond the wonted cruelties of those times, even to flaying her victims alive. "Violence" was specified by the men of that city themselves, in the hour of their repentance, as their peculiar sin (iii. 8).

In the proclamation of God's judgment to Nineveh, Jonah saw the possibility of mercy for that city, and the sparing of his country's foe; for he had a true knowledge of God's character as a merciful and gracious God, of great kindness (chap. iv. 2). He also may have thought that the one hope for the moral restoration of his own country was the object-lesson of God's judgment on a large scale upon what was then the leading city of the world.

Jonah was God's prophet to Israel, his whole being was bound up in the salvation of his own people, and it was no doubt his intense patriotism which made him question the wisdom of God's command, and made him ready to incur His displeasure and abandon his prophetic office rather than risk the welfare of his country.

Jonah was a diligent student of the Psalms. He knew perfectly well that even if he "took the wings of the morning and dwelt in the uttermost parts of the sea," he could not really flee from God's presence; but, like many a servant of the Lord since, he thought that by a change of circumstances he might get away from the pressure of God's hand upon him or stifle His voice. And so he went down to Joppa. "And he found a ship going to Tarshish: so he paid the fare thereof, and went down into it, to go with them unto Tarshish from the presence of the Lord."

THE STORM. A graphic account of the voyage follows. "The book of Jonah is the most beautiful story ever written in so small a compass, only 1328 English words. In writing it is condensation that declares the master." The violent storm, the efforts of the mariners, the indignation of the shipmaster at finding Jonah carelessly asleep at such a juncture, when even these heathen sailors were crying "every man to his god,"—the whole scene lives before us. They cast lots to discover who was answerable for such an unusually severe storm. The lot, as in the case of Achan, directed by God, fell upon the guilty prophet, and then we can picture the mariners crowding round him and plying him with questions. "Tell us why this evil has come?" cries one. "What is your occupation?" cries another. "Where do you come from?" "What is your country?" "Who are you?" We are told the fear and astonishment of these simple sailors as they learn from his own lips that he serves the God who made the earth and this tempestuous sea, and yet that he is fleeing from His presence. They ask his advice, but shrink from carrying it out when he tells them to cast him into the sea. But all their efforts are useless and they yield at last, earnestly beseeching the Lord not to lay this innocent blood to their charge.

The Gentile Pilate was willing to have released Jesus when the Jews cried "Crucify Him." He washed his hands, saying, "I am innocent of the blood of this just Person."

As Jonah was cast forth into the sea it ceased its raging, and these heathen men were turned to the Lord, and not only offered sacrifices, but made vows for their future life. In Jonah's willingness to be cast into the deep, we have a picture of Him who said of His own life, "No man taketh it from Me, I lay it down of Myself."

"THE LORD PREPARED A GREAT FISH." There is a Hebrew word *manah*, to "appoint" or "arrange," rendered "prepare" in the authorised version, which Jonah uses several times. He who "sent forth a great wind into the sea," "prepared a gourd," "prepared a worm," "prepared a vehement east wind," and in like manner "prepared a great fish" to swallow Jonah.

Those who smile over the story of Jonah and the whale would do well to remember not only that our Lord Himself referred to it, but in what connection. He used it as a most solemn sign regarding the most solemn event of His life on earth. And He has expressly told us that in the great Judgment Day the men of Nineveh shall rise up and condemn the men of this generation, because they repented at the preaching of Jonah, and behold a Greater than Jonah is here. We cannot imagine our Lord using these solemn words of a fictitious people and of a fictitious repentance.

To us who believe in the greatest miracle of all—the incarnation and resurrection of Christ—it is but a little thing to believe that God saved Jonah in this way to be a type of our Saviour's resurrection. We have no alternative to believing Christ's word that He did do so, but, on the other hand, God had many alternatives at His disposal by which He could make such a thing possible. Let us consider a few of them.

The word translated "a great fish" in the Old Testament, and a "whale" in the New Testament, is in both cases "a great sea-monster," the term including whales, sharks, and other varieties. Many believe it to have been the *Carcharias*, or white shark, constantly found in the Mediterranean, often 30 feet long and more; and there are traces of a much larger race, now extinct. The voracity of the shark leads it to swallow whole all it can. Horses, sea calves the size of an ox, a reindeer without horns, have all been found at different times inside sharks. Men have also been found several times—in one instance it was a man in a coat of mail.

In 1758 a sailor fell overboard from a frigate in the Mediterranean, and was swallowed by a shark. The captain had a gun fired at it, and the creature cast the man out of his throat, and he was taken up alive and but little injured. The fish was harpooned, dried, and presented to the sailor, who went round Europe exhibiting it. It was 20 feet long.

The Spermaceti whale has a throat capacious enough to swallow substances much larger than a man, and it is its almost invariable habit to eject the contents of its stomach just before death. A case is related in the *Expository Times* for

August 1906, of a sailor being found inside a whale as it was being cut up. This took place off the Falkland Islands in 1891. But the man, though alive, was unconscious. The miracle consisted in Jonah being preserved alive some thirty-two to thirty-four hours, and, part of the time at least, in a state of consciousness.[1] But the Creator of all is surely as well able so to *prepare* a fish as to make this possible, as our modern engineers are to prepare a submarine for the same purpose.

The Rev. James Neil believes the "great fish" to have been the Arctic Right Whale (*Balæna mysticetus*). This whale has an enormous head and a mouth 12 feet square. To its upper jaw are attached hundreds of *baleen* or whalebone blades, some of them from 10 to 15 feet long, and 8 inches wide, highly elastic, with delicately fringed edges. These blades usually lie up against the palate of the mouth. The whale draws into its mouth an immense quantity of water, filled with small jelly-fish, on which it feeds. It then lets down the baleen bars in front of its wide open mouth and strains the water out through the fringes of hair, retaining the tiny food on which it subsists. The smallness of its throat prevents it from swallowing large fish, and would utterly prevent it swallowing Jonah. This species of whale occasionally wanders into southern seas, and in a warm climate, like that of the Mediterranean, where it has been seen in recent times, is apt to turn sick and lie about on the surface of the water, and all the time it remained on the surface there would be plenty of air in its mouth. In such a prison cell as this, with its "bars," of which Jonah speaks, and "the weeds wrapped about his head," as they would certainly be in the whale's mouth, it may well have been that Jonah was imprisoned. It may be objected to this that our Lord said that Jonah was in the whale's *belly*. But this is rather a confirmation than otherwise, for it must be remembered that He also said that the Son of Man must be "in the *heart* of the earth," whereas His place of burial was in a cave on the very surface of the earth's crust, corresponding exactly to the mouth of the whale. In both cases the figure of synecdoche is used, by which the part of a thing is put for the whole of it; and the same figure is used in the expression "three days and three nights," where, by synecdoche, the whole is put for the part.

---

[1] It is a Jewish saying that "A day and a night make an Onah, and part of an Onah is as the whole." Even in England a prisoner sentenced to three days' imprisonment is seldom more than forty hours in jail, and sometimes only thirty-three—part of a day reckoning by law as a day (Sir R. Anderson).

Jonah's prayer to God from his prison cell is the breathing of one to whom the Psalms had long been familiar. He quotes short fragments from various Psalms, and adapts them to meet his own case. There are allusions in his prayer to the great Messianic Psalms xxii., lxix., xvi. Most striking of all is the application of xvi. 10: "Thou wilt not leave my soul in *hell*; neither wilt Thou suffer Thine Holy One to see *corruption*." Jonah says: Out of the belly of *hell* cried I," and "Yet hast Thou brought up my life from *corruption*."

"And the Lord spake unto the fish, and it vomited out Jonah upon the dry land."

THE COMMISSION REPEATED. "And the word of the Lord came unto Jonah the second time, saying Arise, go unto Nineveh, that great city, and preach unto it the preaching that I bid thee." Twice the word comes unto the prophet from the Lord, "*Arise!*" Once from the shipmaster. Sinners are sleeping, like Jonah, with only a plank between them and eternity, and the call to them is, "Awake thou that sleepest, and arise from the dead, and Christ shall give thee light." But the call to awake came here to God's servant through the heathen shipmaster: He often chooses to send His message through a rough instrument. Let us be ready to hear it, however it comes.

Twice the Lord speaks direct to Jonah "Arise." He did not upbraid him for his disobedience; the sharp lesson he had learnt was enough; and in His goodness He is still willing to use His servant, prepared now to do His bidding. "A 'bent' Jonah was able to bend all heathen Nineveh, so that revival blessing held back impending judgment. Oh that God's people might be 'bent' in like manner now; that revival blessing might be poured out upon London and the whole world!"[1]

The tidings of Jonah's miraculous escape must have spread far and wide. The sailors would tell the news. All Israel would know it. In the constant interchange of thought between those ancient nations the news might well have reached Nineveh itself. Or it may have been left for Jonah to tell the Ninevites of it. Certain it is that they knew it somehow, for Jonah was not only a prophet to them; our Lord tells us that he was a sign, a sign which carried conviction with his preaching.

NINEVEH. "That great city." God Himself calls it great.[2]

[1] *Jonah, Patriot and Revivalist*, p. 19. Rev. W. F. S. Webster.
[2] *Jonah, the Truant Prophet*. Rev. F. B. Meyer.

Until 1841 all that was known of Nineveh was gathered from the Bible and a few scattered fragments of Assyrian history; and sixty or seventy years ago there were those who looked upon Nineveh as a myth. But since that date the excavations have continually been proving the truth of the Bible account. The city is great in its antiquity, founded by Nimrod. It was great in its size. Three chariots could drive abreast on the top of its walls. "A city of three days' journey," Jonah says; and the excavations prove its walls to have enclosed a circuit of sixty miles, just about three days' journey in its circumference. It evidently enclosed a good deal of pasture land besides the actual buildings, which agrees with Jonah's words, "much cattle." As it contained 120,000 little children, too young to know their right hand from their left, the total population would not have been far short of a million. Nineveh was great in its palaces, its fortifications and temples, and in its marvellous works of art—its great stone lions and bulls, with wings and human faces. It was great in its high civilisation, and it was great, above all, in its wickedness.

To this city Jonah was sent the second time, this time with "sealed orders." "Preach unto it the preaching that I bid thee." There was no hesitation this time. Jonah arose and went. The burden of his message was: "Yet forty days, and Nineveh shall be overthrown."

"THE MEN OF NINEVEH REPENTED." Jonah's own soul had been so stripped and prepared by God that his message came with the power of the Spirit. He himself was a sign. God's Spirit worked so mightily that at the end of one day's preaching the city was stirred to its depths. The record is: "So the people of Nineveh believed God." They acted immediately upon their belief, and proclaimed a fast, and put on sackcloth. This repentance evidently began among the people themselves, for chap. iii. 6 should be translated, "And the matter came unto the king," that is the whole account, and he too believed; and he rose up from his throne, and laid his robe from him, and covered himself with sackcloth, and sat in ashes. And the decree went forth from the king and his nobles that there should be a universal fast in Nineveh, extending even to the beasts of the field. Man and beast were clothed in sackcloth, and the cry of repentance—mingled, no doubt, with the lowing of the distressed beasts—went up from the great city into the ears of a compassionate and long-suffering God. God saw that the repentance was sincere; that it did not end with the putting on of sackcloth, but that the people turned from their evil ways. And He heard their cry and spared the city.

The question arises, Is it likely that the state would interfere in such a matter, and that a royal edict would be issued enjoining a long fast? Professor Sayce gives the answer from the monuments of Nineveh, and tells us that in the days of Ezarhaddon II., when the northern foe was gathering against the Assyrian empire, the king issued a proclamation enjoining a solemn service of humiliation for one hundred days.

Again, Is it likely that the beasts should be clothed with sackcloth? Herodotus tells us that when the Persian armies were in Greece, on the occasion of the death of one of their generals, a mourning spread through the camp. They cut off the hair from themselves and their horses and their beasts of burden. Such a custom then was common to a closely neighbouring nation.

God's dealings with Nineveh, and His dealings with His repining prophet in the last chapter, alike show us His merciful loving-kindness. Jonah was angry that the great city, the enemy of his country, should be spared. He was angry at the destruction of the gourd which had sheltered him. Concerning both the Lord asks him with the utmost tenderness, "Doest thou well to be angry?" And Jonah, still not sparing his own character in any detail, hands on the lesson to his countrymen, and hands down the lesson to us, that God's salvation is intended for the whole world.

The book of Jonah is essentially a missionary book, a foreshadowing of our Lord's great commission to go and preach the Gospel to every creature.

When Christ came back from the grave, the message of His Gospel was borne to the Gentiles, and has proved the power of God unto salvation to every one that believeth, the world over.

## 13. MICAH

Micah's home was the village of Moreshah, in the maritime plain of Judah, near the borders of the Philistines.

He was a contemporary of Hosea and Isaiah, and prophesied in the days of Jotham, Ahaz, and the earlier years of Hezekiah, kings of Judah. He prophesied concerning both Samaria and Jerusalem, but the burden of his prophecy was for Judah.

Micah bore the same name, abbreviated, as Micaiah, the son

of Imlah, the prophet of Israel, who stood alone for God against the 400 false prophets, 150 years before this, in the days of Ahab, when he and Jehoshaphat went against Ramoth-Gilead (1 Kings xxii.).  Micaiah had concluded his prophecy with the words, "Hearken, O people, every one of you."  Micah begins his prophecy with the same words.  The three divisions of his book each begins with this call to *Hear* : i. 2, iii. 1, vi. 1. Micaiah had seen "all Israel scattered upon the hills, as sheep that have not a shepherd."  Micah's prophecy abounds in allusions to the Good Shepherd and His pitiful care over His flock.

With much brokenness of heart Micah denounces God's judgments upon Judah for their sins, but he seems to hasten over the words of judgment, and to linger over the message of God's love and mercy, concluding his prophecy with a specially beautiful proclamation of it, with which he identifies his own name, *Micah*, which means "*Who is like God ?*"  "Who is like the Lord, the Pardoner of sin, the Redeemer from its guilt, the Subduer of its power ?  For no false God was ever such a claim made.  This was the one message that he loved above all to proclaim ; and his own name was the herald to the people in his day " (Dr. Pusey).

SAMARIA AND THE CITIES OF JUDAH.  Micah proclaims the coming judgment first upon Samaria, and then upon the cities of Judah.  These were all speedily fulfilled by the armies of Assyria.

The idolatry of Israel had spread to Jerusalem, and the strong city of Lachish seems to have been the connecting link, "the beginning of the sin of the daughter of Zion" (i. 13).  It is this spread of idolatry, and all its attendant evils, to Judah, under king Ahaz, which Micah specially deplores.  He rebukes the extreme oppression of the poor, women and little children being driven from their homes; covetousness and self-aggrandisement, even at the price of blood, which he graphically likens to cannibalism.  He specially denounces the sins of the rulers, bribery among the judges, false weights and balances.

Micah further proclaims the captivity in Babylon (iv. 7), and the destruction of Jerusalem (iii. 12), even to the ploughing up of the city, which was fulfilled by the Emperor Hadrian. We are distinctly told in the book of Jeremiah that this prophecy led to the great turning to the Lord of King Hezekiah and his people, at the beginning of his reign, which averted the destruction of the city, it may be for 136 years, and led also to the great reformation under that king. The elders of Judah reverted to this prophecy of Micah about 120 years after it was uttered, when the priests would have put Jeremiah to death for predicting the same doom.

"BETHLEHEM OF JUDAH." But for us the great interest of the prophet Micah centres round its clear prophecies of the Saviour who was to come. It was from this book that "all the chief priests and scribes of the people," gathered together by Herod, proclaimed unhesitatingly that it was at Bethlehem of Judah that the Christ, the King, should be born. This prophecy proclaims His eternity. He who was to go forth from Bethlehem as the Ruler, was He whose goings forth were "from the days of eternity." Micah v. 3 is closely connected with Isaiah vii. 14.

"He shall stand and feed (or rule) in the strength of the Lord, in the majesty of the name of the Lord His God." Here we have the majesty of the Royal Shepherd caring for His flock.

Micah's picture of the restoration of Zion and many nations flowing to it, and the glory and prosperity of Christ's Kingdom, with its reign of universal peace, was introduced by Isaiah into his prophecy.

## 14. NAHUM

The destruction of Nineveh is the one burden of Nahum. The prophet's name means *Comfort*, and his word of comfort is for Judah, "The Lord is good, a stronghold in the day of trouble, and He knoweth them that trust in Him" (i. 7). "Behold upon the mountains the feet of him that bringeth good tidings and publisheth peace," points forward to the proclamation of the good tidings of the Prince of Peace.

NINEVEH. The rest of the prophecy is wholly concerned with Nineveh. The dwelling-place of the prophet is uncertain. It may have been Capernaum, "the city of Nahum." The time in which he prophesied, from internal evidence, seems to have been between the fall of No-Amon (Thebes) in Upper Egypt, 663 B.C., and the fall of Nineveh, 606 B.C., for he speaks of the one as past (iii. 8-10) and the other as future (i. 8, 14).

"The prophecy of Nahum is both the complement and the counterpart of the book of Jonah" (Dr. Pusey). God revealed

His Name to Moses as showing His two-fold character. "The Lord, the Lord God, merciful and gracious, long-suffering and forgiving iniquity, and that will by no means clear the guilty." Jonah dwells on the first side of God's character (iv. 2), Nahum brings out the second. "A jealous God and Avenger is the Lord. . . . The Lord is slow to anger and great in power, and will not at all acquit the wicked." God had shown His long-suffering to the great city. It had repented at the preaching of Jonah. But though multitudes of individuals were, no doubt, truly turned to the Lord, its repentance as a nation was short-lived, and we find it guilty again of the very sins from which it had repented, violence and insatiable cruelty (ii. 11, 12). But beyond all this, Nineveh seems to have been guilty of an open defiance of the living God, as shown in the blasphemous attitude of Sennacherib, and in the allusions of Nahum i. 9, 11.

The doom of the city was delayed two hundred years, but it fell at last, and Nahum's prophecy was one of unconditional and final destruction. With an over-running flood would God make a full end of her; her name should be utterly cut off, and He would dig her grave. The mustering of the armies round Nineveh, the marshalling of the forces within the city, are described with graphic eloquence.

The destruction of Nineveh was complete. It occurred almost at the zenith of her power. According to Nahum's prophecy, it came true that the Tigris assisted the attacking army of the Medes and Babylonians in its overthrow (ii. 6), and it was partly destroyed by fire (iii. 13, 15). So deep and so effectually did God dig its grave that every trace of its existence disappeared for ages, and its site was not known. But its excavations since 1841 have been confirming the truth of God's Word.

THE CITY OF THEBES. Among other revelations, we have the actual fall of the city of Thebes, No-Amon, alluded to by Nahum, described on the monuments in the words of Assur-banipal, the Assyrian king, who was its conqueror. He tells us how completely he took the city, carrying off its gold and silver and precious stones, and two lofty obelisks, covered with beautiful sculptures, weighing 2500 talents (over 90 tons), which he raised from their place and transported to Assyria, with a great and countless booty.

## 15. HABAKKUK

Habakkuk is the prophet of faith.    His name means "*Embrace,*" or "*one who strongly enfolds.*"    Through all the mystery of sin and its apparent success, through the mystery of suffering and of God's judgments, he lays hold of God's promises, and clings to Him with faith triumphant.

He tells us nothing about himself except that he was a prophet, and we may infer from chapter iii., which is evidently a Psalm for the Temple, that he had to do with arranging its services, and was probably a Levite, as he speaks of "*my* stringed instruments."

Habakkuk opens his prophecy with the cry, "O Lord, how long shall I cry and Thou wilt not hear?" as he looks round upon the iniquity which prevailed in Judah.

The Lord's answer is that He is about to bring a punishment upon this sinful nation in the form of the terrible Chaldean invasion.

The Chaldeans were noted for their cavalry (i. 8); they were noted also for scoffing at their captive kings (i. 10). Jeremiah's prophecy was fulfilled that Jehoiakim should be "buried with the burial of an ass," that is, "cast forth beyond the gates of Jerusalem," as food for the vultures (Jer. xxii. 19).

Having seen in vision the destruction of his people, Habakkuk again brings his questionings in confidence to God (i. 12): "Art Thou not from everlasting, O Lord, my God, mine Holy One? we shall not die."

"THE JUST SHALL LIVE BY FAITH."    Habakkuk's next question is, How is it that He who is of purer eyes than to behold iniquity will execute His vengeance upon Judah by a people even worse than themselves?    He then resolves to wait for God's answer to his complaint.

As he waits upon God on his watch-tower God speaks again, and tells him to make plain, so that he that runs may read it, this glorious message for all time, "*The just shall live by faith.*" "This motto became the centre of Paul's teaching (Rom. i. 17; Gal. iii. 11; Heb. x. 38).    In Romans JUST is the emphatic word; in Galatians FAITH; in Hebrews LIVE" (Dr. Pierson). Habakkuk speaks of an immediate vision, but he looks on to the end.    "At the end it shall speak . . . though it tarry wait for it; because it will surely come, it will not tarry."    In Hebrews the quotation, "The just shall live by faith," is preceded by the words, "For yet a little while, and He that shall come will come, and will not tarry." "Surely I come quickly" are our Saviour's last words in the Bible.

Then God shows Habakkuk that the Chaldeans will be destroyed themselves for their iniquity. God had used Babylon as His hammer to punish the nations, and He was about to break the hammer itself in pieces (Jer. l. 23). And He points forward to the Day of Christ when the earth shall be full of the knowledge of the glory of the Lord, as the waters cover the sea (ii. 14).

HABAKKUK'S PRAYER. Then follows the prayer of Habakkuk. His description of the majesty of God is as fine as any in the whole Bible. He describes the wonderful history of God's dealings with His people in bringing them into Canaan. Here again there are foreshadowings of a greater salvation yet to come, as we catch glimpses of the working of Him who is the brightness of His Father's glory.

Three times in this prayer he uses the exclamation *Selah*, found elsewhere only in the Psalms. It is a call to pause and be silent that the soul may "listen to the divine illuming," as in the last verse of chapter ii., "The Lord is in His holy temple, let all the earth keep silence before Him," and the words of ii. 1, "I will watch to see what He will say unto me." How much we need this silence of soul before the Lord in these days, that we may give Him time to speak to us, that we may "listen to the divine illuming." As we saw in studying the book of Job, the rays of light are vocal, but it needs a finely-tuned ear indeed to hear them.

Though the prophet trembles at the revelations of the Lord, yet he stays himself upon Him in quiet confidence, knowing that he can rest in the day of trouble. He sums up in the finest poetical language the failure of everything of earth, and when all nature and every seeming hope is dead, he adds, "Yet will I rejoice, as with exulting joy, in the God of my salvation." It is almost the name of Jesus, for Jesus is 'Jehovah—Salvation," or "Jehovah is Salvation," whence the words are here rendered, even by a Jew, "in God the Author of my redemption," and by Augustine, "In God my Jesus.'

### 16. ZEPHANIAH

This short book has been called "The Compendium of all prophecy." It is a survey of the universal government of Jehovah, His judgment of the whole earth.

Zephaniah ("*the watchman of Jehovah*") gives his own genealogy to the fourth generation, showing his descent from Hizkiah, who is probably identical with King Hezekiah. He prophesied during the early part of the reign of Josiah, before idolatry had been put away by the reforms of that king.

Zephaniah's prophecy is marked by the emphasis he lays upon the Day of the Lord. The final application is to the Day of Christ. The impressive language can only find its fulfilment in the great Day of His wrath, described in Revelation vi. "A day of wrath, a day of trouble and distress, a day of wasting and desolation, a day of darkness and gloominess, a day of clouds and thick darkness, a day of trumpet and alarm" (Zeph. i. 14-16).

But meanwhile, a day of judgment was near for Judah on account of her sins. He urges her to seek the Lord while there is still time. He then proclaims God's judgment upon various nations which have oppressed God's people — upon Philistia, Moab, Ammon, Ethiopia, Assyria, prophesying the fall and utter desolation of Nineveh.

The third chapter shows God's coming judgment upon Judah and Jerusalem, and the future restoration and joy of God's people in the day of the Messiah.

THE LORD IN THE MIDST. The third chapter contains a beautiful lesson, taken spiritually. It describes the sinful condition of a soul apart from Christ—ver. 1, sins of commission; ver. 2, sins of omission. Those who should have been leaders in righteousness are leaders in iniquity — princes, judges, prophets, priests. Then the Lord Himself takes the place of these leaders, and we see Him "in the midst," fulfilling each office in turn. First He comes to our hearts as Judge, and convicts us of all that is sinful there, bringing His judgment to light (5-7). Second, He comes as Prophet, teaching us with pure lips to call upon His name—still "in the midst," dealing with the pride of heart, and bringing us low into the place of blessing, in the presence of His holiness (8-13). Third, He comes "into our midst" as King, to reign in undisputed sway in the heart that is surrendered to Him. When the Lord reigns thus the song begins (14-16). Fourth, He is "in the midst" as our Great High Priest, bringing us into the place of communion with Himself. Here we know Him as the Beloved of our souls. "He will rejoice over thee with joy, He will rest in His love, He will joy over thee with singing."

The chapter closes with six beautiful "I wills" of what the Lord will do for us.

## 17. HAGGAI

Haggai, Zechariah, and Malachi are the three prophets to the restored remnant that returned from Babylon. They all make frequent use of the title "The Lord of Hosts."

Haggai and Zechariah were probably among the first exiles who returned with Zerubbabel. From his words in ii. 3 it is thought that possibly Haggai himself had seen the glory of Solomon's Temple, in which case he would be an old man at this time, while Zechariah was quite young (Zech. ii. 4).

The burden of Haggai's message was, "*I am with you, saith the Lord of Hosts*" (i. 13).

To the prophet Haggai is given the privilege—along with Zechariah—of stirring the people by his few concise words to the work of rebuilding the Temple. His message may be summed up in the words, "Seek ye first the Kingdom of God and His righteousness, and all these things shall be added unto you." He uttered four short prophecies during the last four months of the second year of Darius.

In the first he endeavoured to shame the people out of their apathy in beautifying their own houses while the house of the Lord lay waste; and he tells them that all the drought on crops and cattle had its source in this neglect. This prophecy produced the desired effect, and Zerubbabel, the governor of Jerusalem, and Joshua the High Priest, and the residue of the people rose up and began the work of rebuilding the Temple, which had been interrupted by their surrounding enemies, chiefly the Samaritans.

A month later discouragement seems to have beset the workers at the contrast between the glory of the former house and the poverty of this latter. Haggai exhorted them to be strong and build, for the Lord was with them, His Spirit would remain among them, and, moreover, a time was coming when the Lord of Hosts would shake the heavens and the earth, and the Desire of all nations should come, and His glory should fill the Temple, so that the glory of this latter house should be greater than that of the former, and in this place would the Lord of Hosts give peace.[1]

[1] Herod's Temple, to which our Lord came, was not a new Temple, but a renovation of this second Temple, with splendid additions and improvements. In Haggai's words, "The silver is Mine and the gold is Mine, saith the Lord of Hosts," we probably have a prophecy of its magnificence when adorned at the

A SIGNET. The fourth prophecy was addressed to Zerubbabel, and through him to Christ. Zerubbabel was a prince of the house of David, he had led back the people from captivity, he had built the Temple. In all this he was a type of Christ, who is the Servant of the Lord, chosen of Him, set as signet or seal upon the hand of the Father, the "express image of His person." This word in Hebrews i. 3 means the impression made as by a seal upon wax.

Haggai's message is full of stirring words to us to-day. If, as a Church, we thought more of the Lord's work of saving souls than of our own comfort, there would be no lack of means to carry it forward.

"Consider your ways," said Haggai; if we so adjust our ways as to make them fall into line with God's will for us, we have the certainty of His promise, "I am with you, saith the Lord of Hosts." And if His Spirit remaineth among us, we need fear neither opposition from without, nor discouragement from within.

## 18. ZECHARIAH

We have already seen the connection of this prophet with Haggai. He was probably a priest as well as a prophet. (See Neh. xii. 16.)

His first prophecy occurred just after the time of discouragement, when the people had begun to rebuild the Temple, and he warns them not to disappoint God, as their fathers had done. He has a special word of encouragement to the ruler Zerubbabel, who must have been conscious of his own weakness, and that it was indeed a "day of small things." "Not by might, nor by power, but by My Spirit, saith the Lord of Hosts" (iv. 6-10). He promised that the mountains of difficulty should be removed, and that he who had laid the foundation should have the joy of bringing forth the headstone with rejoicing, crying, "Grace, grace," unto it.

Christ is both the Foundation-stone and the Headstone of the corner.

EIGHT VISIONS. Zechariah's second prophecy consists of eight visions concerning God's final dealings with Israel. First, of Myrtle Trees, a picture of Israel to-day, outcast but never

cost of many millions by Herod, so as to make it a glorious house, just before He whose house it was came to it, as it were in preparation for His august presence. Yet the true glory was the presence of the "Great King" in His deep disguise as a peasant of Galilee (Rev. James Neil).

forgotten by Jehovah. Second, of Horns and Smiths, fore-telling the overthrow of Israel's enemies. Third, of the Measuring Line. This shows the future prosperity of Jeru-salem. The presence of Jehovah as a wall of fire round about His people will make walls *unnecessary*, the extent of the city will make them *impossible*. Fourth, of Joshua, a picture of Israel cleansed and restored to the priestly position of access to God. Fifth, of the Candlestick, or, as it should be, lamp-stand, Israel as God's light-bearer. The two olive-trees in this vision refer in the first place to Zerubbabel the ruler and Joshua the priest, and thus through them to both offices ful-filled in the person of the Messiah. Sixth, the Flying Roll, government of the earth. Seventh, the Ephah, restriction of wickedness. Eighth, the Chariots, the administrative forces of righteousness (Dr. Campbell Morgan, *Westminster Record* for September 1907).

Then follows the symbolic act of crowning the High Priest (vi. 9-11). By this act the two great offices of priest and king are united in his person, type of the person and work of the Man whose name is the Branch (ver. 12, iii. 8), who shall sit on His throne of glory as a Priest, the Builder of the eternal Temple of the Lord, and " bear the glory."

" THY KING COMETH UNTO THEE." More than any other of the Minor Prophets, Zechariah foretells the Saviour. Twice He is announced as the Branch; God speaks of Him as My Servant (iii. 8). We have the prediction of His entry into Jerusalem, riding upon an ass's colt (ix. 9). In contrast to the false shepherds we see Him as the *Good* Shepherd, saving His flock, caring for the poor of the flock (ix. 16, xi. 11). We see Him as the *Smitten* Shepherd, with the sheep scattered (xiii. 7). In the words " Awake, O sword, against My Shepherd, and against the Man that is My fellow, saith the Lord of Hosts," we have a specially clear revelation of Christ, both in His Divine and human nature; the Man, the smitten Shepherd, is spoken of by God as His fellow, on an equality with Him and yet distinct in His personality.

Zechariah speaks of " the blood of the Covenant " (ix. 11), which our Lord applied to His own blood. " This is My blood of the New Covenant, which is shed for many unto remission of sins " (Matt. xxvi. 28, R.V.). We have the prophecy of His betrayal by Judas for thirty pieces of silver, even to the fact that the money was " cast to the potter in the house of the Lord " (xi. 12, 13).

Zechariah prophesies the conversion of his people to the Lord in the day that the Spirit is poured out upon them, and when they shall look on Him whom they have pierced, and the sin of the nation shall be washed away through that fountain opened through their Messiah's death on Calvary (xii. 10, xiii. 1). He speaks of the wounds with which He was wounded in the house of His friends (xiii. 6). The third part of the remnant shall be brought through the fire and purified in the time of Jacob's trouble (xiii. 9).

The last chapter foretells the Great Day of the Lord, which is always associated with the coming of Christ to judgment. He who ascended from the slopes of Olivet shall so come in like manner as those who watched Him saw Him go. "And His feet shall stand upon the mount of Olives . . . and the Lord my God shall come, and all the saints with thee. . . . It shall be one day which shall be known to the Lord . . . at evening time it shall be light. . . . And the Lord shall be King over all the earth: in that day shall there be One Lord. and His name One."

## 19. MALACHI

Malachi—"*the Messenger of the Lord*"—wished to be known by this name only. Like the Forerunner, of whom he prophesies, he was but a voice. Speaking of Levi, as an example of the true priesthood, he says "He is the *messenger* of the Lord of Hosts" (ii. 7). He speaks of John the Baptist as God's "*messenger*," and of our Lord Himself as "the *Messenger* of the Covenant" (iii. 1).

And what is the "burden" of the Lord's message by Malachi? "*I have loved you, saith the Lord.*" What a message to a people who were disappointing God's love !

Malachi bears the same relation to Nehemiah that Haggai and Zechariah bear to Zerubbabel. He lived either at the time of Nehemiah or directly after, for he rebukes the very same sins among the people that Nehemiah dealt with on his second visit to Jerusalem :—(1) The corruption of the priesthood (Neh. xiii. 29 ; Mal. ii. 8). (2) The alliance with idolatrous wives (Neh. xiii. 23-27 ; Mal. ii. 10-16). (3) The neglect of the tithe (Neh. xiii. 10-12 ; Mal. iii. 10). Eliashib the priest was allied unto Tobiah the Ammonite, and had allowed him the use of a great chamber in the courts of the House of God. Eliashib's grandson also had married a daughter of Sanballat, the Horonite (Neh. xiii. 1-9).

"WHEREIN?" Malachi's message is to the priests who ought to have been the leaders in righteousness, and also to the people who followed their lead in neglecting and dishonouring God. His book is marked by its straightforward, plain words of rebuke, by which he brings home their sins to a self-satisfied people, who had a form of godliness, but were denying the power thereof.[1] Every rebuke of the prophet was disputed by the people with the question " *Wherein?*" or " *What?*"[2]

(1) i. 2 : " *Wherein* hast Thou loved us ? "
(2) i. 6 : " *Wherein* have we despised Thy name ? "
(3) i. 7 : " *Wherein* have we polluted Thee ? "
(4) ii. 17 : " *Wherein* have we wearied Him ? "
(5) iii. 7 : " *Wherein* shall we return ? "
(6) iii. 8 : " *Wherein* have we robbed Thee ? "
(7) iii. 13 : " *What* have we spoken so much against Thee ? "
(8) iii. 14 : " *What* profit is it that we have kept His ordinance ? "
(9) ii. 14 : " *For what?*" or " *Wherefore?*" (referring to what Malachi had said in ver. 13).

Malachi describes the coming of Christ to His Temple. He came as a little babe to the expectant gaze of Simeon and Anna. He came to overturn the tables of the money-changers. He comes to the temple of our hearts. His coming is as purifying fire. With the patience of the Refiner of silver He *sits* till He sees His own image reflected in the molten metal. And when He takes up His abode in our hearts He is a "swift Witness there against sin." Our Lord calls Himself "the faithful and true Witness."

"THE WHOLE TITHE." This book contains the secret of spiritual blessing. "Bring ye the whole tithe into My store-house." The tithe was the outward recognition that everything belonged to God. We are to bring Him our whole selves, body, soul and spirit, all that we have and all that we are, all that we know about in our lives and all that we do not know about yet. If we thus honestly keep nothing back from Him we may be certain that He will accept us and will open the windows of heaven, and pour us out such a blessing that there shall not be room enough to receive it, but it shall flow out to all around. "All nations shall call you blessed, for ye shall be a delightsome land, saith the Lord of Hosts."

[1] *Studies in Malachi*. Rev. G. Campbell Morgan.
[2] In questions 1 to 6 it is the Hebrew word *bemah*, "in what," or "wherein." In questions 7 and 8 it is the Hebrew word *mah*, "what." In question 9 it is the Hebrew word *atmah*, "for what," or "wherefore."

Amidst all the hypocrisy and formalism there was a little remnant who feared the Lord. His ear was bent down to hear them as they spoke together of Him. He promised that they should be His own special treasure in the coming Day of the Lord. That Day should be as an oven and consume the wicked as stubble, but it should arise upon this faithful remnant as "The Sun of Righteousness with healing in His wings."

The Old Testament closes with the word "*curse*." But it is expressive of the great desire of God's love to avert it, for He says "*Lest* I come and smite the earth with a curse."

The New Testament closes with *blessing*. "The grace of our Lord Jesus Christ be with you all. Amen."

A silence of 400 years lay between the voice of Malachi and the voice of one crying in the wilderness, "Prepare ye the way of the Lord." "But there is a remarkable link between the two Testaments: the last figures on the inspired page of Malachi, and the first on the inspired page of Matthew, are the Angel of the Covenant and His Forerunner" (Dr. Pierson).

# VI. CHRIST IN HIS LIFE ON EARTH

## The Gospels

THE Sun of Righteousness has arisen with healing on His wings. In our previous studies we have been watching the unfolding of the dawn of that day which Abraham rejoiced to see, of the Star prophesied by Balaam, of the great Light foretold by Isaiah. We have, as it were, been watching one cloud after another lit up by the coming glory, and now the King of Glory Himself has come. "We have seen His star in the east, and are come to worship Him." We have "seen the Lord's Christ." "Mine eyes have seen Thy salvation which Thou hast prepared before the face of all people, a Light to lighten the Gentiles and the glory of Thy people Israel."

Wherever the Light of Christ has shone it has brought a higher ideal of human life to the individual, a higher moral law than was known before. The Gospel of Christ is the only religion which has a ray of hope for the lost, the sinful, the oppressed and the weak, or a message for the woman and the little child.

The Christ who, for nineteen centuries, has won the victory over sin and darkness and moral degradation is the Christ of the New Testament. Except the bare fact of His existence, all we know of Him is from the Bible. It is vain for men to say to-day, we believe in Christ, but reject the Bible. It is the preaching of Christ as He is revealed in the Bible—"God incarnate, perfect Man, Saviour by the way of the Cross, and Lord by the resurrection"—that has produced this transformation in the hearts and lives of men (Campbell Morgan).

In the Gospel of Christ according to Matthew, Mark, Luke and John, we see God's purpose in giving us a fourfold picture of Him, which brings out the majesty of His person and work.

A statue has this advantage over a picture, that it enables us to see the one represented from all sides. So this fourfold presentation of Christ exhibits from each point of view some fresh beauty in Him.

The four evangelists have been compared with the four cherubim of Ezekiel and Revelation. Matthew shows us our Lord in His kingly aspect as the *Lion* of the Tribe of Judah; Mark exhibits Him as the faithful Servant of Jehovah, the *ox*, ready alike for service or for sacrifice; Luke presents Him as the Son of Man, full of human sympathy, as the emblem of the *man* suggests; whereas, with John, we see Him as the Son of God, the *eagle*, soaring into the heavenly blue with a majesty that transcends all our thought and imagination.

Dr. Monro Gibson has pointed out the beautiful unity of plan between the Old and New Testaments, as shown in the following table :—

| | | | |
|---|---|---|---|
| O.T. | LAW | Law | *Giving of the Law.* |
| | | Historical Books | *Application.* |
| | PROPHETS | Poetical Books | *Experience.* |
| | | Prophetical Books | *Outlook beyond.* |
| N.T. | CHRIST | Gospels | *Giving of the New Covenant.* |
| | | Acts | *Application.* |
| | APOSTLES | Epistles | *Experience.* |
| | | Revelation | *Outlook beyond.* |

## MATTHEW

### CHRIST THE KING

In this Gospel we see the royal majesty of our heavenly King. The Gospel by Matthew was written for the Jews. It sets forth the Law, and refers constantly to the Old Testament Scriptures, showing how both have been fulfilled by Christ.

This Gospel opens thus: "The book of the generations of Jesus Christ, the Son of David, the Son of Abraham" (i. 1). This shows His covenant position as Son of Abraham, and His royal position as Son of David. "David the King," in ver. 6, emphasises our Lord's position as David's royal Heir.

His wondrous divinity is announced in His birth through the power of the Holy Ghost, in His personality as Saviour (Jesus), and in His absolute Godhead as revealed in the name Emmanuel—*God with us.*

Matthew alone recounts the visit of the Magi. The whole world at this time was expecting the advent of some Great One. "Where is He that is born King of the Jews?" Their adoration foreshadowed His universal dominion. Matthew alone tells us how Herod, the usurper of David's sovereignty, sought to slay the heir.

In this Gospel John the Baptist introduces the Lord Jesus as the mighty Judge, Who shall purge His floor with tremendous judgment. Matthew's account of the temptation, instead of following the chronological order of Luke, gives the account of the temptation on the mountain last, as if to emphasise it. Our Lord is the world's King. Satan has usurped the dominion; he offers to surrender it on one condition. It means escape from Calvary for the Saviour, and escape from centuries of suffering for His Church. But we see the victory of the King.

"From that time Jesus began to preach, and to say, Repent, for the Kingdom of Heaven is at hand." The word Kingdom occurs fifty-five times in Matthew; thirty-five times it is "the Kingdom of Heaven," an expression found nowhere else in the Gospels. John uses the word Kingdom only five times.

The Sermon on the Mount (chaps. v.-vii.) gives us the Laws of the Kingdom. We have the seven parables of the Kingdom in chapter xiii., each beginning with "The Kingdom of Heaven is like," except that of the Sower, where we have the word Kingdom in verse 11. Almost all our Lord's parables in Matthew begin thus, whereas in Luke it is nearly always "A certain man." Compare also the two accounts of the Marriage Supper. It is Matthew who tells us that the host was a King. The parables of the Day of Judgment set forth especially the royal dignity and power of Christ.

In common with Mark and Luke, Matthew tells us of the unveiled glory of the King in the transfiguration. He adds this touch, "His face did shine as the sun," and these words, "in whom I am well pleased," showing how perfectly our Lord fulfilled God's Law. In his account of the Resurrection he tells of the great earthquake, the angel whose face was like lightning, for fear of whom the keepers did shake and become as dead men.

Finally, this Gospel gives us, as no other, our Lord's last royal Commission. "All authority hath been given unto Me in heaven and on earth, go ye therefore and make disciples of all the nations."

## MARK

### CHRIST THE SERVANT

Mark gives us the picture of Christ as the willing Servant, yielding active, prompt obedience at every moment of His life.

This Gospel is believed to have been written in Italy for the

Romans, and that Mark received his information from Peter. Peter's words to Cornelius form a perfect summary of this book: "God anointed Jesus of Nazareth with the Holy Ghost, and with power; who went about doing good, and healing all that were oppressed of the devil: for God was with Him" (Acts x. 38). Instead of opening with any record of our Lord's birth or early years, Mark begins at once with His ministry. His introduction again supplies the key to the book: "The beginning of the Gospel of Jesus Christ, the Son of God." The *beginning*, but not the *end*,—through all eternity, it may be, we shall never come to the end of the Gospel of Jesus Christ, the Son of God.

One half of this Gospel is occupied with narrative, and only half with our Lord's utterances; while in Matthew the latter occupy three-fourths, in Luke two-thirds, and in John five-sixths.

The words *immediately, forthwith, anon, straightway* meet us constantly.[1] The lesson for us is a like prompt obedience. Matthew and Luke tell us that our Lord was "led" of the Spirit into the wilderness; but Mark's words are, "The Spirit *driveth* Him into the wilderness." From him too we learn that the temptation lasted the whole of the forty days, and that the Lord was "with the wild beasts." The four parables of chapter iv. tell us the working of the Gospel. The parable of the Lord's return is given only by Mark, and here the Gospel of service is plainly emphasised.

Everywhere Mark gives us the idea of stress of service. Multitudes crowd to hear Christ. The whole city was gathered to the door; so many came and went at times that He could not even eat, or could not enter into the city; men from all the cities ran together on foot to see Him; wherever He went they placed the sick before Him, and as many as touched Him were made whole. Though prompt action ever characterised His ministry He was never hurried in His dealing with those in need. Mark alone tells in two cases of healing, that our Lord took the deaf man and the blind man apart with Himself when He healed them. He alone tells us that He took the little children up in His arms when He blessed them.

These little graphic details are a feature of this Gospel, adding some fresh touch to almost every narrative. Peter's quick eye had evidently noted them.

[1] These are all one in the Greek, and it is deeply to be regretted that our translators and revisers have not rendered the original uniformly in this and countless other places.

In each Gospel we have the record of the great Sacrifice by which sin is put away. But when our Lord rises from the grave and gives His final commission to His disciples, there is a marked contrast here to the record in Matthew; it rings with the urgency of service: not a corner of the world is to be left unvisited, not a soul to be left out.

The book opened with the words "the beginning of the Gospel of Jesus Christ, the Son of God." Here we have *the continuation*. The Lord is still carrying on His work, and we are co-operating with Him. "So then, after the Lord had spoken unto them, He was received up into heaven, and sat on the right hand of God. And they went forth, and preached everywhere, *the Lord working with them*, and confirming the word with signs following."

## LUKE

### CHRIST THE SON OF MAN, THE SAVIOUR

This is the Gospel for the sinner. It brings out the compassionate love of Christ in becoming Man to save us. It was probably written for the Greeks. It traces our Lord's descent back to Adam, and shows Him as the Son of Man and the Son of God, the Saviour for the whole human race. The "Son of the Highest," and the Son of the lowly virgin.

Instead of the visit of the Magi, Luke tells us of the humble shepherds to whom was announced the tidings of peace to all people, "to *you* is born a Saviour," and there, among the cattle, the Saviour's first guests would feel themselves at home.

"Mine eyes have seen Thy Salvation," said the aged Simeon, as he took the Holy Child in his arms. And Anna "spake of Him to all that looked for Redemption in Israel."

Here, in His baptism, we see Him taking His place among the multitudes; Luke omits the words with which Matthew proclaimed Him as the coming Judge. Again, instead of the words, "Repent, for the Kingdom of Heaven is at hand," we find Him beginning His ministry by taking His place in the synagogue at Nazareth, and applying to Himself the gracious words of Isaiah which proclaimed His ministry of mercy to the broken-hearted.

Luke records his compassion to the Widow of Nain, and the depths of His mercy to the woman that was a sinner; the story of Zaccheus with the murmuring of the Pharisees because He had gone to be a guest with a man which was a sinner. The parables of this Gospel bring out in the same way His compassion and His saving power. They generally begin "a certain man." Such are the Good Samaritan, the Pharisee and the Publican, the Importunate Widow, and, above all, the three parables of the central chapter, the fifteenth, the Lost Sheep, the Lost Coin, and the Lost Son, in which His joy over the lost found is so marvellously represented. In the parable of the Great Supper it is Luke who records the Lord's command to go out into the highways and hedges and compel them to come in. And the words "Yet there is room" has been the Gospel motto through all the ages.

Luke alone tells us that when our Lord beheld the city He wept over it; of the bloody sweat in Gethsemane; of the Lord showing mercy to the dying thief even in His agony, and gathering from the very Cross the first-fruits of His sufferings. Luke alone tells of the walk to Emmaus, he himself, very possibly, being one of the two disciples. He tells of our Lord deigning to eat the piece of broiled fish and of the honey-comb, in order to show us His perfect humanity even after His resurrection; of His leading them out as far as to Bethany, and that, *as He lifted up His hands and blessed them*, He was parted from them.

## JOHN

### CHRIST, THE SON OF GOD, THE DIVINE FRIEND

John wrote to reveal the Son of God as our Divine Friend. The first chapter shows Him to us as "the only-begotten Son of God, which is in the bosom of the Father." One of the closing chapters shows us "the disciple whom Jesus loved" "lying on Jesus' breast." He came right *from* the heart of God, right *to* the heart of man.

"I bare you on eagles' wings, and brought you to Myself" (Exod. xix. 4). The object of this Gospel is to bear us as upon the eagle's wings of our Divine Saviour, right into the presence of the Father Himself. "Father, I will that they also whom Thou hast given Me be with Me where I am; that they may behold My glory, which Thou hast given Me: for Thou lovedst Me before the foundation of the world" (xvii. 24).

These words in the seventeenth chapter take us back to the introduction to this Gospel, "In the beginning was the Word." Our thoughts are turned back to the first words of the Bible, and unite the great work of creation with the glorious revelation of the Son of God. "And the Word was God. All things were made by Him, and without Him was not anything made that was made." Jesus is the Creator; He meets the need of all created life; He meets the need of man by giving Himself to be each man's greatest, nearest Friend (Rev. John Urquhart).

In accordance with this, one of the chief features of John's Gospel is our Lord's personal interviews with individuals. The first disciples in chapter i., Nicodemus, the Woman of Samaria, and others right through the book, to the very end, where He revealed Himself to Thomas, and said to Peter, "Lovest thou Me?" In all these He disclosed Himself as the Friend of the soul. The close union between Christ and the Church is set forth in this Gospel under the figure of the Bridegroom (iii. 25-29), of the Vine and the branches (xv.), of partaking of His flesh and blood (vi. 48-57), and of the living water. We see His friendship with the beloved disciple, and in the home at Bethany. It comes out again in His last discourse with His disciples, which is introduced by the words, "Having loved His own which were in the world, He loved them unto the end." "Greater love hath no man than this, that a man lay down his life for his friends. Ye are My friends, if ye do whatsoever I command you. I have called you friends." It is revealed in His prayer, where His desire is in all things their oneness with Himself. The love of Christ is limitless to each soul.

The "I AM" in this Gospel shows how perfectly He meets the world's need.

*I AM He, the Christ,* iv. 26, meets our need of a Divine Saviour, who is also human.

*I AM the Bread of Life,* vi. 35, meets our soul-hunger.

*I AM the Light of the World,* viii. 12, meets our darkness.

*I AM the Door of the Sheep,* x. 7, meets our homelessness.

*I AM the Good Shepherd,* x. 11, meets our helplessness.

*I AM the Resurrection and the Life,* xi. 25, meets our death.

*I AM your Master and Lord,* xiii. 13, meets our dependence.

*I AM the Way, the Truth, and the Life,* xiv. 6, meets our need of salvation.

*I AM the True Vine,* xv. 1, meets our need of union with Himself.

*I AM Jesus of Nazareth,* xviii. 5, meets our need of a human Saviour, Who is also Divine.

These words I AM (ἐγώ εἰμι) identified our Lord with the covenant name of Jehovah in the Old Testament. The Jews recognised that He claimed deity in applying it thus emphatically to Himself, for it was when He said, "Before Abraham was, I AM," they took up stones to stone Him, considering it blasphemy, which by the law was punishable by death.

John wrote his Gospel that men "might believe that Jesus is the Christ, the Son of God; and that believing they might have life through His name" (xx. 31). Accordingly, we find the word "*believe*" occurring nearly a hundred times through this Gospel, and the word "*witness*" nearly fifty times. For, beginning with the Baptist (i. 6, 7), John called in one witness after another to give evidence in proving the case. See especially chapter v. 31-40.[1]

[1] *Studies in the Gospel of John.* Prof. W. W. White.

# VII. CHRIST IN RESURRECTION POWER

## ACTS

### THE RISEN CHRIST

IN the Acts we see the risen, ascended, glorified Christ, still living and working on by the power of the Holy Spirit through His Church on earth. The Epistles, likewise, are the continuation of His teaching through the Holy Spirit, according to His promise (John xvi. 12-14). There is no fundamental truth revealed in the Epistles which is not contained in germ in the Gospels. For instance, the Epistle to the Hebrews is one long commentary upon our Lord's words : "This is My blood of the New Covenant, which is shed for many for the remission of sins."

The teaching of the Epistles is one. The great theme is salvation through Christ. Like the Gospels they have the advantage of giving us different aspects of our Lord's work by different writers. There is, moreover, a certain correspondence between the Gospels and Epistles. James reminds us of Matthew, especially the Sermon on the Mount. The teaching of Peter is grounded mainly on the example of Christ, and reminds us of Mark's Gospel. There is an affinity between Paul and his companion Luke, whose Gospel is emphatically the Gospel for the sinner. "John in his Gospel tells us how the Divine life is exhibited in the person of Christ. In his Epistle he shows how it is imparted, and how it manifests itself" (Moorehead).

This book might be called "The Acts of the Holy Spirit," or "The Acts of the Risen Saviour." Luke, in his Gospel, told us what Jesus "*began*," and here what He *continued* both to do and to teach by the Holy Ghost, through the disciples.

Our Lord told His disciples that He would send the Spirit, "And He shall bear witness of Me ; and ye also shall bear witness, because ye have been with Me from the beginning" (John xv. 26, 27). Our Lord fulfilled His promise on the day

230

of Pentecost, and poured forth the Holy Spirit upon His disciples (Acts ii. 16, 17, 33), and from that moment, as they bore witness to the Saviour, the Holy Spirit bore witness at the same time in the hearts of the hearers, and multitudes were converted to the Lord.

"We are His witnesses of these things," said Peter, "and so is also the Holy Ghost, whom God hath given to them that obey Him" (v. 32). Throughout the book of Acts we see the mighty working of the ascended Saviour through this twofold witness. It was He who shed forth the Holy Spirit at Pentecost (ii. 33). It was He who chose the workers and selected their various fields of service. His last words to His Church before He ascended were, "Ye shall be witnesses unto Me both in Jerusalem, and in all Judea, and in Samaria, and unto the uttermost part of the earth" (i. 8). The infant Church was slow to recognise the breadth of this commission and to lay aside its Jewish prejudices. They confined their preaching to Jerusalem till persecution was allowed to scatter them. The blood of the first martyr, Stephen, proved indeed the seed of the Church. It was one of the means used in preparing the great Apostle of the Gentiles.

Those that were scattered abroad went everywhere preaching the Word. Philip preached Christ in Samaria, with the result of a great ingathering. Cæsarea (viii. 40), Phenice, Cyprus, Antioch (xi. 19), Damascus (ix. 2), heard the Word. The direct intervention of the risen Saviour is seen in the admission of the Gentiles to His Church. He used Peter to open the door of the Gospel to the Jews at Pentecost, and to the Gentiles in the house of Cornelius, and so fulfilled His promise concerning the keys (Matt. xvi. 18, 19).

The risen Saviour appeared to Saul of Tarsus to make him "a minister and a witness" (xxvi. 16), to send him "far hence unto the Gentiles" (xxii. 21); and at every step of his three great missionary journeys he made known His will with unmistakable clearness. The record of the book of Acts mainly clusters round these two Apostles : Peter, the Apostle to the dispersed of Israel ; Paul to the Gentiles. It deals chiefly with the devoted labours of the Apostle Paul, the last called but most honoured of the Apostles, and shows us that it is his name, and not that of Matthias, that we must look for among "the twelve Apostles of the Lamb" (Rev. xxi. 14). The book opens with the preaching of the Gospel in Jerusalem, the great centre of the Jewish nation. It closes with its preaching in Rome, the great centre of the world-power.

The book of Acts is the best guide-book to missionary enter-
prise. It tells us the true motive, the best plans, and the
source of power. Guided by their risen Lord, the Early Church
pursued a definite programme in its extension, always selecting
some great radiating centre of population for its operation,
whence the influence might spread to the surrounding district—
Jerusalem, Samaria, Antioch, Cyprus, Iconium, Lystra, Derbe,
Philippi, Thessalonica, Berea, Athens, Corinth, Ephesus, Rome.
Their methods were simple, straightforward, and successful.
They went forth in dependence on the living God, with un-
quenchable zeal and undaunted courage. Their one aim was to
bring men to a saving knowledge of Christ. He was their one
theme and the Word of God their efficient weapon. Christ was
always and everywhere the centre of their testimony, and the
Holy Spirit their power for service (Moorehead).

## ROMANS

### THE GOSPEL OF CHRIST

This Epistle, which Luther called "The perfect Gospel," and
Coleridge "The most profound work in existence," stands first
of all the Epistles as setting forth the great truths of man's
fallen state, and of justification by faith in the person and work
of our Lord and Saviour Jesus Christ.

By birth a Hebrew, by citizenship a Roman, by culture a
Greek, Paul was well fitted naturally to write it; but it was in
the grace and apostleship received direct from Jesus Christ (i. 5)
that he trusted alone for his qualification. "*Thy faith hath
saved thee, go in peace,*" may be taken as the Gospel germ of the
Epistle to the Romans.

The clue to the Epistle is to be found in i. 16: "I am not
ashamed of the Gospel of Christ: for it is the power of God
unto salvation to every one that believeth; to the Jew first, and
also to the Greek. For therein is the righteousness of God
revealed from faith to faith: as it is written, THE JUST SHALL
LIVE BY FAITH." He was not ashamed of the Gospel, for he had
proved its power.

The Epistle naturally divides itself into three parts: (1)
Justification; (2) Sanctification; (3) Application of the foregoing to daily life, each of which are associated with one of the
great Apostle's irresistible "THEREFORES."

(1) *Justification by faith* for access. Rom. v. 1: "*Therefore,
being justified by faith, we have peace with God, through our*

Lord Jesus Christ." Throughout the Epistle we hear the challenge, " Where shall righteousness be found ? " It is found alone in Christ. It was while we were yet " without strength," " ungodly," " sinners," " enemies," that God commended His love toward us and Christ died for us (v. 6, 8, 10). We are justified " by grace," " by His blood," " by faith." The results of justification are peace, access, joy in God.

(2) *Sanctification by faith* in Christ, through the power of the indwelling Spirit (viii. 1-2, R. V.) : " There is *therefore* now no condemnation to them that are in Christ Jesus. For the law of the Spirit of life in Christ Jesus hath made me free from the law of sin and death." Chapter vi. shows us our position as having been crucified and raised with Christ, that we should henceforth walk in newness of life. Chapter vii. shows us the religious self seeking deliverance from the power of indwelling sin. The personal pronoun " I " which abounded in chapter vii. disappears in chapter viii., and the word " Spirit " takes its place, showing Him as the active agent of God, in revealing Christ for our sanctification, making us " more than conquerors through Him that loved us."

(3) *Application. The dedication of heart and life* to God's service (xii. 1): " I beseech you *therefore*, brethren, by the mercies of God, that ye present your bodies a living sacrifice, holy, acceptable unto God, which is your reasonable service."

In this practical and personal appeal, and in his clear words in chapter vi. 1-2, he for ever refutes the charge that the doctrine of justification by faith countenances laxity in life ; and it is a remarkable fact that the Epistle of Faith begins and ends with OBEDIENCE (i. 5, xvi. 26). See also the frequent repetition of the word " obedience " throughout the Epistle. The Apostle turns aside in chapters ix.-xi. to show us that the cause of Israel's fall is unbelief, that their rejection is neither total nor final, and that the conversion of the world awaits the conversion of Israel.

## 1 AND 2 CORINTHIANS

### THE MINISTER OF CHRIST

The first Epistle to the Corinthians was called forth by the state of things in the Corinthian Church—by party factions, by the neglect of administering discipline upon offending members, and by certain questions regarding worship and conduct, upon which the believers sought light.

The second Epistle to the Corinthians contains more of Paul's personal history than any other of his Epistles, and reveals his courage and self-sacrificing love.

The main subject of both Epistles is *the minister of Christ.* "Woe is me if I preach not the Gospel" (1 Cor. ix. 16).

We see the *urgency of the message.* He points to the judgment seat of Christ and the shortness of the time (2 Cor. v. 9, 10, 20, vi. 1-2, yii. 10, 11; 1 Cor. vii. 29). He ever remembers that his work will be tried by fire (1 Cor. iii. 13). Whether his message is accepted or rejected he is a sweet savour of Christ unto God (2 Cor. ii. 15, v. 9). He recognises the work of Satan in blinding men's eyes to the Gospel (2 Cor. iv. 3, 4, xi. 3, 14).

1. *The foolishness of the message.* Christ crucified, to the Jews a stumbling-block; to the Greeks foolishness.

2. *The power of the message.* Christ the power of God to those who are saved.

3. *The foolishness of the messenger.* His weakness from the human side.

4. *The power of the messenger.* The all-sufficiency of Christ.

Right through both Epistles Paul's theme was:

(1) *Christ Crucified* (1 Cor. i. 13-24). He determined to know nothing else among them (1 Cor. ii. 2). Christ the only Foundation (iii. 11). Christ our Passover sacrificed for us (v. 7). Christ our smitten Rock (x. 4). One Lord Jesus Christ (viii. 6). The blood of the New Covenant (x. 16, xi. 25). His death for our sins, according to the Scriptures (xv. 3). We preach Christ Jesus the Lord (2 Cor. iv. 5). Always bearing about in the body the dying of the Lord Jesus, that the life also of Jesus may be manifested (iv. 10, 11). Christ died for all (v. 15). Yea, He was made *sin* for us, that we might be made the righteousness of God in Him (v. 21).

(2) *Christ Risen.* Nowhere are the glorious facts of the Resurrection set forth more fully than in 1 Cor. xv. The chapter contains the believer's future hope and present victory through our Lord Jesus Christ. Even here the thought of service is ever present with Paul (xv. 58).

(3) *The foolishness of the messenger* (1 Cor. i. 27, 28). The five ranks in God's army:—The weakness of the messenger (1 Cor. ii. 1, 3; 2 Cor. x. 10, xi. 6, xii. 7-11, xiii. 9), and yet his fervent love (1 Cor. iv. 14, 15; 2 Cor. ii. 4, xi. 2, 3; xii. 15). The self-abasement of the messenger (iv. 9-13, ix. 19-27; 2 Cor. vii. 2-9, x. 1). His sufferings, hardships, and perils (1 Cor. iv. 7-18; 2 Cor. i. 4, 5, 8-10).

(4) *The power of the messenger.* This is seen in the all-sufficiency of Christ, and His grace made perfect in weakness (2 Cor. xii. 9). Christ Jesus is made unto him Wisdom, etc. (1 Cor. i. 30). His preaching is in demonstration of the Spirit and of power (ii. 4-16). In Christ he finds the yea and the amen, to all the promises of God (2 Cor. i. 20). A personal sight of Christ constituted his first call (1 Cor. ix. 1). Daily beholding the face of Christ is his transforming power (2 Cor. iii. 18, iv. 6). The love of Christ is his constraining power (v. 14). His glory is to be Christ's ambassador (v. 20). The meekness and gentleness of Christ is his strength (x. 1).

## GALATIANS

### THE CROSS OF CHRIST

The error which had crept into the Galatian Church was vital, affecting the foundations of faith. Judaisers had come, introducing legalism and ritual, adding the works of the Law to the pure Gospel of justification through the free grace of God, through faith in Christ.

On account of this, Paul first asserts his apostleship, as derived direct from Christ, and then sets forth the power of the Cross of Christ, in its various aspects, as the only ground of our salvation.

(1) *The power of Christ's Cross to deliver from sin* (i. 4, ii. 21, iii. 22).

(2) *The power of Christ's Cross to deliver from the curse of the Law* (iii. 13).

(3) *The power of Christ's Cross to deliver from the self-life* (ii. 20, v. 24).

(4) *The power of Christ's Cross to deliver from the world* (vi. 14).

(5) *The power of Christ's Cross in the new birth* (iv. 4-7).

(6) *The power of Christ's Cross in receiving the Spirit* (iii. 14).

(7) *The power of Christ's Cross in bringing forth the Spirit's fruit* (v. 22-25).

Paul describes his own preaching as having so fully set forth the Cross that it was as if they had seen Christ crucified in their midst (iii. 1). Therefore he was able to "minister to them the Spirit" (iii. 5). He speaks of "the offence of the Cross" (v. 11, vi. 12), and of bearing the brand marks of Christ in his own body (vi. 17). He repeats once more his central motto : "THE JUST SHALL LIVE BY FAITH" (iii. 11).

## EPHESIANS

### HEAVENLY PLACES IN CHRIST

In this Epistle the teaching of Paul reaches its spiritual climax. He unfolds God's purpose of blessing to the Church, the body of Christ, redeemed and brought nigh by His blood (i. 7, ii. 13, v. 23-32), built upon one foundation, an holy temple in the Lord, with no middle wall of partition between Jew and Gentile.

Its Key-note is *Heavenly Places in Christ.*

(1) *The Heavenly place of Blessing* (i. 3). (Notice the words "all" and "in.") Christ the Inheritance of the Church (i. 11). The Church the Inheritance of Christ (i. 18).

(2) *The Heavenly place of Power* (i. 19, 20). The same power of God which raised Christ from the dead is to work in the believer.

(3) *The Heavenly place of Rest* (ii. 6). In Christ we enter our heavenly Canaan here below. This Epistle corresponds with the book of Joshua.

(4) *The Heavenly place of Manifestation* (iii. 10). The Church is to manifest Christ, His riches, wisdom, love, unity, fulness.

(5) *The Heavenly place of Victory* (vi. 12). The "wiles of the devil" (vi. 11), the enmity of the "prince of the power of the air" (ii. 2), is, as we might expect, manifested in this Epistle, and is provided for in the Christian's armour.

The length and breadth and depth and height of the love of God in Christ comes out in every chapter (i. 4, 6, ii. 4, 7, iii. 17-19, iv. 2-6, 15, 32, v. 2, 25, vi. 23, 24).

Chapter ii. 1-13 is a complete epitome of the Gospel.

Chapter ii. 14, 15, 17, Christ *is* our Peace. He *made* peace. He *preached* peace.

Chapter iii. contains the fullest and deepest of Paul's prayers.

Study the subject of Paul and Prayer throughout his Epistles.

## PHILIPPIANS

### REJOICING IN CHRIST

This is the Epistle of joy in Christ Jesus. The word *joy* or *rejoice* occurs sixteen times. Throughout it is rejoicing in the midst of tribulation. Thus had Paul rejoiced in the jail at

Philippi, when at midnight, with bleeding backs, he and Silas sang praises. Thus he rejoiced now, chained to a Roman soldier, for his very bonds furthered the spread of the Gospel. Thus he exhorted his beloved Philippian converts to rejoice because they were allowed to suffer for Christ (i. 29). He rejoiced in his converts, his joy and crown (iv. 1). In their growth (i. 3-6). In their again ministering to his necessities, even in Rome (iv. 10-19). Above all he rejoiced in Christ (iv. 4).

Chapter ii. 5-11 describes the grace of Christ, the eternal Son of God, descending, step by step, to the death of the Cross for our salvation, and His glorious exaltation to eternal glory and universal homage.

Chapter iii. contains the heart of the Epistle. Paul first *counted* all things but loss for Christ, and then actually *suffered* the loss of all things for Him, to be found in Him, and to know the power of His resurrection, and the fellowship of His sufferings, being made conformable unto His death.

## COLOSSIANS

### CHRIST OUR HEAD

The real dangers which threatened the Church at Colossæ— the deceitful philosophy of the Gnostics which set God on one side, worship of angels, legalism, forced asceticism—called forth this marvellous description of the Lord Jesus Christ.

Ephesians dwells on the Church, the body ; Colossians on Christ the Head. Christ is the image of the invisible God the Son of His love (i. 13), the abode of His fulness (i. 15, 19, ii. 3, 9).

Christ is the sovereign Creator of the universe (i. 16, 17).

He is from all eternity, and has all pre-eminence (i. 17).

He is the Reconciler of the universe through the blood of His Cross (i. 20-22, 14, ii. 14).

He is the Head of all principality and power (ii. 10, 15).

He is the Head of the body, the Church (i. 18, 24, ii. 19, iii. 4).

He is All in All (iii. 11).

The Church's position is united to Christ, complete in Him, dead, buried, risen with Him ; therefore she is to put off the old and to put on the new (i. 27, ii. 10, 12, iii. 1-10).

Like Paul's other Epistles, the doctrinal section is followed by practical rules for daily life. As if he said, "Here is the principle, now see how it works out."

## 1 AND 2 THESSALONIANS

### CHRIST OUR HOPE

The personal coming again of the Lord Jesus Christ is the hope of the Church, and the main subject of both these Epistles, being mentioned in every chapter.

### 1 *Thessalonians*

Chap. i. 9, 10, *Christ's Coming an incentive to conversion.* This was mainly a Gentile Church; they turned to God from idols, to serve the living God and to wait for His Son from heaven.

Chap. ii. 19, 20, *Christ's Coming an incentive to faithful ministry.* Paul's conduct had commended his preaching. The Thessalonians became an eager Missionary Church.

Chap. iii. 12 13, *Christ's Coming an incentive to Christian love.* They were already "taught of God to love one another" (iv. 9); but Paul's prayer for an increase of that love was answered (2 Thess. i. 3).

Chap. iv. 13-16, *Christ's Coming the ground of comfort in bereavement.* When Christ comes those that have fallen asleep believing in Him will be the first to rise to meet Him. The majesty of His Coming is set forth. Compare 1 Cor. xv. 51, 52.

Chap. v. 4-6, *Christ's Coming an incentive to watchfulness.* Compare Mark xiii. 33-37.

Chap. v. 23, 24, *Christ's Coming an incentive to holiness.* Compare 2 Peter iii. 14.

### 2 *Thessalonians*

Chap. i. 7-10, *Christ's Coming supplies comfort under persecution.* "Rest with us." This was a much persecuted Church. This passage also foretells the judgment of the impenitent.

Chap. ii., *Christ's Coming in connection with the growth of apostasy* and revelation of the man of sin, who shall be destroyed by the brightness of Christ's Coming.

Chap. iii. 5, *Practical preparation for His Coming.*

## 1 AND 2 TIMOTHY

### THE DOCTRINE OF CHRIST

1 and 2 Timothy and Titus are "Pastoral Epistles," addressed to ministers in charge of important Churches. Both Timothy

and Titus seem never to have disappointed the full trust Paul reposed in them. Timothy, young and sensitive, is exhorted to endure hardness and fight the good fight of faith, and to be an ensample to the believers.

(1) *A pure Gospel.* Paul emphasises the need of true doctrine. The false teaching of the first century which Timothy was exhorted to arrest, bears a close resemblance to that of the twentieth.

(2) *A pure worship.* Teaching with regard to prayer, etc.

(3) *A faithful ministry.* The supreme duty of devotion to the Lord's service. An unqualified promise (1 Tim. iv. 16).

(4) *The importance and authority of the Scriptures* (1 Tim. vi. 3; 2 Tim. iii. 15-17, iv. 1-4).

*Christ our Saviour* (1 Tim. i. 15, ii. 3, iv. 10). Christ our Mediator (ii. 5). Christ our Ransom (ii. 6). Christ our Teacher (vi. 3). Christ our King (vi. 15). Christ our Captain 2 Tim. ii. 3).

The second Epistle to Timothy is of special interest as being the last Paul wrote, written from the dungeon in Rome in the near expectation of his execution. His zeal and faith are unabated. He is able to say : "I have fought a good fight, I have finished my course, I have kept the faith."

These two Epistles contain two prophecies of coming peril for the professing Church : (1) 1 Tim. iv. 1-5, bearing a close resemblance to the errors of the Church of Rome ; (2) 2 Tim. iii. 1-5, probably relating to the great apostasy of the last days before the Coming of our Lord, and giving a photographic picture of the evils of our own day.

## TITUS

### CHRIST OUR SAVIOUR

This Epistle was addressed to Titus, the Bishop of Crete, a hard post (i. 12, 13). To him had been committed the difficult task of settling the differences at Corinth (2 Cor. ii. 13, xii. 18, vii. 6-15). Paul's second Epistle to the Corinthians proves how successfully he had accomplished the mission.

The Epistle deals with the qualifications of a Bishop or Elder (i.); with the need of sound doctrine (ii.); with the need of good works (iii.).

The words "God our Saviour" and "Christ our Saviour" both occur in the same order in each of the three chapters of this Epistle, as if to emphasise the deity of our Lord.

The Epistle embodies two rich and comprehensive outlines of salvation by grace (ii. 11-14, iii. 4-8).

Chap. ii. 11-14, God's grace brings salvation (ver. 11). *Past.*—Christ gave Himself to redeem us from all iniquity (ver. 14). *Present.*—To purify unto Himself a peculiar people, "zealous of good works" (ver. 14, 12). *Future.*—"Looking for the appearance of the glory of our great God and Saviour Jesus Christ." Christ's personal, pre-millenial Coming, of which Paul wrote to the Thessalonians about thirteen years before, was still his blessed hope as he neared the close of his life. See also 1 Tim. vi. 14 and 2 Tim. iv. 8, almost his last word.

## Philemon

### THE BONDS OF CHRIST

This beautiful personal letter from God's aged servant, in bonds for the Gospel, foreshadows the time when the bonds of Christ's love should break the bonds of slavery.

The story it contains "is an exquisite picture of what the Lord Jesus Christ does. He not only intercedes for us with Him from whom we have departed, and against whom we have sinned; but, knowing to the full how much we have wronged God, and how much we owe Him, He says, 'Put that on Mine account'" (F. R. Havergal, *Morning Bells*).

## Hebrews

### CHRIST OUR HIGH PRIEST

The glories of our Saviour are exhibited in this Epistle; it is one of the most precious books in the Bible. It has been called "The Fifth Gospel." Four describe Christ's ministry on earth, this describes His ministry in heaven.

It was written to Hebrew disciples, probably of Jerusalem, to avert the danger of their drifting back into Judaism. They are exhorted to *let go* everything else, in order *to hold fast* the faith and hope of the Gospel. The Epistle is attributed to Paul, and though many question this, there is abundance of evidence in its favour. To give one example only, the concluding salutation, "Grace be with you all," is Paul's "sign-manual" in every Epistle.

The Key-note is *the High-Priesthood of the Lord Jesus.*

Chaps. i. and ii. *Christ better than the angels* both in His deity and His humanity.

Chap. iii. *Christ better than Moses.*

Chap. iv. *Christ better than Joshua.*

Chaps. v., vi., vii. *Christ better than Aaron.*

Chap. viii. *A better Covenant.*

Chap. ix. *A better Tabernacle.*

Chap. x. *A better Sacrifice.*

Chap. xi. *Examples of Faith's better choice.*

Chap. xii. *Call to follow this glorious company* and the great Captain Himself in the path of outward loss for eternal gain.

Chap. xiii. *Call to go forth unto Him without the camp* bearing His reproach.

*Christ's twofold nature.* Perhaps no other short space in the Bible so emphasises *both* our Lord's deity and humanity as chaps. i. and ii. As our great High Priest, Christ is able to *understand* all our need, because He is perfect Man. He is able to *meet* all our need, because He is perfect God.

The central point is Christ's eternal Priesthood and all-availing sacrifice for sin. The Epistle dwells upon the supreme importance and power of the blood of Christ in obtaining eternal redemption for us, in purging the conscience, in opening to us the heavenly sanctuary.

Throughout this Epistle we note that whatever Christ touches He makes eternal. Trace the word "eternal" throughout. Also the words—*Perfect—Once—Blood—Without —Better*, and the expression *We have . . . therefore let us.*

## JAMES

### THE LAW OF CHRIST FOR DAILY LIFE

This beautiful Epistle of holy living was possibly the first of the New Testament writings, a patriarchal letter, addressed to the twelve tribes, reminding us of some Hebrew prophet in its denunciation of the oppression of the rich, the hire of the labourers kept back by those who give themselves up to live in pleasure.

It is a superficial reading of Paul and James which counts them to be at variance as to the relative importance of faith and works. Paul uses the word *justify* in the sense of "acquitted," "accounted righteous." James uses it in the sense of being *proved righteous* by the works which are the result of faith.

It is a remarkable fact that while Paul uses the expression "rich in good works" (1 Tim. vi. 18), James uses "rich in faith" (ii. 5). James exalts faith; its trial worketh patience (i. 3); his Epistle opens and closes with strong encouragement to pray the prayer of faith (i. 6, v. 14-18). He exposes the spurious faith which does not produce works by the question so emphatically rendered in the R.V. "Can *that* faith save him?" Paul is one with him in this when he says we are "created in Christ Jesus *unto good works*" (Eph. ii. 10).

James compares God's Word to a mirror, revealing the natural depravity of the heart of man. His description of the sins of the tongue is unequalled: "The tongue can no *man* tame"; but *God* can, for He can bring every *thought* into captivity to the obedience of Christ (2 Cor. x. 5).

## 1 AND 2 PETER

### CHRIST OUR PRECIOUS CORNER STONE

These are the Epistles of joy in suffering. 1 Peter chiefly the suffering of persecution; 2 Peter chiefly the suffering of temptation and of the surrounding apostasy. He speaks of himself as a witness of the sufferings of Christ (1 Pet. v. 1), and as an eye-witness of His majesty (2 Pet. i. 16); of partaking of Christ's sufferings, and partaking of His glory (1 Pet. iv. 13, v. 1).

Peter dwells on the sufferings of Christ and the sufferings of His followers. He to whom our Lord gave the commission "Feed My sheep," delights in this Epistle to speak of Christ the Chief Shepherd (1 Pet. ii. 25, v. 4), and of His servants as under-shepherds (v. 2, 3).

He speaks of Christ the precious Corner Stone, and of believers as living stones in the same Temple (1 Pet. ii. 4-8). By implication he speaks of Christ as our great High Priest by whom we offer spiritual sacrifices, and of the royal priesthood of all believers (1 Pet. ii. 5, 9).

Peter brings out very fully the atoning work of Christ through His death, and precious blood shed for us (1 Pet. i. 18-20, ii. 24, iii. 18; 2 Pet. i. 4, ii. 20), and he closes his writings where Paul, in his Epistle to the Thessalonians, began —the blessed hope of the Coming of the Lord (2 Pet. iii.).

He throws radiant light on the inspiration of the Scriptures (see 1 Pet. i. 10-12; 2 Pet. i. 4, 16-21, iii. 15). He also includes Paul's writings under the same title as the Old Testament Scriptures, and shows that he wrote not in his own wisdom, but by wisdom given from above.

Note the use of the word *Precious* in both Epistles.

## 1 John

### FELLOWSHIP WITH CHRIST

John wrote his Gospel in order that men might believe that Jesus is the Christ, the Son of God, and that *believing they might have life through His Name* (John xx. 31).

He wrote his Epistle in order that those who believed on Christ *might know that they have eternal life* (v. 9-13).

Consequently, as we find the word *believe* running through and characterising the Gospel, so here we have the word *know* running through this Epistle.

John gives the evidence for his own knowledge, that he has heard and seen and handled the Word of Life—Christ Jesus. He seeks to bring his hearers into intimate knowledge and fellowship with the Father and the Son, that their joy may be full (i. 3, 4, 7, ii. 13, 14).

*This fellowship rests on salvation through the atoning work of Christ* (i. 7, 9, ii. 1, 2, 12, iii. 5, 16, iv. 9, 10, 14, v. 11-13). It is received by faith (iii. 23, v. 1, 13).   This faith results :

(1) *In the new birth* (ii. 29, iii. 1, 2, 9, iv. 7, v. 1).

(2) *In forgiveness of sins* (i. 7, 9, ii. 12).

(3) *In deliverance from the power of sin* (i. 6, ii. 1, 6, iii. 3, 5, 6, 9, v. 18).

(4) *In deliverance from the love of the world* (ii. 15, v. 4, 5).

(5) *In victory over the devil* (ii. 13, 14, iii. 8, iv. 4).

(6) *In keeping His commandments* (ii. 3-8, v. 2, 3).

(7) *In love of the brethren* (ii. 9-11, iii. 10-19, 23, iv. 7, 8, 11, 12, 20, 21).

(8) *In the fulness of the Holy Spirit* (ii. 20, 27, iii. 24, iv. 2, 13, v. 6).

(9) *In Divine enlightenment and knowledge*, by which we may know truth from error (ii. 20, 21, 27, iv. 1-3, 6, v. 20).

(10) *In answered prayer* (iii. 21, 22, v. 14-16).

### AND 3 John

### CHRIST THE TRUTH

The words *truth* and *true* occur twelve times in these two short personal Epistles.   Both distinguish between the Truth and the errors which had already spread so widely in the Church, against which John warns his friends in the strongest terms.

## JUDE

### CHRIST OUR KEEPER

*First, we are to keep the faith.* "*Contend earnestly* (the word is the same as *strive, agonise,* in Luke xiii. 24) for the faith once for all delivered to the saints" (ver. 3, R.V.).

*Second, we are to keep ourselves in the love of God,* that He may be able to keep us (21). Jude uses the word *kept* ironically in verse 6 : the angels which *kept* not their first estate are *kept* in chains unto judgment. In verse 13 the same word *kept* is used : to sinners is *kept* the blackness of darkness for ever.

*Third, the Lord is able to keep us from falling.* It is a stronger word used here, *guard,* showing Christ's power to protect us from the perils Jude has been enumerating, and, finally, to present us faultless before the presence of His glory in that great day.

# VIII. CHRIST IN FUTURE GLORY

## REVELATION

### CHRIST THE LAMB OF GOD

THE majestic presence of the eternal Son of God fills the last book of the Bible with the glimpse it gives us of His glory throughout the eternal future, Jesus Christ, the same yesterday, and to-day, and for ever; one with the Father and with the Holy Spirit. "Holy, holy, holy, Lord God Almighty, which was, and is, and is to come." "The Lamb is all the glory of Immanuel's Land."

Rev. xiii. 8 takes us back to the earliest ages: "The Lamb slain (in the purpose of God) from the foundation of the world."

Rev. v. 6. John's vision of the future shows us till all eternity "a Lamb as it had been slain."

Between these two records lies the progressive teaching of the whole Bible with regard to the Lamb of God. Abel's lamb; Abraham's words, "God will provide Himself a Lamb," prefigured in the sacrifice of his beloved son; the ram caught in the thicket, sacrificed in his stead. The Passover Lamb; the two goats on the day of the Atonement. The Lamb of Isaiah liii. is seen to prefigure a person, the coming Messiah The words of John the Baptist, recorded by this same John in his Gospel: "Behold the Lamb of God, which beareth away the sin of the world!" God's eternal purpose for our salvation is seen behind all these Scriptures. "It is this book which contains the title of 'Lamb' no less than twenty-six times, emphasising thereby the increasing value of the sacrificial nature of Christ in the last dark times."[1]

Rev. v. 6. The Lamb is one with the Lion of the tribe of Judah. John looked up, expecting to see a Lion, and he saw a Lamb as it had been slain. The same thought is brought out in that remarkable expression "the wrath of the Lamb" (vi. 16). In connection with this we may note that the strongest words,

*The Spiritual Grasp of the Epistles.* Rev. Chas. Fox.

relative to the future judgment, fell from the lips of Him who was perfect love.

Rev. vii. 14. *Salvation through the blood of the Lamb.*

Rev. xii. 11. *Victory through the blood of the Lamb.*

Rev. v. 12, 13. The new song of eternity will be " *Worthy is the Lamb that was slain.*"

Rev. v. 8. *The worship of the Lamb.*

Rev. vii. 17. *The Lamb* identified with the *Good Shepherd* of John's Gospel.

Rev. xiii. 8. *The Lamb's book of life* (xxi. 27, xxii. 19).

Rev. xiv. 1-4. *The faithful followers of the Lamb.*

Rev. xvii. 14. *The victory of the Lamb* over all His enemies.

Rev. xix. 13, 16. *The Lamb* is identified with the *Word of God* of John's Gospel.

Rev. xix. 7, 9 and xxi. 1-9. *The bride of the Lamb,* and the *Marriage Supper of the Lamb,* identifying Him with the *Bridegroom* of John's Gospel.

Rev. xxi. 22. *The Lamb and the Lord God Almighty are the Temple of the New Jerusalem.*

Rev. xxi. 23. *The Lamb is the Light of the heavenly city,* identifying Him with the *Light of the World* in John's Gospel.

| GENESIS. | REVELATION. |
| --- | --- |
| Paradise lost. | Paradise regained |
| Creation of heaven and earth. | A new heaven and a new earth. |
| The curse enters—Sin, Sorrow, Suffering, Death. | No more curse—No more Sin, Sorrow, Suffering, Death. |
| Tree of Life guarded. | Tree of Life restored. |
| Four rivers watering the garden. | A pure river of water of life. |

The last chapter contains Christ's thrice uttered word, His last recorded word to His Church, "Behold, I come quickly." "Amen. Even so, come, Lord Jesus."

# INDEX

247